Letter-Perfect:
The Accurate Secretary

How to Proofread Letters to Get Them Perfect for Mailing

Contents

Introduction   7

    How *Letter-Perfect* Is Arranged   7

Letter Styles   9

    Block or Modified Block   9
    Semiblock   11
    Complete or Full Block   11
    Special Notes About Business Letters   11
    Punctuation and Capitalization in Business Letters   14
    How to Close Business Letters   15
    Enclosure Notice   16
    Carbon Copy Notations   16
    Two-Page Letter   17

Spelling   19

    General Rules   19
    Individual Words   20
    Cities and States   20

How to Proofread Successfully   23

    Proofreading Checklist   23
    Master Spelling List   24
    Two-Letter State Abbreviations   26

Before You Begin   31

    The Types of Errors You Must Look For   31
    Word List—Letters 1–10   33

Verb Endings   47

    Word List—Letters 11–20   56

The Apostrophe   69

    Word List—Letters 21–30   79

Rules for the Correct Use of Punctuation Marks   93

    Colon   93
    Semicolon   94
    Dash   94
    Hyphen   95
    Exclamation Mark   96
    Parentheses   96
    Period   97
    Question Mark   98
    Quotation Marks   98
    Word List—Letters 31–40   103

Rules for Commas—Part 1   117

    Word List—Letters 41–50   123

Rules for Commas—Part 2   137

    Word List—Letters 51–60   143

Rules for Commas—Part 3   157

    Word List—Letters 61–70   167
    Word List—Letters 71–100   181

Now That You Have Reached This Point   217

Corrected Letters 1–100   219

INTRODUCTION

When your employer dictates a letter to you, he expects you to put the letter on his desk, ready for signature—letter-perfect.

A letter is really letter-perfect when:

1. It is a word-for-word repetition of what the employer has dictated.
2. It has been set up attractively on the page with even margins. The letter style should be the one that is preferred by your employer or by your company.
3. It is clean, with no finger marks, smudges, or poor erasures or other corrections.
4. It has no spelling errors.
5. It has no typographical errors.
6. It has no errors in punctuation or in grammar.

Only if all of these conditions have been met is your work *Letter-perfect.*

How *Letter-Perfect* Is Arranged

This book is arranged so that you can make your work letter-perfect every time you type a letter.

The major part of this book consists of one hundred letters. Each of these letters has many errors in it. With all the help you will get from the various sections in the book, you will be able to find all the errors in the letters and make the necessary corrections. After you have made the corrections, you will check your corrections with the corrected letters which appear at the back of the book. This will enable you to see whether or not you have overlooked any errors. Then you will type the letters correctly, proofread them carefully, and again check with the correct copy at the back of the book.

To help you, there are preliminary instructions on how to use this book. There is a review of the correct styles used in typing business letters. Instructions and hints on how to spell words precede a section on proofreading. This section gives the procedures to be followed so that all errors can be found. A Master Spelling List of the words which are most frequently misspelled in business correspondence also includes some cities in the United States whose spelling causes difficulties. Then there is a list of all the states and their correct two-letter abbreviations. A sample letter with many errors is given, and then the necessary corrections are indicated. This letter is shown in typewritten form after all the errors have been corrected. Hints on how to find errors are given, and you will be ready to begin the exciting job of making one hundred letters perfect in every way.

Each group of ten letters is preceded by a list of words which are used in these letters for the first time. In addition, there is a review of some of the rules of grammar and punctuation. These rules will have examples and are followed by exercises which will apply the rules which have just been given. The corrected exercises are shown so that you can see whether or not you have made all the necessary corrections.

LETTER STYLES

Three styles of letters are commonly used in business. (See pp. 10, 12, and 13.)

Block or Modified Block

The style most often used is called *Block* or *Modified Block.* Listed below is a summary of how the parts of the letter are typed when this style of letter is used:

Date

The date line may be typed in three ways:

1. It may be pivoted from the right margin. *Pivoting* means that the last digit of the year ends at the right margin. Pivoting is done by backspacing from the right margin once for each letter or space.

2. It may start at the center of the typing line. When a typewriter with elite type is used, the center is usually 50 or 51. When a typewriter with pica type is used, the center is usually 42 or 43.

3. It may be centered. In order to center, backspace once for every two letters and spaces from the center of the typing line (50 or 51; 42 or 43).

NOTE: When typing the date, do not abbreviate the month or add **st** or **rd** after the date. Type: November 1, 19—, not Nov. 1st, 19—.

Inside Address, Salutation, Paragraphs, and Identifying Information

Each of these letter parts is blocked at the left margin with no indentions. The *identifying information* includes initials, enclosures, and notation of carbon copies. There also may be a postscript (P.S.) which is also typed at the left margin.

Complimentary Close, Firm Name, Typewritten Signature, and Title

Each of these letter parts usually starts at the center of the typing line (50 or 51; 42 or 43).

SAMPLE OF LETTER TYPED IN "BLOCK" OR "MODIFIED BLOCK" STYLE

November 1, 19--

Mr. Thomas Benson
321 Middle Road
Bethel, CT   18017

Dear Mr. Benson:

On October 23 I spoke to you and wrote to you regarding your truck which was parked on our property at 437 Johnson Avenue in Hartford. In our conversation on that date, you assured me that the truck would be removed by October 26. For your information I am enclosing a copy of my letter.

As of this date, the truck is still parked on our property.

We are now advising you that if this truck is not removed by Saturday, November 4, at noon, we will have it towed away at your expense. You will not be able to get possession of the truck until all legal and towing costs have been paid.

Please make this action unnecessary and have the truck removed by that time.

Very truly yours,

POLAND CONSTRUCTION COMPANY

EP:YOI   Ella Poland,
Enclosure   Vice President

cc: Walter Gibson

NOTES

The date is pivoted with the right margin. It could also have been centered, or it could have started at the center.

The inside address, salutation, paragraphs, and identifying information (initials, enclosure notice, and notation of carbon copy) are typed at the left margin.

The complimentary close, firm name, typewritten signature, and dictator's title start at the center of the typing line.

Semiblock

The *Semiblock* style of letter is also frequently used. It is exactly like the *Block* or *Modified Block* style except that the paragraphs are indented, usually five spaces from the left margin. See page 12 for sample letter.

Complete or Full Block

The third style of letter in common use is the *Complete Block* or *Full Block.* In this style, everything, including the date and the closing information starting with the complimentary close, is typed at the left margin. See page 13 for sample letter.

Special Notes About Business Letters

In addition to the parts of business letters which appear in every business letter (date, inside address, salutation, body, complimentary close, and identifying information), there are some other parts which may be used. The following information will help you type these parts correctly.

Attention Line

When a letter is written to a firm, it is sometimes advisable to make a notation so that the letter goes to a specific person or department. This is called an *attention notice* or *attention line.* This notice may be typed as the second line of the inside address (where it appears on envelopes according to United States Postal Service requirements), or it may be typed between the last line of the inside address and the salutation. A double space is left before and after the *attention line* when it is typed after the inside address.

There are various correct forms for typing the *attention line.*

1. It may be typed at the left margin, it may be typed after indenting five spaces from the left margin, or it may be centered.

2. The word **attention** may have an initial capital letter, it may be in full capitals, or it may be underscored. It may be followed by a colon, it may be followed by the word *of,* or it may be followed by neither. **Attention** may also be abbreviated **ATT.**

All of these examples are typed in correct, acceptable form:

Attention: Mr. Smith	Attention Mr. Smith
ATTENTION: Mr. Smith	Attention of Mr. Smith
ATT: Mr. Smith	Attention Mr. Smith

3. Even though there is an *Attention line* with a person's name, the letter is being written to a firm, and **Gentlemen:** must be the salutation.

SEMIBLOCK

The "Semiblock" style is exactly like the "Block" or "Modified Block" style except that the paragraphs are indented, usually five spaces from the left margin.

SAMPLE OF LETTER TYPED IN "SEMIBLOCK" STYLE

May 27, 19--

Mr. Peter Lerange
136 Euclid Avenue
Chicago, IL   60605

Dear Mr. Lerange:

    I have reviewed the contents of your letter of May 19. We are now in the process of correcting the deficiencies in the drainage system of the first nine holes of the golf course. Mr. Williams' estimate of $5,529 for the rest of the work to be done was very low. I would guess that the costs will approach $15,000 for this work.

    If you need a more detailed breakdown of the work actually performed up to this point and the costs, I shall be happy to furnish it.

    Please let me know if you need this information.

                          Very truly yours,

                          JAMES CONSTRUCTION COMPANY

MW:YOI   Martin Weston,
                          Planning Department

NOTES

The date is centered. It may also be pivoted with the right margin, or it may start at the center.

The paragraphs in the body of the letter are indented five spaces from the left margin.

COMPLETE BLOCK OR FULL BLOCK

The third style of letter is the "Complete Block" or "Full Block." In this style, everything, including the date and the closing information starting with the complimentary close, is typed at the left margin.

SAMPLE OF LETTER TYPED IN "FULL BLOCK" OR "COMPLETE BLOCK" STYLE

April 14, 19--

Mr. George Peck
Institutional Advisers, Inc.
143 Broadway
New York, NY   10009

Dear Mr. Peck:

In accordance with your request, I am enclosing the Tax Information Data Sheet prepared for our newest development, Heritage Harbor.

The information has not changed since the last Data Sheet I sent to you, but we expect that there will be a revision very soon.

As soon as the revision is made, I shall let you know.

I am sending a copy of this letter to Charles Mackey for his guidance.

Very truly yours,

SUNRAY BUILDERS, INC.

Milton Chancy,
Treasurer

MC:YOI
Enclosure

cc: Charles Mackey

NOTE

Every part of the letter begins at the left margin.

Subject Line

A *subject line* is sometimes used to identify the subject or purpose of a letter. It is typed a double space after the salutation, and a double space is left before beginning the body of the letter. Like the *attention line,* it may be typed at the left margin, indented five spaces, or centered. It, too, has many correct variations in style. Sometimes instead of the word **Subject,** the word or abbreviations **Reference: Re:** or **In Re:** are used. (The abbreviations mean **in reference to, in regard to,** or **regarding.**) The word **Subject** may be in solid capital letters, or it may have just an initial capital letter. Sometimes, the word **Subject** is omitted when the purpose of this additional line is clear.

All of these examples are typed in correct, acceptable form:

Subject: Increase in Orders	SUBJECT: Increase in Orders
Re: Increase in Orders	In Re: Policy # 4,734,672
SUBJECT: Increase in Orders	Reference: Policy # 3,734,672
RE: Increase in Orders	Increase in Orders

Punctuation and Capitalization in Business Letters

Although there will be a review of punctuation later in this book, this summary of how to punctuate and capitalize the parts of a business letter will be especially helpful to you.

Date

There is always a comma between the date and the year.
Example: November 7, 19—

Inside Address

1. If there is a person's title as part of the first line of the inside address, the title is separated from the name by a comma.
Example: Mr. Fred Harper, President

2. The city and the state are separated by a comma. The state is written with the two-letter state abbreviation and is followed by the five-digit ZIP Code. There is no comma after the state abbreviation; there is no period after the state abbreviation. The ZIP Code is usually typed two or three spaces after the state.
Example: Chicago, IL   60601

3. Abbreviations in the inside address or salutation are followed by periods, but words which are spelled out do not have a period.
Examples: Mrs.   Ms.   Mr.   Dr.   Miss
Messrs.
(NOTE: "Messrs." is used when a letter is written to two men.)

Salutation

1. The salutation is always followed by a colon.
    Examples: Gentlemen: Dear Mr. Haynes:

2. If a salutation is composed of three or four words, with the second word **dear,** all words have initial capital letters except the word **dear.**
    Examples: My dear Sir: My dear Mrs. Smith:

3. The first word of the salutation always begins with a capital letter.
    Examples: Gentlemen: Dear Mr. Brown:

Complimentary Close

1. A comma after the complimentary close is optional; it is correct to have the comma or to omit it.
    Examples: Sincerely yours   Sincerely yours,

2. Only the first word of a complimentary close is capitalized.
    Examples: Yours truly   Yours very truly,   Cordially yours

Identifying Initials

1. The identifying initials of the dictator and the typist are separated by a colon or a diagonal with the dictator's initials first. The initials may be capitalized, they may be in small letters, or there may be any combination of capitalization.
    Examples: GWG:YOI   gwg:yoi   GWG/YOI   GWG:yoi   GWG/yoi

2. Some firms prefer that only the typist's initials appear.
    Examples: YOI   yoi

How to Close Business Letters

1. When a firm name is included, it is usually typed in solid capital letters two spaces after the complimentary close. Four to six spaces are generally left after the firm name before the typewritten signature or title. If there is no firm name, the typewritten signature or title is typed four to six spaces after the complimentary close. Four to six spaces are left before the typewritten signature or title because that is where the handwritten signature is placed, and sufficient space is required.
    Example a: Very truly yours,

    CHASE EQUIPMENT COMPANY (all capitals: two spaces from the complimentary close)

    Paul Chase, President (four to six spaces from the firm name)

Example b: Very truly yours,

Paul Chase, President (no firm name; typewritten signature typed four to six spaces after the complimentary close)

2. When there is a typewritten signature, **Mr.** is never typed.
    Example: Yours truly,

Paul Chase

The first example is correct. The following is INCORRECT.
    Example: Yours truly,

Mr. Paul Chase

Enclosure Notice

1. When something is being included, enclosed, or attached to the letter, an *enclosure notice* must be typed under the initials. Sometimes the enclosure is described. The *enclosure notice* may be spelled out, or it may be abbreviated. Both *enclosure* and *inclosure* are considered correct, but **enclosure** is the preferred form. It is important that there be consistency between the way it is spelled in the body of the letter and the way it is spelled when it is placed under the initials. It cannot be spelled *enclosure* in the body and *inclosure* under the initials.
    Examples: Enclosure   Enclosures (2)   Enclosure—Invoice   Inclosure

2. If the word **Enclosure** or **Enclosures** is abbreviated when it is placed under the initials, the abbreviation is followed by a period, not a colon.
    Examples: Enc.   Encl.   Encs.   Encls.   Inc.   Incl.

Carbon Copy Notations

1. If carbon copies are being sent to others, the abbreviation **cc** is used and is either followed by a colon, or there is no punctuation after it. The **cc** note is typed below the initials. If there is an enclosure, the **cc** note is typed below the *enclosure notice*. The carbon copy notations may be typed with small letters or with capital letters.
    Examples: cc: Mr. Hayes   CC: Mr. Hayes   cc Mr. Hayes
                     Mr. Chase   Mr. Chase   Mr. Chase

2. When the dictator wants a carbon copy sent to a person other than the person to whom the original is being sent and does not want the recipient to know that a carbon

copy is being sent, a special notation is made on the file carbon copy but not on the original. Instead of typing **cc,** the notation **bcc** is typed. This means *blind carbon copy*. This notation may be typed in the same ways as the **cc** notation.

Examples: bcc: Mr. Hayes   BCC: Mr. Hayes   bcc Mr. Hayes
                       Mr. Chase   Mr. Chase   Mr. Chase

Two-Page Letter

1. A long letter requires more than one page. The first page is typed on letterhead paper, and the second page is typed on plain bond paper. The first page should have at least six blank lines on the bottom.

2. The second page starts six lines from the top of the page and has a heading consisting of the name of the person or firm to whom the letter is going, the page number, and the date. This heading may be typed in several ways.

Example a:
Mr. Tom Healy   2   November 1, 19—

NOTE: In this example, the name appears at the left margin, the page number is at the center of the line, and the date is pivoted from the right margin.

Example b:
Mr. Tom Healy
Page 2
November 1, 19—

NOTE: In this example, the lines all begin at the left margin.

3. The continuation of the body of the letter should start three spaces from the heading. A minimum of three lines of the body should be typed on the second page.

SPELLING

Most of us spell nearly all words correctly. Just a few words give us trouble. These are words we have to concentrate on in order to avoid unnecessary and embarrassing errors.

There are certain steps you can take to improve your spelling. Read through the suggested procedures with care and follow them. Your spelling ability must then improve.

1. Pronounce the word silently and aloud. Use it correctly in a sentence. Look at it very carefully. Say the word. Say it by syllables. Say the letters in order. Build the word up by letters and syllables; break it down by letters and syllables.

2. Close your eyes and spell the word. Check your thinking with your eyes open to see that every letter and every syllable is correct.

3. Copy the word with a pen or pencil, or type it. Cover the word, and rewrite or retype it. If the spelling is correct, write or type the word once again. If the spelling is incorrect, start the steps over again, and write or type the word correctly three or four times.

4. If there are words that ALWAYS seem to give you trouble, try to see why you are getting them wrong. Are you putting letters in reverse order (**ie** for **ei**)? Are you putting single letters where double letters belong (one **c** instead of two **c**'s)? Are you putting double letters where single letters belong (two **c**'s instead of one **c**)? If you make errors like these, write or type the word in a special way while you are practicing the spelling. This will help you focus on the difficult parts of the word.

    a. Try underscoring the difficult parts: rec<u>ei</u>ve, re<u>c</u>o<u>mm</u>end, a<u>cc</u>o<u>mm</u>odate

    b. Try CAPITALIZING the difficult parts: recEIve, reCoMMend, aCCoMModate

5. Think of special ways to remember the correct spelling of words you ALWAYS have difficulties with. Here are some simple memory devices which will help you spell these words correctly.

General Rules

These few general rules cover many words which are often misspelled.

    a. Use **i** before **e** except after **c**—relieve, believe, receipt, receive

    b. Words ending in the syllable **ful** have only one **l**—hopeful, helpful, grateful, useful

    c. All words beginning with **over** are one word—overdue, overcoat, overcome, overlook

    d. All words with the prefix **self** are hyphenated—self-control, self-conscious, self-satisfied, self-reliant

    e. Double the **r** in the past tense if words with **er** and **ur** have the accent on the last syllable—prefer, preferred; occur, occurred; defer, deferred; infer, inferred; transfer, transferred; incur, incurred

BUT

f. Do not double the **r** in the past tense if the words with **er** do not have the accent on the last syllable—offer, offered; answer, answered; differ, differed; suffer, suffered

Individual Words

accommodate—two **c**'s and two **m**'s; compare with *recommend* which has one **c** and two **m**'s

bookkeeper—a book keeper; therefore, two **k**'s

catalog—think of *cat on a log* and cross out the **on**

committee—two of everything: two **m**'s, two **t**'s, and two **e**'s

congratulate—a t in the middle, not a **d**

describe, description—both words start with **des** and not **dis**

disappoint—think of *appoint;* therefore, one s and two **p**'s

dissatisfaction—think of *satisfaction;* therefore, two s's because of *dis*

embarrass—two **r**'s and two s's

exceed, proceed, succeed—the only three words in the English language that end in **ceed**

exercise—no c after the **x**

familiar—ends with *liar;* compare with *similar* which ends with *lar*

government—an **n** in the middle

hear—you hear with your *ear*

inasmuch as—two words (*inasmuch* is one word)

nevertheless—one word

occasion—two **c**'s and one **s**

price list—two words

principal—**a** as in main; the principal of a school is your *pal*

principle—this spelling means rule

privilege—there are two **i**'s and two **e**'s with no **d**

procedure—one **e** in the middle; compare with *proceed* which has two **e**'s

questionnaire—two **n**'s and a final **e**

recommend—one **c** and two **m**'s; compare with *accommodate* which has two **c**'s and two **m**'s

separate—the **r** is separated by two **a**'s

similar—ends with *lar;* compare with fami*liar* which ends with *liar*

somewhat—one word

stationary—this spelling means stand still; think of **a** in *stand*

stationery—this spelling means paper; think of **er** in *paper*

supersede—the only word in the English language which ends in **sede**

there—the opposite of *here*

unnecessary—think of *necessary;* therefore, two **n**'s because of **un**

whenever—one word

withhold—think of *with hold;* therefore two **h**'s

Cities and States

Albuquerque—two **que**'s

Asheville—an **e** in the middle; compare with *Nashville* which has no **e** in the middle

Berkeley—three **e**'s
Cincinnati—think of *1 2 1;* one **n,** two n's, and one **t**
Harrisburg—ends in **g;** compare with *Pittsburgh* which ends with **gh**
Indiana, Indianapolis, Louisiana—each contains **ana**
Nashville—no **e** in the middle; compare with *Asheville* which has an **e** in the middle
Pittsburgh—ends in **gh;** compare with *Harrisburg* which ends with **g**
Wilkes-Barre, Winston-Salem—each is hyphenated

HOW TO PROOFREAD SUCCESSFULLY

When you proofread a letter, you are trying to find all mistakes. You want to be sure that the dictator's thoughts and words have been faithfully reproduced. You want to be certain that no words have been added or omitted.

Proofreading is a combination of the mind and sight. When you proofread, it is not sufficient to look at the entire word. Instead, each separate letter must be carefully checked. After each word has been carefully checked letter by letter, the entire sentence must be read to make sure that the content makes sense and that there are no errors in grammar. In some cases, it is necessary to read the entire letter to make sure that there are no inconsistencies between sentences or paragraphs.

Use the checklist below to be certain that you have not overlooked the answers to any of these questions:

Proofreading Checklist

1. Are letters in a word omitted? Are there single letters where there should be double letters?

2. Are letters added in a word? Are there double letters where there should be single letters?

3. Are letters transposed in a word?

4. Are there missing **ed** or **ing** endings?

5. Have the **s**'s in plurals been omitted?

6. Are letters properly spaced both within words and between words?

7. Are words properly capitalized?

8. Are words properly divided into syllables at the ends of lines? If I am in doubt about syllabication, have I consulted the dictionary?

9. Are proper names spelled the same way in all parts of the letter? Have I checked the spelling of proper names ending in a silent **e** to make sure that I have spelled them correctly?

Examples: Greene, Green   Brown, Browne   Read, Reade, Reed, Reid

10. Have I considered the context to make sure that the entire sentence, paragraph, and letter make sense?

11. Have I checked small words as carefully as I have checked the longer words?

12. Are words transposed?

13. Are words repeated? Have I checked very carefully to see that the beginning of the line does not start with a repetition of what appeared at the end of the previous line?

14. Are there no more than two consecutive divisions at the end of lines?

15. Have I remembered to place the closing quotation mark or the closing parenthesis?

16. Have I checked that homonyms (words that sound alike) have been used correctly?
     Examples: coarse, course   to, too, two   dying, dyeing

17. Have I placed the apostrophe correctly when one is needed? Have I remembered to omit the apostrophe when it is not needed, as in the following words: **hers, its, ours, yours, theirs**?

18. Have I checked the punctuation at the end of each sentence to make sure that it is correct?

19. Have I checked the correctness of hyphens between words in the middle of lines?

Refer to this checklist as you proofread. If you find that you are not correcting all the errors, review this checklist again.

The importance of checking a dictionary immediately cannot be overemphasized. If you are in doubt, do not *guess* or allow a spelling about which you have doubts to go through until you have checked it in your dictionary.

Master Spelling List

This Master Spelling List contains the words which are most commonly misspelled in business correspondence. These are the words which writers and typists are most likely to have wrong.

All of the words on this list occur more than once in the letters. Read the instructions for learning how to spell a word before studying the words on this list. Note that before each group of letters is a listing of the words which occur for the first time in those letters. Practice spelling those words and use this list as a resource list or as a mini- dictionary. If you are not sure of the spelling of a word and it does not appear on this list, be sure to consult your dictionary immediately.

Added to this list of spelling words, you will find a list of cities which are often misspelled. Since many of the street names and cities in the inside addresses of the letters are misspelled, this list of cities must also be consulted.

Words

absent	accuracy	address	affect	aloud
accept	achievement	adequate	agreeable	already
acceptance	acknowledgment	advantage	all right	also
accidentally	across	advertisement	allotted	altogether
accommodate	ad	advertising	allowances	always
accordance	add	advice	allowed	among
account	addition	advise	almost	amount

analysis
analyze
annual
answered
anxious
apologize
apparent
appearance
appointment
appreciate
arrangement
assistance
assistants
attempt
attendance
attorneys
August
available

balance
bankruptcy
bargain
beginning
believe
benefit
benefited
bookkeeper
brochure
budget
bulletin
bureau
business
buy
by

calendar
cancellation
cannot
catalog
certain
choose
chose
column
coming
commercial
committee
confident
congratulate
conscious
contract
controversy
convenience

convenient
cordially
correspondence
courteous
courtesy
criticism
criticize
customer

December
decided
decision
defendant
deferred
definite
dependent
describe
description
develop
development
device
devise
die
difference
disappoint
dissatisfied
district
dye

edition
effect
efficiently
eligible
eliminate
embarrass
emphasize
encourage
envelope
equipment
equipped
essential
exceed
excellent
except
exercise
existence
expense
extension

fair
familiar
fare

February
financial
find
fine
forfeit
formally
formerly
forty
forward
fourth
freight
friend
further
future

Gentlemen
genuine
government
grateful
guarantee

hear
helpful
here
hoping
immediately
improvement
inasmuch as
incidentally
incurred
indebtedness
independent
indispensable
inquiry
institute
insurance
interest
investigate
it's
its

January
judgment

know

library
loose
lose

magazine
may be
maybe

merchandise
Messrs.
minimum
miscellaneous
mortgage

necessary
nevertheless
ninety
ninth
no
noticeable
November

occasion
occurred
occurrence
occurring
October
of course
offered
omission
omitted
one
opinion
opportunity
organization
original
overdue

paid
pamphlet
partial
passed
past
permanent
personal
personnel
persuade
planning
pleasant
possession
possible
practical
precede
preference
preferred
prejudice
premium
previous
price list
principal

principle
privilege
probably
procedure
proceed
products
promptly
proof
prove
pursue

questionnaire

realize
reasonable
receipt
receive
recent
recognize
recommend
reference
referred
regret
remittance
remove
repetition
representative
requirements
resent
response
responsibility
responsible
restaurant

Saturday
secretary
separate
September
several
sew
shipment
shipped
shipping
similar
sincerely
so
some
somewhat
sponsored
stationary
stationery
strictly

substantial	their	too	vacuum	withhold
succeed	then	transferred	valuable	won
success	there	truly	volume	yield
sufficient	therefore	two	weather	you're
suggest	they're	undoubtedly	Wednesday	your
sum	thorough	unnecessary	whenever	
superintendent	though	unpaid	whether	
surprise	through	until	who's	
than	to	usually	whose	

Cities

Akron	Detroit	Memphis	Phoenix	Springfield
Albuquerque	Duluth	Miami	Pittsburgh	Syracuse
Asheville	Gary	Milwaukee	Racine	Toledo
Baton Rouge	Harrisburg	Minneapolis	Raleigh	Topeka
Beaumont	Hartford	Mobile	Rochester	Tucson
Berkeley	Honolulu	Nashville	Sacramento	Washington
Bridgeport	Indianapolis	New Haven	St. Louis	Waterbury
Buffalo	Jersey City	New Orleans	St. Paul	Wilkes-Barre
Chattanooga	Knoxville	Niagara Falls	San Francisco	Wilmington
Chicago	Lincoln	Oklahoma City	Savannah	Winston-Salem
Cincinnati	Los Angeles	Omaha	Schenectady	Worcester
Cleveland	Louisville	Paterson	Seattle	
Des Moines	Macon	Philadelphia	Shreveport	

Two-Letter State Abbreviations

Listed below are all the states (plus the District of Columbia and Puerto Rico) and their two-letter state abbreviations. Refer to this list for the correct spelling and abbreviation.

Alabama	AL	Louisiana	LA	Oklahoma	OK
Alaska	AK	Maine	ME	Oregon	OR
Arizona	AZ	Maryland	MD	Pennsylvania	PA
Arkansas	AR	Massachusetts	MA	Puerto Rico	PR
California	CA	Michigan	MI	Rhode Island	RI
Colorado	CO	Minnesota	MN	South Carolina	SC
Connecticut	CT	Mississippi	MS	South Dakota	SD
Delaware	DE	Missouri	MO	Tennessee	TN
District of Columbia	DC	Montana	MT	Texas	TX
Florida	FL	Nebraska	NE	Utah	UT
Georgia	GA	Nevada	NV	Vermont	VT
Hawaii	HI	New Hampshire	NH	Virginia	VA
Idaho	ID	New Jersey	NJ	Washington	WA
Illinois	IL	New Mexico	NM	West Virginia	WV
Indiana	IN	New York	NY	Wisconsin	WI
Iowa	IA	North Carolina	NC	Wyoming	WY
Kansas	KS	North Dakota	ND		
Kentucky	KY	Ohio	OH		

SAMPLE LETTER

1

2   Novembre 3, 19--

3 Mr. Herbert Laine

4 376 Philidelphia Street

5 Pittsburg, PA 15201

6 Dear Mr. Lane

7   I was ver happy to learn form you letter of Januery 7 that you

8 are planing a trip ot our city the at begining of next year. Youcan

9 be sure that everywon in our office will be please to welcome you and

10 will extent what ever curtesies posible.

11   In you lettre you refered to the fack thta you woud preferr to

12 see sum of the govenment offices an we shall make all the nesessary

13 arrangments to recieve passes.

14   The volumn of my work in Januery is less then it is during o-

15 ther months of the year. I shall, therefor have a fare ammount of

16 time to be of assistants to you.

17   As you no, it is allways a pleasure to see you, an Im looking

18 foward to your visit with great pleasure

19   Yours Sincerly

20   WILLS EQUIPTMENT COMPANY

21 AW:YOI   Mr. Alfred W. Wills

22

23

24

25

26

SAMPLE LETTER

~~Novembre~~ *November* 3, 19--

Mr. Herbert Laine

376 ~~Philidelphia~~ *Philadelphia* Street

~~Pittsburg~~, *Pittsburgh,* PA 15201

Dear Mr. ~~Lane~~ *Laine:*

    I was ~~vet~~ *very* happy to learn ~~form~~ *from* ~~you~~ *your* letter of ~~Januery~~ *January* 7 that you are ~~planing~~ *planning* a trip ~~ot~~ *to* our city ~~the~~ at, *the beginning* ~~begining~~ of next year. You *can* be sure that ~~everywon~~ *everyone* in our office will be ~~please~~ *pleased* to welcome you and will ~~extent~~ *extend* ~~what ever~~ *whatever* ~~curtesies~~ *courtesies* ~~posible.~~ *are possible.*

    In ~~you~~ *your* ~~lottre~~ *letter* you ~~refered~~ *referred* to the ~~fack~~ *fact* ~~thta~~ *that* you ~~woud~~ *would* ~~proferr~~ *prefer* to see ~~sum~~ *some* of the ~~govenment~~ *government* offices, ~~an~~ *and* we shall make all the ~~nesessary~~ *necessary* ~~arrangments~~ *arrangements* to ~~recieve~~ *receive* passes.

    The ~~volumn~~ *volume* of my work in ~~Januery~~ *January* is less ~~then~~ *than* it is during ~~o~~ther *other* months of the year. I shall, ~~therefor,~~ *therefore,* have a ~~fare~~ *fair* ~~ammount~~ *amount* of time to be of ~~assistants~~ *assistance* to you.

    As you ~~no,~~ *know,* it is ~~allways~~ *always* a pleasure to see you, ~~an~~ ~~Im~~ *and I'm* looking ~~foward~~ *forward* to your visit with great pleasure.

Yours ~~Sincerly~~ *sincerely*

WILLS ~~EQUIPTMENT~~ *EQUIPMENT* COMPANY

~~Mr.~~ Alfred W. Wills

~~AW:YOI~~ *AWW:*

SAMPLE LETTER

(Typed correctly)

November 3, 19--

Mr. Herbert Laine
376 Philadelphia Street
Pittsburgh, PA   15201

Dear Mr. Laine:

I was very happy to learn from your letter of January 7 that you are planning a trip to our city at the beginning of next year. You can be sure that everyone in our office will be pleased to welcome you and will extend whatever courtesies are possible.

In your letter you referred to the fact that you would prefer to see some of the government offices, and we shall make all the necessary arrangements to receive passes.

The volume of my work in January is less than it is during other months of the year. I shall, therefore, have a fair amount of time to be of assistance to you.

As you know, it is always a pleasure to see you, and I'm looking forward to your visit with great pleasure.

Yours sincerely

WILLS EQUIPMENT COMPANY

AWW:YOI   Alfred W. Wills

BEFORE YOU BEGIN

You are now ready to begin working on the one hundred letters.

The first step to be taken is to look at the Master Spelling List (p. 24) and the list of two-letter state abbreviations (p. 26) so that you can check for the correct spellings.

Each group of letters is preceded by a word list which contains words which occur for the first time in the letters. Study these words, using the section on spelling for hints on how to remember spelling "demons." While you are making the corrections in the letters, refer to these lists if you are not certain of the spelling of a word. If the word does not appear on the spelling lists, check your dictionary immediately.

As you can see, each letter is numbered so that you can easily find the corrected letter with the same number in the back of the book. Each line of the letter is numbered, too, to make the checking easier for you.

When you are ready to begin Letter 1, tear out the page at the perforation.

Make corrections in pencil. Write the corrections above the error carefully and legibly. You will have to read your own corrections.

Check your corrections with the corrected letters in the back of the book. If there are additional corrections to be made, write them on the original letter in ink or with a colored pencil. By writing the additional corrections in ink or with a colored pencil, you will be able to see how many errors you did not find the first time. Keep score of the number of overlooked errors. These should decrease as you progress throughout the book. If your score does not improve, work more slowly and carefully. Review the Master Spelling List, the word lists which precede each group of letters, and the section on How To Proofread Successfully. If you are not finding missing **ed** endings, apostrophe errors, or punctuation errors, review the rules for their correct use and do the exercises once again.

Type the letter correctly, using one of the acceptable letter styles. Proofread carefully before you remove the letter from the typewriter. It is much easier to make corrections if the paper has not been removed from the machine. Proofread by reading out loud, letter by letter, word by word, and line by line. If you cannot read the letter out loud, say the individual letters to yourself so that your mind can "hear" them.

If you follow all of these steps, you should have letters that are really *letter-perfect*.

The Types of Errors You Must Look For

In order to assist you to find errors, the following listing of the types of errors in each part of the letter should be used as a guide:

Date

Check the spelling of the month.
Make sure that there is a comma between the date and the year.

Inside Address

Check to see that the first word has a period if it is an abbreviation (**Ms., Mrs., Messrs., Dr.**) but no period if it is not an abbreviation (**Miss**).

Many of the streets are city or state names. Check to see that they are spelled correctly.

Check to see that the city is spelled correctly and that there is a comma before the state and none after it.

Check to see that the two-letter state abbreviation is correct and that there is no period after it.

Salutation

Make sure that the salutation agrees with the first line of the inside address. (If there is a variation, assume that the correct word or abbreviation is in the inside address and not in the salutation.)

Make sure that the words are capitalized correctly (**Dear Sir:, My dear Sir:**).

If there is an *attention notice,* make sure that the salutation is **Gentlemen**.

Check to see that a colon follows the salutation.

Body of the Letter

Use the checklist in the section on How To Proofread Successfully.

In addition, check to see that dates and amounts agree. (If there is a variation, assume that the date or amount which appears first is the correct one.)

Complimentary Close

Check to see that each word is spelled and capitalized correctly.

Note that the comma is optional after the complimentary close and may or may not be included.

Firm Name

If there is a firm name, check the spelling of each word.
Check to see that the firm name is in solid capital letters.

Typewritten Signature and Title

Check to see that each word is spelled correctly.

Check the punctuation. If the typewritten signature and the title are on the same line, they must be separated by a comma. If they are on separate lines, the comma after the typewritten signature is optional.

Note that the word **Mr.** does not appear in the typewritten signature.

Identifying Initials

Check to see that the dictator's initials are the same as the initials in the name in the typewritten signature.

Note that sometimes the dictator's initials are omitted. This is an acceptable style and should not be considered an error.

Note that in all of the letters **YOI** is an abbreviation for *your own initials.* Substitute your own initials for **YOI**.

Enclosures

If there is an enclosure, make sure that there is an *enclosure notation.*

If there is no enclosure and there is an *enclosure notation,* it is incorrect, and the enclosure notation should be eliminated.

If the word is spelled **enclosing, enclosed,** or **enclosure** in the body of the letter, the enclosure must be spelled with either a small or a capital **E** when it appears under the initials.

If the word is spelled **inclosing, inclosed,** or **inclosure** in the body of the letter, the inclosure must be spelled with either a small or a capital **I** when it appears under the initials.

If the expression in the body of the letter is **Attached** or **We are sending you with this letter,** the enclosure may be spelled with either an **e** or an **i.** However, the **e** spelling for **enclosure** is preferred.

It is permissible to abbreviate the enclosure notation; but the abbreviation, like all abbreviations, must end with a period. The following are all acceptable abbreviations:

Examples: Enc.   Encl.   enc.   encl.   Inc.   Incl.   inc.   incl.

Word List—Letters 1–10

The words on this list occur in Letters 1-10. Following the suggestions for learning how to spell words, study the spelling of these words before correcting letters. When correcting the letters, refer to this list. If you are not sure of the spelling of a word and it does not appear on this list, be sure to consult your dictionary immediately. The starred (*) words are repeated in the Words Often Confused section of this list. Brief definitions are given, and the part of speech is indicated in parentheses.

advantage	customer	know*	personnel*	their*
advice*		merchandise	privilege	then*
advise*	decided		products	there*
also	dissatisfied	ninth	promptly	therefore
always		no*		to*
appreciate	February		receive	too*
	find*	occasions	recent*	truly
bargains	fine*	of course	resent*	two*
beginning	friend	opportunity		
believe	further	organization	sincerely	usually
benefit			some*	
	hear*	passed*	sum*	whenever
choose	helpful	past*		
committee	here*	personal*	than*	

Words Often Confused

advice (n.)—a suggestion
advise (v.)—to recommend

find (v.)—to discover by chance; opposite of *lose*
fine (adj.)—superior in quality

hear (v.)—to listen
here (adv.)—in this place; opposite of *there*

know (v.)—to be certain of
no (adv.)—not so; opposite of *yes*
    (adj.)—not any, not one

passed (v.)—gone by; exceeded; past tense of the verb *to pass*
past (adj.)—finished; done with; over; ended

personal (adj.)—concerning a particular person; not general or public
personnel (n.)—persons employed in a business

recent (adv.)—modern; fresh; new
resent (v.)—to be indignant at

some (adj.)—moderate; limited in degree or amount
sum (n.)—entire quantity

than (conj.)—when, as, or if compared with
then (adv.)—at that time

their (pron. adj.)—the possessive case of the pronoun *they*
there (adv.)—in, at, or about that place; opposite of *here*
they're—contraction for *they are*

to (prep.)—in a direction toward
too (adv.)—in addition; also; excessive
two (n.)—the sum of one and one

1

2   Febuery 8, 19--

3   Mr. Fred Kelley

4   439 Illinoise Avenue

5   Chicargo, IL   60601

6   My Dear Mr. Kelly:

7   Do you thing it might be a good idea to solve the prolbems of

8   of the world? If so, come to teh nest meeting of our organazation.

9   We woud consider it a priviledge if you would bring a freind. We no

10 that you will both have a good time, and we allso think that our mem-

11 members allways learn someting.

12   We sometimes give advise where it is needed, and we fine thta

13 our members do not recent the words of wisdom which they here at teh

14 monthly meetings. Of cause, if you cannot be there promply, try to

15 come when ever you are able to do so. We look forward to seeing you

16 often, and we hope taht we will here from you telling us that you are

17 going to be the at next gatherin.

18   Yours truely,

19   WORLD PROLBEMS, INC.

20 AE:YOI   Albert D. Evans

21

22

23

24

25

26

1

2   . Febuary 18, 19--

3   Miss Judith Brown

4   1492 Niagra Falls Avenue

5   Buffallo, NY   14202

6   Dear Miss. Browne:

7   It woud be very fortunate and helpfull if you could work for us

8   during the Christmas season. We usully have a sale than, and we need as

9   as much help aswe can get. On some occassions, we call on retired men

10   and woman, but this year we have desided to look for younger persons.

11   We are, threfore, writing to you to ask if you woud be willing to

12   to be at our store on thursday nights during the months of December.

13   Their are many benifits to be gained from being their, and we hope

14   hope you will take avantage of all of them. For example, you can buy

15   many of our producks at a find discount. Of cause, you can chose

16   them after you have looked at all our merchandize.

17   Sincerly Yours,

18   MARTIN'S DEPARTMENT STORE

19   JM:YOI   Jack Mason,

20   Personal Department

21

22

23

24

25

26

1

2   Febuary 9, 19--

3   Miss Joan Flowers

4   454 Nineth Avenue

5   Los Angoles, CA   90003

6   Dear Mrs. Flowers:

7   I no that you will fine it a pleasure and a priviledge to shop

8   at our store becuse we have many bargins. We have a find selection

9   of clocks and watchs, and I belive you will want to pick up one or

10 to the nex time you are in in our store.

11   Whenever you come in, you will be mor then welcome becuase our

12 salesman treat there costumers very well. We thing you will apprecite

13 what we have to offer since we try very hard to stock a line of mer-

14 chandize which is attractive in every way.

15   Come in promptly and give yourselves a treat. We beleive taht

16 you will want to take our advise and buy a watch or clock.

17   Sincerly your,

18   ROTH JEWELRY STORE

19 JR:YOI   James A. Roth

20   Pressident

21

22

23

24

25

26

1

2   Febuery 3, 19--

3   Mr. John Brown

4   14 Minnisota Avenue

5   Mineapolis, MN   55404

6   Dear Dr. Browne:

7   We are veyr sorry that resently you were disatisfied with

8   with the treatment you recieved at our Mineapolis store.

9   In the passed we have alwasy considered it a privelege to serve

10   you becusase we honestly beleive that we have the findest merchandize

11   available inthis sity. We no tha t you agree with us because we have

12   checked our records and note that you have usualy taken avantage of our

13   special bargin days in the months of Febuery and March. Of cause, we

14   hope that you will continue to do so. We now have a new selection of

15   of find clothing on sale begining nest Monday, Febuary 10.

16   We shall investi gate the rudeness of one of are salesman. Since

17   our Personal Deaprtment gives full training to our salesmen on how to

18   treat costumers, we are upset that she treated you reudely.

19   As soon as we have completed our investigation, you shall here

20   from us. In the meantime, we are enclosin a special listing of sum

21   of the itmes which will be on sale.

22   Yours Truely,

23   ADAMS DEPARTMENT STORES

24   JB:YOI   James Adams

25   Custommer Service

26

1

2   Febuery 6, 19--

3   Mrs Kay Welles

4   245 Connecticutt Avenu

5   Hardfort, CT   06105

6   Dear Miss Wells,

7   Their is an espression that you can allways depend upon your

8   freinds for good advise.

9   I bleieve that you have been shoping at my store for so long

10   long that you consider me a freind. I no that I feel thatway about

11   you. I am, therfore, giving advise too you now.

12   If you shop at the store befor the end of Febuery, you will be

13   able to chose many table linens at bargin prices. During this season

14   of the ear, their are many occassion which you like to celebrate by

15   having a small dinner party for to or three freinds. We have new

16   cloths with matching napkins in various colors adn size. The patter-

17   ns are even more attractive than those we have carried in tsock in teh

18   resent passed.

19   I woud advice you to visit the store promptly so that you can

20   can chose what you need while we have a cojplete stock. Even if you

21   deside that you donot want to buy anything at thsi time, please stop

22   in to visit me. We will have a freindly chat.

23   Sincerely your,

24   DAVIS LINEN SHOP

25   VAD:YOI   Vera Davis

26

1

2   Febuery 1, 19--

3   Mrs. Alice Sharp

4   2345 Wisconcin Avenue

5   Raseen, WI   53406

6   Dear Miss Sharpe:

7   We have jus recieved a letter from Mr Herbert Black, advicing us

8   that you have resently purchased a house in Milwakee and will be movi-

9   ng to our city withing the nest too monthes. Of cause, we wish to

10   to welcom you and to wish you many hears of happyness in your home.

11   As Mr. Blake may have tole you, we are the oldest bank in the

12   city, and we invite you to become a depositor as soon as possible.

13   You will fine that their are many benifits to be gained by doing you

14   banking business with you. You can chose from many different types of

15   accounts. We have a special savings account which gives you interest

16   from the first of teh month if you deposit you money by the nineth. We

17   have too different kinds of personnel checkin accounts that are real

18   bargins, to.

19   Our entire organzation will allways be in a possession to offer

20   offer you freindly advise. All our personal in every department will

21   be helpfull, and we hope that you will deside to take advantige of

22   there expert opinions after you have moved into you new home.

23   Sincerly your,

24   FIRST FEDERAL BANK

25   TS:YOI   Thomas A. Smith, President

26

1

2   Mya 6, 19--

3   Mr. Robert Nelson

4   4725 Nerbraska Avenue

5   Linclon, NE   68507

6   Dear Dr. Nelson:

7   I should like to take tihs oportunity to invite you to become

8   a sponsor of our annual benifit concert wich will be held on Munday,

9   Februery 12, at the Municipal Opera House. Details of the consert

10 are enclosed with this letter.

11   I sincerely beleive that you will recieve great pleasure on this

12 this occassion. After teh comitee desided to have a concert to raise

13 funds for cultural activities, it wuz difficult to chose the artists

14 who would preform. Therfore, the comittee asked the advise of the

15 National Opera Society, the largest such organixation in this area.

16   The personal in there offices, freindly as usul, helped by cons-

17 ulting the schedules of sum of there famous artists. They adviced

18 us of the availability of John Thomas and Ella Browning. Of cause, we

19 we promply got in tuch with there agents, and contracts for this joint

20 recital hav been signed. It will be a priviledge to here these too

21 find artists becusase they have never appeared together in this city.

22   You will fine that the advantiges of being a sponsor are many.

23 In the first place, you will be intitled to too tickets in the orc-

24 hestra. You can allso secure tickets fro you family and freinds

25 before teh sale of tickets the to general public. You will recieve

26 the ticket locations well in advance, and if you are disatisfied in

27   any way, tthe tickets can be exchanged for seats in another section of

28   the Opera House. Secondly, sponsors are invited to the suppr whitch

29   will follow teh concert.

30   Please let us here from you promptly so that we can be sure to

31   include you name on teh printed program.

32   I no that you will want to join the many other outstanding citis-

33   ens of the city who are allways willing to do more then their share in

34   supporting the cultural activities wich we think truely make this a

35   a wonderful city in which to live.

36   I hope you will take advantige of this special oportunity to

37   render service to our city.

38   Yours Sincerly,

39   LINCLON CULTURAL COMITTEE

40   MJ   Mary A. Johnstone

41   Chairperson

42

43

44

45

46

47

48

49

50

51

52

1

2   Februery 1, 19--

3   Mrs. Helen Morse

4   398 Conneticutt Avenue

5   Waterberry, CT   06708

6   Dear Mr. Morse:

7   People rarely recent advise about how to save money, and that is

8   why I am takin the liberty of writing too you. Our records show that

9   you have not shopped atour store for almost to years although befor

10 that time you shopped often in many of our department.

11   I am, therefor, writing to you to urge you to tak the advise of

12 the manager of our Fancy Food Department, Mrs. Gladys Smith. She say

13 that the items in that department is better then ever befor. You will

14 be able to fine all the famous brands allways carried their. You also

15 will fine that their are new bands, and you will now have a wider sele-

16 ction form which to choose then ever befor. The advantige of shopping

17 before to much time has past is that you will benifit from low prices.

18 Miss Smith aksed us to write you to tell you that the bargin prices you

19 will fine will save you more money then you would think possible. Of

20 cause, the personnel advise that she gives will be helpfull, to.

21   I believ that know other Fancy Food Department can mach ours for

22 the high quality of the merchendise and the low prices.

23   Your truely,

24   WATERBURY DEPARTMENT STOR

25 EW:YOI   Edgar Waters, Manger

26

1

2   March 8, 19--

3   Mister Richard Defranco

4   89 Pensylvania Avenue

5   Pittsburg, PA   15209

6   Dear Mr. De Franco:

7   I am writing this letter in answer to you letter of Febuary 27

8   concerning you disatisfaction with the merchandize you ordered from

9   the Amerigo Distributing Company. We have written to taht company on

10   on many occassions in the passed, but the company has never responded

11   to our letters. Sinse there offices are not in this city, we have

12   have no way of taking furthur action.

13   If you deside that you would like to bring this situation to teh

14   attention of the authorities, we belive that the bes way to do this is

15   to write to the Attorney General in Harrisburgh. We hav done so, and

16   he has assured us that she is doin all taht he legally can.

17   It is the advise of our organzation that consumers shoud be more

18   careful befor buying merchandize from a company about whom they no

19   nothing. We beleive, to, that it is generally too your advantige to

20   see what youare buying rather then to depend only on literature.

21   It is allways a privelege for our organzation to be helpfull. I

22   am sorry that we can do little in thsi instance.

23   Yours Very Truely,

24   FEDERAL BUSINESS BUREAU

25   YOI:JM   Jane Milton, Legal Department

26

1

2   February 12th, 19--

3   Mr. Louis Rivera

4   876 Massachusettes Avenue

5   Springfeild, MA   01110

6   Dear Mr. Rivers:

7   I am very much pleased that you desided to buy your new color

8   television set at our store. I am sincerly happy taht you allways

9   allways choose to buy your radios and television sets hear.

10   We no that personnel service is important to please our freinds.

11   Taht is why we aks you to call our Service Department promptly if you

12   are in any way disatisfied with our producks. This benifits us bec-

13   ause we than can fine the cause for the unappiness and remedy it. Un

14   Unless we here from you promply, we cannot no that their is anything

15   wrong. We, therefor, ask you to advice us when their is the slightes

16   difficult wit any of you pruchases.

17   It gives me great satisfaction to no that you are such a regular

18   costumer. I am enclosing to copies of the service contract. As you

19   can see, there are know changes in the benefts to be gained by chosing

20   Plan A, and it is my advise thatyou chose this plan rather then Plan B.

21   After you have desided which plan you want, please sign one copy and

22   retrun it to me promply. The second copy is fro you.

23   Very truly your,

24   MASSACHUSETTES RADIO SHACK

25   JAB   John Burrell, Manger

26

VERB ENDINGS

Very often errors are made because the writer or typist is unsure of whether certain words must end in **ed**. To help you avoid making these errors, this section contains rules and examples of sentences in which **ed** endings may or may not be needed.

Here are two simple rules which will help you decide when an **ed** ending is required:

Rule 1: When there is a verb which has a helping word or helping words such as, "is, are, may be, will be, was, were, has, have, had," the verb must add an **ed.**

    Examples: I have checked.   It was finished.   It may be planned.

Rule 2: With regular verbs, the past tense showing action that was started and completed in the past ends with **ed.**

    Examples: I shall check this now.   BUT: I checked it last night.
                I shall finish it soon.   BUT: I finished it yesterday.

Beginning with Letter 11, there will be words with missing **ed** endings. Before you correct the letters, complete the following exercises to make sure that you understand the rules and can apply them. After you have completed the exercises, check them with the corrected copy. If you have made errors, study the rules again, and do the exercises once more.

If, when checking your letters, you see that you are making errors with the **ed** ending, review the rules, and do the exercises once more.

DIRECTIONS: Cross out the **incorrect form of the verb** in each of the
              following sentences:

1. I have (finish, finished) this job.

2. I may (check, checked) your work.

3. This has to be (plan, planned) very carefully.

4. I will (furnish, furnished) the information.

5. I have (turn, turned) the work in to my teacher.

6. I shall (study, studied) my lesson well.

7. I have (study, studied) my lessons.

8. I may (walk, walked) there soon.

9. I have (walk, walked) there.

10. I (work, worked) there last Saturday.

11. I have (work, worked) there on Saturdays.

12. I (stop, stopped) at her house the day before yesterday.

13. I (step, stepped) off the train yesterday.

14. I have (step, stepped) off the platform many times.

15. I was all (choke, choked) up.

16. We have (return, returned) home.

17. The books may be (return, returned) soon.

18. Jack (learn, learned) his lesson well.

19. I have (burn, burned) my hand on the matches.

20. She (stamp, stamped) her foot in anger.

21. I may (stamp, stamped) the envelope.

22. I have (groan, groaned) at the decision.

23. She (talk, talked) with him yesterday.

24. She will (talk, talked) with him today.

25. She (cross, crossed) the street.

26. She (passed, past) the test.

27. Have you (spell, spelled) these words correctly?

28. She (sprain, sprained) her foot.

29. I (mark, marked) your paper yesterday.

30. I shall (mark, marked) your paper today.

31. She (stop, stopped) her at the door.

32. I may (step, stepped) in with my cousin.

33. We (talk, talked) with him yesterday.

34. We have (cross, crossed) that bridge many times.

35. He has (complete, completed) the book.

36. She has (enter, entered) the room quietly.

37. Last year the children (learn, learned) how they were (suppose, supposed) to act.

38. On my first day at work, I was (suppose, supposed) to find the supervisor before I could be (assign, assigned) to my job.

39. During the winter, people (use, used) to (line, lined) up to punch their time cards five minutes before quitting time. Then the boss (crack, cracked) down, and they had to wait until 5 o'clock.

40. While I was getting into my uniform, my shoelace (snap, snapped). I (tie, tied) the broken ends together, but the loose shoe (annoy, annoyed) me throughout the game.

41. Richard (notice, noticed) the sign of a fortuneteller in a window, and he (decide, decided) to have his fortune told.

42. It may be said that Chicago was (settle, settled) in 1803 when Fort Dearborn was (establish, established) on the river.

43. As a Boy Scout, Bill (work, worked) hard to get his badges, and at last he (receive, received) the awards he (earn, earned).

44. We have (learn, learned) many things this term.

45. Yesterday I (check, checked) my work; today it will not be necessary to (check, checked) it.

46. Tomorrow I may (look, looked) at the book; an hour ago I (look, looked) at the bulletin.

47. I (pass, passed) my driving test last Tuesday.

48. I have (pass, passed) my driving test, and now I have my license.

49. I may (pass, passed) my driving test when I take it tomorrow.

50. I (doubt, doubted) his word last week, and now I am sorry.

51. When I (arrive, arrived) at school yesterday, I (pass, passed) my teacher in the hall.

52. Last Thursday I (talk, talked) to him, but I do not think I shall ever (talk, talked) to him again.

53. Why didn't you come to school yesterday when I (ask, asked) you to do so?

54. Many times I have (ask, asked) him to be on time, but he is always late.

55. I should have (look, looked) at this paper more carefully.

56. I (walk, walked) to work yesterday, but I do not think I will (walk, walked) tomorrow.

57. According to that old dog, it was too late to (learn, learned) new tricks.

58. He (learn, learned) some new tricks.

59. I have (learn, learned) many new jokes, but I have to (check, checked) them with my friend before I tell them.

60. He (jump, jumped) over the hurdles and won the track meet for his school.

61. When do you think that you will have (purchase, purchased) the goods?

1. I have (~~finish,~~ finished) this job.

2. I may (check, ~~checked~~) your work.

3. This has to be (~~plan,~~ planned) very carefully.

4. I will (furnish, ~~furnished~~) the information.

5. I have (~~turn,~~ turned) the work in to my teacher.

6. I shall (study, ~~studied~~) my lesson well.

7. I have (~~study,~~ studied) my lessons.

8. I may (walk, ~~walked~~) there soon.

9. I have (~~walk,~~ walked) there.

10. I (~~work,~~ worked) there last Saturday.

11. I have (~~work,~~ worked) there on Saturdays.

12. I (~~step,~~ stopped) at her house the day before yesterday.

13. I (~~step,~~ stepped) off the train yesterday.

14. I have (~~step,~~ stepped) off the platform many times.

15. I was all (~~choke,~~ choked) up.

16. We have (~~return,~~ returned) home.

17. The books may be (~~return,~~ returned) soon.

18. Jack (~~learn,~~ learned) his lesson well.

19. I have (~~burn,~~ burned) my hand on the matches.

20. She (~~stamp,~~ stamped) her foot in anger.

21. I may (stamp, ~~stamped~~) the envelope.

22. I have (~~groan,~~ groaned) at the decision.

23. She (~~talk,~~ talked) with him yesterday.

24. She will (talk, ~~talked~~) with him today.

25. She (~~cross~~, crossed) the street.

26. She (passed, ~~past~~) the test.

27. Have you (~~spell~~, spelled) these words correctly?

28. She (~~sprain~~, sprained) her foot.

29. I (~~mark~~, marked) your paper yesterday.

30. I shall (mark, ~~marked~~) your paper today.

31. She (~~stop~~, stopped) her at the door.

32. I may (step, ~~stepped~~) in with my cousin.

33. We (~~talk~~, talked) with him yesterday.

34. We have (~~cross~~, crossed) that bridge many times.

35. He has (~~complete~~, completed) the book.

36. She has (~~enter~~, entered) the room quietly.

37. Last year the children (~~learn~~, learned) how they were (~~suppose~~, supposed) to act.

38. On my first day at work, I was (~~suppose~~, supposed) to find the supervisor before I could be (~~assign~~, assigned) to my job.

39. During the winter, people (~~use~~, used) to (line, ~~lined~~) up to punch their time cards five minutes before quitting time. Then the boss (~~crack~~, cracked) down, and they had to wait until 5 o'clock.

40. While I was getting into my uniform, my shoelace (~~snap~~, snapped). I (~~tie~~, tied) the broken ends together, but the loose shoe (~~annoy~~, annoyed) me throughout the game.

41. Richard (~~notice~~, noticed) the sign of a fortuneteller in a window, and he (~~decide~~, decided) to have his fortune told.

42. It may be said that Chicago was (~~settle~~, settled) in 1803 when Fort Dearborn was (~~establish~~, established) on the river.

43. As a Boy Scout, Bill (~~work~~, worked) hard to get his badges, and at last he (~~receive~~, received) the awards he (~~earn~~, earned).

44. We have (~~learn~~, learned) many things this term.

45. Yesterday I (~~check~~, checked) my work; today it will not be necessary to (check, ~~checked~~) it.

46. Tomorrow I may (look, ~~looked~~) at the book; an hour ago I (~~look~~, looked) at the bulletin.

47. I (~~pass~~, passed) my driving test last Tuesday.

48. I have (~~pass~~, passed) my driving test, and now I have my license.

49. I may (pass, ~~passed~~) my driving test when I take it tomorrow.

50. I (~~doubt~~, doubted) his word last week, and now I am sorry.

51. When I (~~arrive~~, arrived) at school yesterday, I (~~pass~~, passed) my teacher in the hall.

52. Last Thursday I (~~talk~~, talked) to him, but I do not think I shall ever (talk, ~~talked~~) to him again.

53. Why didn't you come to school yesterday when I (~~ask~~, asked) you to do so?

54. Many times I have (~~ask~~, asked) him to be on time, but he is always late.

55. I should have (~~look~~, looked) at this paper more carefully.

56. I (~~walk~~, walked) to work yesterday, but I do not think I will (walk, ~~walked~~) tomorrow.

57. According to that old dog, it was too late to (learn, ~~learned~~) new tricks.

58. He (~~learn~~, learned) some new tricks.

59. I have (~~learn~~, learned) many new jokes, but I have to (check, ~~checked~~) them with my friend before I tell them.

60. He (~~jump~~, jumped) over the hurdles and won the track meet for his school.

61. When do you think that you will have (~~purchase~~, purchased) the goods?

Word List—Letters 11–20

The words on this list occur for the first time in Letters 11-20. Following the suggestions for learning how to spell words, study the spelling of these words before correcting the letters. When correcting the letters, refer to this list and to the list preceding Letters 1-10. If you are not sure of the spelling of a word, be sure to consult your dictionary immediately. The starred (*) words are repeated in the Words Often Confused section of this list. Brief definitions are given, and the part of speech is indicated in parentheses.

Some dictionaries give alternate spellings for the words indicated with a plus sign (+). These alternate spellings are shown on this page. However, when these words are given in the letters, use the spelling on the list since this is the preferred spelling.

absence	add*	edition*	loose*	recommend
accept*	addition*	equipment	lose*	shipped
acceptance	almost	familiar		similar
accidentally	amount		manufacturer	so*
accommodate	appointment	hoping		stationery*
accordance		immediately	necessary	substantial
accuracy	cannot+	interest	ninety	
achievement	catalog+		possible	undoubtedly
acknowledgment+	convenient	January	premium	
across	cordially	judgment+	probably	weather*
ad*	correspondence	library	receipt	Wednesday
				whether*

Words Often Confused

accept (v.)—to receive with favor
except (prep.)—with the exclusion of

ad (n.)—an advertisement
add (v.)—to join or unite

addition (n.)—an increase
edition (n.)—the form in which a literary work is published

loose (adj.)—not fastened; opposite of *tight*
lose (v.)—to part with and be unable to find; opposite of *find*

sew (v.)—to make with needle and thread
so (adv.)—to this or that extent

stationary (adj.)—remaining in one place; standing still
stationery (n.)—writing paper and envelopes

weather (n.)—atmospheric condition of temperature and moisture
whether (conj.)—in case; if

Alternate Spellings

Preferred	*Acceptable*
acknowledgment	acknowledgement
cannot	can not
catalog	catalogue
judgment	judgement

1

2   Januery 21, 19--

3   Pitsburgh Paper Company

4   62 Pensylvania Street

5   Philedelphia, PA   19111

6   Gentlemen:

7   We are the in market for some new stationary. Please send us a

8   a copy of your lastest catolog. We no that it is ver impotant to have

9   new equiptment, but we allso think it is nesessary to give a good ima

10   ge to the public. We, therfore, hope that new paper for our cores-

11   pondance will be helpfull.

12   After you have shipped us your catolog, we shall be able to deside

13   weather or not we can use your producks. If we can do sew, we will get

14   in tuch with you immediatly. We woud apreciate it if you answered us

15   as soon as posible because we usuelly need a substancial ammount of

16   paper at this time of the year, and we are dissatisfied with what we

17   we have on hand.

18   Very Sincerely yours,

19   GENERAL SUPPLY COMPANY

20   JD:YOI   James Brown

21   Manger

22

23

24

25

26

1

2   Februery 4, 19--

3   Springfeild Insurance Company

4   444 Illinoise Street

5   Chicargo, IL   60612

6   Gentlemen:

7   I am enclosin the policy you send me last monthe. I have look

8   at them very carefully, and I fine that it will not be suitable for

9   my needs. Allso, the premims are to high in my judgement.

10   Waht I am looking for is a policy wich will give me a substancial

11   income after I have retire. The policy you send me did not have the

12   provisions I am seeking, and I am, therefor, returning it to you at

13   this time. Please have your agent call me so that we can make a

14   apointment to discuss what I have in mind. I can see him at any time

15   that is convient for him during the next week or to.

16   In edition, one of my partners expressed an intrest in a similiar

17   policy, and we can both recieve the advise of your agent at the same

18   time.

19   Cordialy yours,

20   WORTH & CHAMBERS

21   JW:YOI   James B. Worth

22   Treasurer

23

24

25

26

1

2   Aprill 3, 19--

3   Mister Theodore Johnson

4   145 Ohhio Street

5   Clevland, OH   44113

6   My Dear Miss Johnsen:

7   You are cordialy invite to a anniversary luncheon at the the

8   American Hotel on Wensday, Febuary 5. This lunchen will be held to

9   celebrate the organzation of our club and its achievments throughout

10   the years.

11   At thsi affair, we are, of cause, hopping to have a very good

12   time. I no that you will be able to see sum of you freinds at that

13   time. Therfore, undoubtdly you will want to go.

14   The price of the ticket si only $15, and thsi includes the meal,

15   checking, and tipping. Please reply as soon as posible becuase we

16   expect more then one hundred resopnses to tihs letter. You are pr-

17   obabley familar with the fact that wen we had a similiar affair five

18   year ago, we were unable to acommodate all who want to come. Therfore,

19   we woud reccommend that you answer promply. We will send you a

20   acknowldegment and you reciet by return mail.

21   Yours turly,

22   WAS:YOI   Walter Scott

23   Pres dent

24

25

26

1

2   Juen 4, 19--

3 Ms. Shirley Rogers

4 4372 Calafornia Lane

5 San Fransisco, CA   94114

6 Dear Mrs. Rogers:

7   We are planning an exhibit of the works of teh noted Calafornia

8 artist, John Fischer. He has reccommend you to write the cataloge of

9 teh exhibit, and we hope you will except this invitation.

10   Mr. Fisher says that you are well aware his of achievments and

11 and beleives that you woudl be the pest posible art critic to do thsi

12 work for us.

13   The exibition wil be in the University Libary during the month

14 of Januery and Febuary. We anticipate a substancial ammount of int-

15 rest in the ehxibit becuse it is the judgement of many gallery owners

16 that Mr. Fischer has outstanding talent.

17   I woud appriciate it if you would sent me a letterof acceptence

18 or telephone me as soon as posible. Upon reciept of word form you,

19 we can set up a apointment allmost immediatly sew that we can fill you

20 in on the details of the exhibit and waht we would like include in the

21 cataloge. I need not ad that this apointment will be hel at a time

22 mutually convient. I hope to here from you shortly.

23   Your sincerely,

24   CALAFORNIA ART STUDIOS

25 WD:YOI   William Davis

26

1

2   October 15, 19--

3   Johnson and Johnson

4   4576 Indianna Road

5   Indiannapolis, IN   46215

6   Dear Mr. Hojnson:

7   I am going to be working on the preparation of a new addition of

8   a book on styles of correspondance currently being use. I came acros

9   the name of you company in a add in a recent magazine, and I am, there-

10   fore, writing you for your judgement on the various kinds of stationary

11   now in use.

12   In the absense of one outstanding style of letter form, I belive

13   that the book shoud include samples of letterhead papre wich can be

14   use easily with all style.

15   Since you are a manufacture of paper which is use for cor-

16   respondance, I thought it woud be to me avantage to communicate with

17   with you. I have made inquiries in the field, and I donot have to ad

18   that you have a find reputation.

19   Please let me no weather you would be able to make a apointment

20   to see me promply. If not, can you recomend someone or some company

21   wich in you judgement might be helpfull. Since this is a job wich mus

22   be completed by nest Januery or Febuery, I am eager not to loose any

23   time. I should apreciate hering from you as quickly as possable.

24   Cordialy yours,

25   WISCONSAN PUBLISHING COMPANY

26   MF:YOI   Martin A. Fine, Editor

1

2   Januery 3, 19--

3   Dr. Ted Shanley

4   604 New Youk Avenue

5   Skenektady, NY   12314

6   Dear Mr.. Schanley:

7   I wish that we coud accomodate you request that we repair you

8   camera without charge, but we are unable todo sew. A examination of

9   of the camera indicates that it was probable drop accidently.

10   In acordance with the terms of your pruchase, equipement can be

11   repair at know charge only if the fault is wiht the manufacturor. In

12   this case, this is evidently not sew.

13   I woud recommend that you have the camera ship to us promply.

14   Our Service Department looses not time in checking cameras quickly and

15   with acuracy. Taht department will be albe to inform you wheather the

16   camera can be repair cheaply enough to warrant repair. If this can

17   not be done, they will adviceyou of this fact, to.

18   In you letter you wrote that you know lenger haveyou reciept. In

19   the absense of a reciept, we request that you send us a copy of your

20   check or something similiar so that we will no the date of purchase.

21   We are sory that we can not repair this camra without charge, but

22   we mus adhere to our usul policy.

23   Yous very truly,

24   TARGO CAMERA COMPANY

25   YOI   James Targo, Service Departtment

26

1

2   Febuery 28, 19--

3   Mrs William Crane

4   1235 Kantucky Street

5   Louieville, KY   40217

6   Dear Mrs. Williams:

7   Now that warmer whether is begining to cover a substancial section

8   of the country, you are probable thinkin of making editions to you

9   garden supplies.

10   We are encolsing a copy of our lates catolog of garden tools an

11   machinery. We reccommend that you look at it veyr carefully and order

12   whatever you need with out loosing any time. After you have look at

13   at the catolog, fill out the order blank. Ad $1 to the total only if

14   the supplies ordered come to less then $10. The merchandize will be

15   shiped so that you will be albe to recieve it intime to take care of

16   palanting you garden early.

17   In acordance with our usul policy, we shall sent you a refund

18   immediatly if you return any equiptment with wich you are dissatisfy.

19   We no that you hav been pleased with the items we have send you in the

20   passed, and we are hopping that you will have same the reaction wen you

21   order the new equipement.

22   Cordialy yours,

23   GRASSO GARDEN SUPPLY COMPANY

24   TG:YOI   Thomas Alex Grasso

25   Sales Manager

26

1

2   Juyl 5, 19--

3   Mr. Lee Kotter

4   251 Misouri Avenue

5   Saint Louis, MO   63118

6   Dear Mr Kottre:

7   To find out why you are dissatisfy with the acuracy of your watch

8   which you ship us last week, we have examine it carefully. A lose

9   mainspring is the cause of teh difficult. In the absense of any rep-

10   ort from you, we muss assume that the watch were damage accidently.

11   Although we donot usualy repair watches when the difficulty is

12   caused by a accident, we shall do sew in you case in order to accom-

13   odate you. We are doin this because you have been such a loyal cos-

14   tumer for many years. The repairs should be finish promply, and you

15   you shoud have the watch withing a week or to.

16   Wit this letter we are sending a you new addition of our price

17   list which we have just publish. This gives the prices of our new

18   line of clocks and watchs. We belive that you will fine that they

19   are better then ever from the point of you of style and price. We

20   thing it is a great achievment that we have been able to keep the

21   prices of are watches at the same level as in passed years. The

22   prices of material has gone up. Labor costs have allso been much

23   higher this year then in the past to years, but we are trying to hold

24   hold the line on priceas as much as possibel.

25   Needless to say, we apreciate you patronage and hope that we

26   will continue doing business with you for many years to come.

27   As in the passed, we shall offer the personnel touch wich we

28 have always bin able to give to you and to all our costumers. Although

29 our organzation is large, we allways try to act like the small, frei-

30 ndly firm that we were when we started more then ninty years ago.

31   Of cause, if you fine that you are not happy with your watch

32 after it has been return to you, please do not hesitate to let us no.

33   Allso, we woud apreciate it if you would examin our new price

34 list with care. Their may be some clocks or watches wich would just

35 meet your needs as gift items at tihs time.

36   Sincerly yours,

37   JASPER WATCH COMPANY

38 HAJ:YOI   Harold Jasper

39   Pressident

40

41

42

43

44

45

46

47

48

49

50

51

52

January 5, 19--

Swanson Hardware Company

4244 Hawaai Boulevard

Honolllulu, HA   96819

                    Attention: Mr. Robin Swanson

Dear Mr. Swanson:

     Of cause, we appriciate the business you have given us in the
resent passed, and we hope it will continue to grow. However, in checking our records, we note that their is a substancial ammount owing
ot us, $4,510.09. Our Accounts Payable Departtment has ask me to write
to you so taht you can check the acuracy of your records against ours.
The ammounts out standing have never aded to more then $2,000, and we
we are concern by this large increase.

     We no that the equippment we have shiped has allways please you
because you evidently sold it and reordered it. In edition, we have
rushed shipments to you on a emergency basis when ever you have re-
quisted us to do sew.

     Pleas send us a acknowledgement of this letter and a statement of
how soon you intend to settle this account of $4,510.08. Weather you
can pay us immediatly is unimportant. We would apreciate hearring
form you promply.

                              Cordially Yours,

JTH:YOI   Jeffrey Hartman,

                              Collection Manager

1

2   Janurary 4, 19--

3   Miss Sandra Colon, Personal Department

4   Bell Telephone System

5   623 Arazona Street

6   Phenix, AZ   85020

7   Dear Ms. Colon:

8   We certainly apreciate you willingness to acommodate a group of

9   35 pupils your at offices on Monday, Aprill 18. I no that our pupils

10   will benifit from this visit becase they wil see some of the modern

11   equipement which they have herd about in class but have not seen. They

12   are particularly interest in seeing the Corespondence Department since

13   most of the 36 pupils are preparing to be typists. In edition, the

14   film you usualy show'them in you libary will be most helpfull.

15   I beleive that you are familar wiht the type fo student we have

16   at our school becuse you have arrange similiar trips in the passed to

17   or three year. You will fine that they will asked your advise about

18   the Bell telephone System and the posibilities of job placement in you

19   offices. There skills are good, and I feel that they will make exc-

20   ellent employees.

21   In acordance with you request, we are filling out the acknowledge-

22   ment form for this visit and are enclosing it with thsi letter.

23   Sincerly yours,

24   HC:YOI   Hattie Chambers, Instructor

25   Incl.

26

THE APOSTROPHE

The incorrect use of the apostrophe is another frequently occurring error in business correspondence. In this section, the two uses of the apostrophe are explained, and examples are given. A thorough study of this section should help you avoid errors in the placement of apostrophes.

Beginning with Letter 21, some letters will have words with missing or incorrectly placed apostrophes. Before you correct the letters, complete the exercises which follow the rules to make sure that you understand the rules and can apply them. After you have completed the exercises, check them with the corrected copy. If you have made errors, study the rules again, and do the exercises once more.

If, when checking your letters, you see that you are making errors in the placement of apostrophes, review the rules, and do the exercises once more.

Rule 1. The apostrophe is used in contractions. It shows that a letter has been left out.
    Examples: don't represents do not
                  they're represents they are
                  let's represents let us
                  doesn't represents does not

Rule 2. The apostrophe is also used to indicate possession. Here is a simple way to learn how to place the apostrophe easily: Think of three key words: a. SIGNAL b. RESPONSE c. RESULT

    a. The SIGNAL is: When there are two consecutive nouns, the first of which ends in **s** (as in a secretarys day), an apostrophe will be needed.

    b. The RESPONSE is: Transpose or reverse the two nouns and separate them in your mind with of, of the, or belonging to.

        day of the secretary
                or
        day belonging to the secretary

    c. The RESULT is: Place the apostrophe after the last letter of the transposed word, and you are correct.

        a secretary's day

Other Examples

SIGNAL	RESPONSE	RESULT
the childrens books	the books of the children	the children's books
everybodys interest	the interest of everybody	everybody's interest

<u>Dickens novels</u>	novels <u>of</u> Dickens	<u>Dickens</u>' novels
mens coats	coats <u>belonging to</u> men	<u>men</u>'s coats
a <u>mans</u> voice	voice <u>of a</u> man	a <u>man</u>'s voice

NOTE: Sometimes the two nouns may be separated by an adjective. Just ignore the adjective. In the words "<u>this countrys outstanding citizens</u>," ignore the word "<u>outstanding</u>," and follow the same procedure as above.

SIGNAL	RESPONSE	RESULT
this <u>countrys</u> outstanding <u>citizens</u>	citizens <u>of this</u> country	this <u>country</u>'s outstanding citizens
the <u>mans</u> black <u>hat</u>	the hat <u>of the</u> man	the <u>man</u>'s black hat
the <u>worlds</u> tallest <u>building</u>	building <u>of the</u> world	the <u>world</u>'s tallest building

Cautions: Although the following pronouns are possessive, they are never written with an apostrophe: <u>ours</u>, <u>yours</u>, <u>hers</u>, <u>its</u>, <u>theirs</u>, <u>whose</u>.

Be careful of the following pairs of words:

<u>its</u>	possessive pronoun; no apostrophe
<u>it's</u>	contraction for <u>it is</u>; apostrophe needed
<u>theirs</u>	possessive pronoun; no apostrophe
<u>there's</u>	contraction for <u>there is</u>; apostrophe needed
<u>whose</u>	possessive pronoun; no apostrophe
<u>who's</u>	contraction for <u>who is</u>; apostrophe needed

DIRECTIONS: Cross out the incorrect form in each of the following
              sentences:

1. (Your, You're) perfectly right.

2. It could have been (her's, hers).

3. (Whose, Who's) going to tell him the results?

4. May I borrow (your, you're) hat?

5. It is all (yours, yours').

6. The cat raised (its, it's) injured paw for me to examine.

7. (There's, Theirs) no answer to that question.

8. They said that it was (our's, ours).

9. They just borrowed (your, you're) (father's, fathers') hammer.

10. May I know when (it's, its) time to watch the baseball game.

DIRECTIONS: The following sentences may or may not need apostrophes.
              After you have studied the rules for apostrophes, supply
              the missing apostrophes.

1. The childrens books were found on the radiator.

2. I believe that my two students essays were lost.

3. The three radio stations broadcasts were excellent.

4. We saw the boys at the game; their accounts of the ride were funny.

5. W. C. Fields movies are funny; the movies plots are also amusing.

6. The growth of the cities is discussed in Marys report.

7. Last Octobers weather was poor, but we hope that next October the
   rains will not be so heavy.

8. The womens clothing sale will take place on Mondays.

9. The salesmans reports were made at the meeting last night.

10. Five years sales are summarized on this sheet.

11. Tomorrows luncheon will take place at the Hilton Lounge.

12. I appreciate the salesmens interest in their behavior.

13. That ladys hat was bought for the Easter Parade.

14. I did what my teachers said, and I passed all my tests.

15. The artists paintings were beautiful, and he sold them for a high price.
16. Tomorrow is my twin daughters birthday, and they will celebrate it with a party.
17. That colleges faculty is interested in each students progress.
18. I bought two envelopes in the stationery store.
19. Help was given to the mens children.
20. Central High Schools new teams are doing well.
21. Womens styles change too frequently to suit my fathers budget.
22. Its just not right.
23. Didnt you just finish reading Dickens A TALE OF TWO CITIES?
24. Judge Jacksons verdict lowered the single prisoners hope, and Judge Jackson is considered a fair judge.
25. Wasnt it theirs?
26. Theyre my best buddys books.
27. Do our stores sell mens suits?
28. I heard a mans voice calling for help somewhere in the distance.
29. Did you say that this isnt a womans world?
30. The policemens whistles broke the stillness of the night.
31. All of the many applicants letters were carefully read.
32. This book discusses childrens games.
33. Two special citizens committees will hold meetings this evening.
34. We ask that many creditors claims be filed by February 12.
35. This debtors assets and liabilities are shown on the sheet.
36. Interest is added on all 5,000 depositors books on January 1.
37. All of our salespersons wages have been increased.
38. We ought to have that information at our fingers ends.
39. The company is now in its fortieth year.
40. We sell janitors supplies throughout the country.
41. We have inspected every retailers stock of shoes.
42. In this sale, we shall offer mens ties at special prices.
43. Please give me five minutes time.
44. A new nurses home is being built.
45. When you hear the operators voice, answer her immediately.
46. Please come to the salesmens meeting on February 10.

47. Subscribers telephone numbers are subject to change at any time.

48. Nearly all the stockholders were represented.

49. The annual stockholders meeting will be held next Tuesday.

50. I have joined the two taxpayers associations.

51. The checks were theirs.

52. Accuracy should be the first goal in every typists mind.

53. Have you signed the Visitors Book?

54. Two weeks vacation will do you a great deal of good.

DIRECTIONS: Many apostrophes are missing in the following paragraphs. After you have studied the rules for apostrophes, supply the missing apostrophes.

1. I am going to see a childrens play with the boys and girls. The girls interest is in a comedy, but the boys would prefer seeing a mystery. I hope the ladies and gentlemen who produce the play select a subject that meets everybodys interest.

2. In my opinion, a secretarys job is not difficult if she is willing to work with her employer and her fellow employees. The other employees preferences must be met if they have been working for the firm for a long time. The firms personnel department is interested in harmony on the job. The employers standards must be met, or he will not be happy with his secretary.

3. The company I work for has a liberal vacation policy. The companys procedure is to allow three weeks vacation after the first year and four weeks vacation after that. One weeks vacation was all I received on my first job.

4. Roberto Clementes death was very distressing to me. I remember seeing Clemente play in Pittsburghs ball park and also at Shea Stadium. He was the National Leagues most exciting player and, in addition, was one of this countrys outstanding citizens.

5. Mens barbershops are now getting as fancy as womens hairdressing establishments. New Yorks beauty parlors were always famous though Paris is considered the center of the worlds fashions.

6. Harold Jacksons store, which is the citys biggest store, is having
a sale next month to celebrate the companys 25th anniversary. The
stores hours will be longer, and the salesmens salaries will be increased. They will get two hours pay for every overtime hour and
an extra days vacation for all merchandise sold above their quota.
The prices of mens suits and boys overcoats have been reduced 40%.
Womens and girls clothing, as well as childrens and babies furniture, has also been marked down. Mr. Jackson says that every
customer will surely get his moneys worth.

7. Since New York is the countrys busiest port, problems relating to
freight shipments frequently come to the secretarys desk. If a
companys foreign trade is great, it may pay to use a freight service.
If not, it may be the shipping departments responsibility to handle
foreign as well as domestic shipments. At a traffic managers convention recently, it was pointed out that knowledge of shipping
forms was among the executive secretarys duties in any export-import
firm. Many shipping lines offices are helpful in supplying sample
forms and instructions.

8. The secretarys first day on a job will sometimes influence her
employers future attitude toward her. Her first weeks experience
will definitely tell him whether she is the person he needs. Here
are some facts which will help to insure that the employers decision
will be the right one.

9. During the personnel managers first talk with her, she should be sure
to find out what is covered in a days work. Is she expected to be
able to take several hours dictation at once? Is it the dictators
responsibility or hers to determine the accuracy of the correspondents
names and addresses? Is there a secretarys manual in the office?
(If it is a large company, there will probably be some kind of
secretarys guide to the companys rules and procedures.) When is a
callers insistence on seeing her employer to be given consideration?
Should she interrupt her employer if he were in the presidents office
or in the executives dining room?

1. (~~Your,~~ You're) perfectly right.

2. It could have been (~~her's,~~ hers).

3. (~~Whose,~~ Who's) going to tell him the results?

4. May I borrow (your, ~~you're~~) hat?

5. It is all (yours, ~~yours'~~).

6. The cat raised (its, ~~it's~~) injured paw for me to examine.

7. (There's, ~~Theirs~~) no answer to that question.

8. They said that it was (~~our's,~~ ours).

9. They just borrowed (your, ~~you're~~) (father's, ~~fathers'~~) hammer.

10. May I know when (it's, ~~its~~) time to watch the baseball game.

1. The children's books were found on the radiator.
2. I believe that my two students' essays were lost.
3. The three radio stations' broadcasts were excellent.
4. We saw the boys at the game; their accounts of the ride were funny.
5. W. C. Fields' movies are funny; the movies' plots are also amusing.
6. The growth of the cities is discussed in Mary's report.
7. Last October's weather was poor, but we hope that next October the rains will not be so heavy.
8. The women's clothing sale will take place on Mondays.
9. The salesman's reports were made at the meeting last night.
10. Five years' sales are summarized on this sheet.
11. Tomorrow's luncheon will take place at the Hilton Lounge.
12. I appreciate the salesmen's interest in their behavior.
13. That lady's hat was bought for the Easter Parade.
14. I did what my teachers said, and I passed all my tests.

15. The artist's paintings were beautiful, and he sold them for a high price.

16. Tomorrow is my twin daughters' birthday, and they will celebrate it with a party.

17. That college's faculty is interested in each student's progress.

18. I bought two envelopes in the stationery store.

19. Help was given to the men's children.

20. Central High School's new teams are doing well.

21. Women's styles change too frequently to suit my father's budget.

22. It's just not right.

23. Didn't you just finish reading Dickens' A TALE OF TWO CITIES?

24. Judge Jackson's verdict lowered the single prisoner's hope, and Judge Jackson is considered a fair judge.

25. Wasn't it theirs?

26. They're my best buddy's books.

27. Do our stores sell men's suits?

28. I heard a man's voice calling for help somewhere in the distance.

29. Did you say that this isn't a woman's world?

30. The policemen's whistles broke the stillness of the night.

31. All of the many applicants' letters were carefully read.

32. This book discusses children's games.

33. Two special citizens' committees will hold meetings this evening.

34. We ask that many creditors' claims be filed by February 12.

35. This debtor's assets and liabilities are shown on the sheet.

36. Interest is added on all 5,000 depositors' books on January 1.

37. All of our salespersons' wages have been increased.

38. We ought to have that information at our fingers' ends.

39. The company is now in its fortieth year.

40. We sell janitors' supplies throughout the country.

41. We have inspected every retailer's stock of shoes.

42. In this sale, we shall offer men's ties at special prices.

43. Please give me five minutes' time.

44. A new nurses' home is being built.

45. When you hear the operator's voice, answer her immediately.

46. Please come to the salesmen's meeting on February 10.

47. Subscribers' telephone numbers are subject to change at any time.
48. Nearly all the stockholders were represented.
49. The annual stockholders' meeting will be held next Tuesday.
50. I have joined the two taxpayers' associations.
51. The checks were theirs.
52. Accuracy should be the first goal in every typist's mind.
53. Have you signed the Visitors' Book?
54. Two weeks' vacation will do you a great deal of good.

1. I am going to see a children's play with the boys and girls. The girls' interest is in a comedy, but the boys would prefer seeing a mystery. I hope the ladies and gentlemen who produce the play select a subject that meets everybody's interest.

2. In my opinion, a secretary's job is not difficult if she is willing to work with her employer and her fellow employees. The other employees' preferences must be met if they have been working for the firm for a long time. The firm's personnel department is interested in harmony on the job. The employer's standards must be met, or he will not be happy with his secretary.

3. The company I work for has a liberal vacation policy. The company's procedure is to allow three weeks' vacation after the first year and four weeks' vacation after that. One week's vacation was all I received on my first job.

4. Roberto Clemente's death was very distressing to me. I remember seeing Clemente play in Pittsburgh's ball park and also at Shea Stadium. He was the National League's most exciting player and, in addition, was one of this country's outstanding citizens.

5. Men's barbershops are now getting as fancy as women's hairdressing establishments. New York's beauty parlors were always famous though Paris is considered the center of the world's fashions.

6. Harold Jackson's store, which is the city's biggest store, is having a sale next month to celebrate the company's 25th anniversary. The store's hours will be longer, and the salesmen's salaries will be increased. They will get two hours' pay for every overtime hour and an extra day's vacation for all merchandise sold above their quota. The prices of men's suits and boys' overcoats have been reduced 40%. Women's and girls' clothing, as well as children's and babies' furniture, has also been marked down. Mr. Jackson says that every customer will surely get his money's worth.

7. Since New York is the country's busiest port, problems relating to freight shipments frequently come to the secretary's desk. If a company's foreign trade is great, it may pay to use a freight service. If not, it may be the shipping department's responsibility to handle foreign as well as domestic shipments. At a traffic managers' convention recently, it was pointed out that knowledge of shipping forms was among the executive secretary's duties in any export-import firm. Many shipping lines' offices are helpful in supplying sample forms and instructions.

8. The secretary's first day on a job will sometimes influence her employer's future attitude toward her. Her first week's experience will definitely tell him whether she is the person he needs. Here are some facts which will help to insure that the employer's decision will be the right one.

9. During the personnel manager's first talk with her, she should be sure to find out what is covered in a day's work. Is she expected to be able to take several hours' dictation at once? Is it the dictator's responsibility or hers to determine the accuracy of the correspondents' names and addresses? Is there a secretary's manual in the office? (If it is a large company, there will probably be some kind of secretary's guide to the company's rules and procedures.) When is a caller's insistence on seeing her employer to be given consideration? Should she interrupt her employer if he were in the president's office or in the executives' dining room?

Word List—Letters 21–30

The words on this list occur for the first time in Letters 21-30. Following the suggestions for learning how to spell words, study the spelling of these words before correcting the letters. When correcting the letters, refer to this list and to the Master Spelling List (p.24). If you are not sure of the spelling of a word, be sure to consult your dictionary immediately. The starred (*) words are repeated in the Words Often Confused section of this list. Brief definitions are given, and the part of speech is indicated in parentheses.

adequate	bulletin	forward	miscellaneous	representative
advertising	buy*	future	mortgage	requirements
affect*	by*			responsible
agreeable		government	nevertheless	
allowances	certain	grateful		sufficient
allowed*		guarantee	occurred	surprised
already*	decision		one*	
annually	definite	independence		though
answered	describing	insurance	paid	through
arrangements	different	it's*	planning	
assistance*	disappoint	its*	pleasant	unpaid
assistants*	district		principal*	until
		may be*	principle*	
	effect*	maybe*		whose*
budget	expense	minimum	reasonable	

Words Often Confused

affect (v.)—to influence
effect (n.)—result
      (v.)—to cause; to accomplish

all ready (adj.)—prepared
already (adv.)—before or by this time

allowed (v.)—permitted to occur
aloud (adv.)—loudly; audibly

assistance (n.)—the act of helping
assistants (n.)—those who help

buy (v.)—to purchase
by (prep.)—next to

it's—contraction for *it is*
its (pron. adj.)—possessive case of *it*

may be (v.)—part of the verb *to be*
maybe (adv.)—perhaps

one (n.)—a single unit
won (v)—gained a victory

principal (adj.)—main; chief
      (n.)—head of a school
principle (n.)—a general rule, truth, or law

who's—contraction for *who is*
whose—possessive case of *who* or *which*

1

2   Januery 2, 19--

3   Midwest Manufacturerrs, Inc.

4   90 Ohhio Avenue

5   Cincinati, OH   45221

6   Dear Sir:

7   Im happy to except your production managers offer for me to visit

8   your organzation at the begining of next month. It can not be after

9   the nineth fo the month because I allready have urgent apointments in

10   Batton Rouge and Shreaveport the second week in Febuary. Wen I have

11   more deffinate plans, I sahall telephone you office to make the necesary

12   arrangments to to give you adaquate time ot be prepare from my visit.

13   I hope to see the new machinery wich you manufacture, and I no that

14   waht Ill see willnot disapoint me.

15   In the near futhure, we are planing to open some new offices ac-

16   cross the country, and we shall require sum new machines. We hope to

17   be abel to acquire them form you becuse we no that you are the manu-

18   facturers of som of the fines equiptment in this area.

19   Im certainly looking foward to seeing you. It will be a find

20   oportunity to talk furthe about this matter. I shall have my assistent,

21   Mr. Walter Burleigh, with me.

22   Yours truely

23   HELLER TOOL COMPANY

24   PH:YOI   Paul Heller, Vice-President

25

26

1

2   Febuary 21, 19--

3   Miss. Elsie Hellman

4   787 North Carolinna Street

5   Ralleigh, NC   27622

6   My Dear Miss. Hellman

7   Untill recent times, ti was impossibel to secure the services

8   of unapid assistent teachers, but now their are many young men an

9   woman amoung resent graduates who's intrest has been stimulated.

10   Its easy to see why colege graduates and studens would be eager

11   to help improve life in there communities. As a result, we think

12   that many wil apply for thes positosn.

13   I shoud appriciate it if you woud get in tuch with me when your

14   recieve this leter. I no that you maybe abel to fine the time to

15   speek to me soon, and we can than make arrangments to plan a program

16   the in near futhure.

17   Our childrens needs must be consider, and its my beleif that

18   this is a resonable method of filling there needs and those of teh

19   the resent graduates.

20   Sincerely your,

21   JSM:YOI   James W. Smith, Principle

22   Enclosure

23

24

25

26

1

2   Januery 4, 19--

3   Ms. Edith Mills

4   89 Road Island Street

5   Worchester, MA.   01623

6   Dear Ms. Miles:

7   We are begining a drive for new members in our organzation. Im

8   writin this letter to you hopping that you may be planing to joinn our

9   club at the minium new rate fo $9 a year.

10   Their are many advantiges to joinin this organzation. In the

11 first palce, you will injoy the company of many young people like you-

12 self. We have sum discussions at are meetings which take place allmost

13 every month, and youll have a chance to taek part. Then, club members

14 mmebers are allso entitle to discoounts wenever they want to go to

15 shows. For esample, a $5 ticket cost only $3.50 if you by it thru

16 the club.

17   A membership blank is enclose. Im sure youll want to join after

18 you have red waht we are sending you.

19   Very truly your,

20   AMERICAN LITERARY CLUB

21 GZ:YOI   Gerald Supp

22 Inclosure   Membership Chairmen

23

24

25

26

1

2   Febuery 6, 19--

3   Mr. Roy Robertson, Chairmen

4   Southern States Comittee

5   704 Floridda Avenue

6   Miammi, FL   33124

7   Dear Mr. Robinson:

8   I want to take this oportunity to thank you for the work you did

9   in making my task somuch easier in planing for this years convention

10   which have just been conclude in Savanna.

11   I new that when I apoint youas my asistant, I wouldnt be dissap-

12   pointed. Their was so many miscelaneous things taht you did that Im

13   unable to express my apreciation adaquately. Its always rewarding to

14   no that their is someone responsable to make sure that their are no

15   no lose ends in planing such a convention. You made certin that all

16   arrangments were taken care fo wiht a minimumm of fiddiculty.

17   It was a real pleasure to work with you on this convention, and Im

18   hoping that this will be the begining of a long and plesent relations-

19   hip. Allready I beleive that I sahll be glad to call on you when ever

20   their is similiar work to be done. Im graetful to you that Im abel

21   to hav this feeling.

22   Very sincerly your,

23   NINETH INSURANCE CO. OF SAVANNA

24   PM:YOI   Patrick Moriarty

25   Presidetn

26

1

2   Januery 31, 19--

3 Ms. Amy Germontt

4 202 Louisianna Street

5 New Orleens, LA   70125

6 Dear Ms. Germont:

7   May be you have not yet started to think about thsi summers vacat-

8 ion plans. Has it occured to you that unless you plan now and begin to

9 make all the nesessary arrangments, you will be dissappointed? Have

10 you past travel agencies in passed summers and aksed yourself why you

11 were still in New Orleens whne you could be in Honollulu, Los Angelos,

12 or San Francico?

13   Higher prices maybe in affect soon, and we cant garantee that

14 the prices quoted in the enclosed bullitin will remain steady. However,

15 we have allways made it a principal to keep our operating costs so low

16 that even tho prices do rise, the total cost to you will not be grately

17 effected.

18   You will be suprised at how resonable a trip will be this summer.

19 Stop in at won of our local office. Our repres005entive will be happy to

20 to make all the nessassary arangements fro you.

21   Cordiall yours'

22   ACE TRAVEL AGENCY

23 YOI   Manager

24

25

26

1

2   May 3, 19--

3   Mr. Allen Lawlor

4   209 Indianna Street

5   Garry, IN   46426

6   Dear Mrs. Lawler:

7   Thankyou very much fro responding to our previous letter, that

8   of Febuary 25, in which you ansered some of the qestions we aksed about

9   waht occur when you were accidently struck by a hit-and-run driever on

10   Wensday, Januery 29.

11   We have gone thru your answers very carefuly, and we beleive we

12   shall soon be able to make defanite arangements to pay for the ex-

13   pences which you payed as a result of thee acident.

14   However, it will be necesary for one of our representative's,

15   Miss Alberta Glenn, to confer wiht yu to make certin that our records

16   is complete and correct. Would it be possable for you to stop buy

17   to see him at our principle office at 112 Nineth Street in Chicargo.

18   There is a few micellanous items' which Miss Glen must discus with

19   you. We would be greatful if you filled in the enclosed card, tellin-

20   g us just wehn a apointment woud be convient for you. Upon reciet of

21   the card, Mr. Glenn will get in touch with you.

22   Yours truely,

23   INDEPENDANCE INSURENCE COMPANY

24   YOI:KW   Kurt Weiss, Districk Manager

25

26

1

2   Marhc 14, 19--

3   Metropolitan Advertizing Agency

4   34 Deleware Road

5   Willmington, DE   19827

6   Dear Mr. Murphy:

7   We are planing a sales drive when we introduce sum new producks

8   to our line of lighting equipement. We are hoping to place these pr-

9   oducks the on market the begining of nest year, and we we are now wri-

10   ting to various advertizing agencies to set up apointments for there

11   representatives' to meet wiht sum of are officers' to see weather our

12   requirments' can be met.

13   Our buget allowences for thsi sales campaign is not yet definate,

14   but we beleive that the some of $50,000 should be sufficent. It maybe

15   that sum more funds will have be to spent. Never the less, this is

16   our companys budget at this time.

17   If youre inteested in bidding for this acount, please have one of

18   you representives get in tuch with me. Im looking wofward to begining

19   to set up apointments as early as posible so that we can see just waht

20   each organzation has to offer.

21   Cordialy yours,

22   LEVITZ ELECTRICAL SUPPLIES, INC.

23   HL:YOI   Henry Levitz

24   Advertizing Depatment

25

26

1

2   Januery 15, 19--

3   Ms. Victoria Grant

4   247 Tenesee Avemue

5   Noxville, TN . 37928

6   Dear Miss Grantt:

7   Thang you for last months correspondenc you send me concerning the

8   budgit we are now discussing in Nasheville. As a member of the Finance

9   Comittee, Ill certinly keep your thoughts in mine. You no that I all-

10   ways make it a principal to take into consideration theviewsof the

11   people in my districk, and only than do I make a desision.

12   This year its very difficult to meet all of our State Governments

13   requirments becuse their are so many more demands on funds then their

14   has been in the passed. However, be assure that our comittee will

15   try it's very best to see that the funds are spend wisely.

16   Im planing to be in Noxville in the near futhure, and, of cause,

17   Im looking foward to seeing you at won of the dinners which I will a-

18   ttend. You can make reservations to attend a dinner thru the regular

19   districk organzation.

20   Very sincerly yours,

21   PM:YOI   Perry A. Miller

22   State Senator

23

24

25

26

1

March 5, 19--

2

3   Dr. Edward Myers

4   333 Wilkes Barre Highway

5   Pittsburg, PA   15229

6   Dear Dr. Meyers:

7   We belive that we have more property to show you then any other

8   real estate agency in this section of Pensylvania. Weather your want

9   a home in the country, in a suburb, or in the city itself, we are cer-

10 tani we can met you requirments.

11   If you want to remain in Pittsburgh, we have to house wich are

12 not allready on the market, but there owners are planint to place them

13 for sale withing the next two months. We have ben their agents in the

14 passed, an they will offered the houses to our costumers first. Both

15 houses are similiar tin that there main features include good location,

16 excellent structure, and a minimun down payment with morgatges easy to

17 obtain. The cost of won house will be about $35,000. The other hose

18 has more rooms, a larger plot, and maybe either $45,000 or $50,000. We

19 have been tole that we will be alloud to see the bouses the first of

20 May.

21   If you think that you woud like to live outside of Pittsburg, we

22 no of to groups of houses being built. Their in this districk but out

23 of the city. The resonable prices will suprise you. Planning for the

24 houses is just about finish, and the building should begin no later

25 then July 1. The affect of the economic situation should result in

26 speedy completion of these houses, and you probable can look foward

27 to moving into the house about a year form July. A definate selling

28 price has not yet been determine, but the two builders representives

29 of these houses have inform us that they will be in the range of

30 $55,000. Each of the houses will be diffrent, the area is a plesent

31 won, and the builders did assure us that these houses will be especia-

32 lly suitable for families similiar to yours.

33   Are you ready for a vacation home in teh mountains? Has it

34 occured to you that a second home is what you want for your familys

35 summers? If sew, I would urge you to olook thru the listings we have

36 in teh special bullitin which we have prepare. Wehn you look at the

37 bullitn, you will see that you do not need a millionaires buget to by

38 won of the cabins in the mountains. May be you have not yet thought

39 thought seriously about such a move, but thsi literature wil show you

40 how agreable country living is and how you can look foward to many

41 vacations for a sprisilngly small sum of money. The prices listed wil

42 be in affect only untill May 30. After that date, prices will probable

43 be much hire.

44   Of cause, we woud consider it a privelege and a pleasure to serve

45 you by discussing the housing oportunities covered in thiss letter.

46 May we here from you shourtly and make arrangments for personnel visits

47 to som of the properties.

48   Cordially your,

49   PENSYLVANIA REAL ESTATE COMPANY

50 ECB:YOI   Eric Blandington,

51   Pittsburg Districk Managerr

52

1

2   Janeary 27, 19--

3 Mrs. Wanda Goldmann

4 2368 Tenesee Street

5 Nasheville, TN   37230

6 Dear Ms. Goldman:

7   Do you feel that time has past you buy? Can you look in to your

8 futhure and no that you will have sufficent resources to enable you

9 to lead a happy life afteryou have stop working? Do you belive that

10 it is very improtant to be planing activities which will make life more

11 intresting and rewarding?

12   These questions answers certinly are not easy wons. However, we

13 think we have someting whichh will be of assistence to you in making

14 making arrangments for a very aggreeable lifestyle after you have

15 retire.

16   We are taking this oportunity to send you corespondence from som

17 other teachers, assistent principles and principles discribing there

18 experiences with our organisation. There comments indicate that that

19 they are greatful for the work that we do.

20   The cost of joining and reciving our monthly bullitins is only

21 $10 annually. Fill out the attached membership blank and rush it ot

22 us as soon as posible. You wont be sorry!

23   Cordilly yours,

24   RETIRED SCHOOL PERSONAL, INC.

25 JAM:YOI   John Marsdent, President

26 Enclsoure

RULES FOR THE CORRECT USE OF PUNCTUATION MARKS

We have already reviewed **ed** endings and the correct use of the apostrophe. In this section, all other punctuation marks, with the exception of commas, will be reviewed. After you have studied the rules, do the exercises which contain examples of these punctuation marks. After you have done the exercises, check with the answers. Note that there are alternate ways of punctuating these sentences. If you find that you have made errors, study the rules again, and do the exercises once more.

Beginning with Letter 31, you will be required to check the punctuation so that you can correct the errors. However, all commas will be correct because the rules for commas have not yet been covered. If, when checking your letters, you see that you have made errors in punctuating the sentences correctly, study the rules again, and do the exercises once more.

Colon

Rule 1. The colon is used after a salutation of a business letter. This is the most common use of the colon in business letters.

  Examples: Dear Sir: Dear Mrs. Smith:
       Gentlemen:

Rule 2. The colon may be used to introduce a long quotation.

  Example: The doctor said: "In my opinion, the medical situation is getting more critical. I would suggest that action be taken immediately."

Rule 3. The colon is used before a listing. The introduction to the listing usually includes the word "following" or the words "as follows."

  Example: The following suggestions will help you proofread better: be careful of spelling, check for typographical errors, and look for inconsistencies.

Rule 4. A special use of the colon occurs with the identification initials in a business letter. The colon separates the dictator's initials from the typist's.

  Example: GWG: YOI (NOTE: **GWG** represents the dictator's initials; **YOI** represents the typist's initials.)

Semicolon

Rule 1. The semicolon is used when there are two complete independent or main clauses with no conjunction separating them. An **independent** or **main** clause can stand by itself as a complete sentence. The conjunctions are **and, or, but, for.** The clauses should be related in meaning so that they can be made into one unified sentence by placing a semicolon between them. Note that this is an optional use of the semicolon because it is just as correct to have two separate sentences.

> *Examples*: Two sentences: I shall be at the office on Wednesday. Mr. Green will be there until Thursday.
>
> One sentence: I shall be at the office on Wednesday; Mr. Green will be there until Thursday.

NOTE: If a comma is used instead of a semicolon, it is incorrect. What results is a run-on sentence. It is always correct to write two separate sentences, and it is safer to do so.

Rule 2. The semicolon is used before explanatory words or phrases, such as: **namely, for example, that is.**

> *Example*: Miss Williams had two important attributes of an excellent secretary; namely, courtesy and good skills.

NOTE: The semicolon comes before these explanatory words or phrases, and a comma follows these words or phrases.

Rule 3. The semicolon is used in long sentences when there are two independent or main clauses separated by a conjunction, and one or both of the clauses has a comma in it.

> *Example*: Mr. Brown, our managing director, may be in Pittsburgh next week; but I do not know whether or not he will be able to see Mr. Arthur, the purchasing agent, then.

NOTE: A semicolon is needed before **but** because both clauses contain commas.

Rule 4. The semicolon separates two independent or main clauses which are joined by adverbs such as **however** or **therefore.**

> *Examples*: The typist was late; however, she was able to finish the work on time.
>
> Mr. Roberts will not be in the office today; therefore, I shall have to see him tomorrow.

NOTE: Once again, a comma instead of a semicolon is not strong enough to separate the two clauses. If a comma is used instead of a semicolon, it is incorrect. What results is a run-on sentence. It is always correct to write two separate sentences, and it is safer to do so.

> *Examples*: Two sentences: The typist was late. However, she was able to finish the work on time.
>
> Mr. Roberts will not be in the office today. Therefore, I shall have to see him tomorrow.

Dash

A dash is made on the typewriter with two hyphens with no spaces before, after, or between the hyphens. The dash is used infrequently in business correspondence. When it is used, it is often used in place of other punctuation marks such as the comma, colon, semicolon, or parentheses.

Rule 1. The dash is used to make points more dramatically and to give emphasis.
    Examples: I was wrong—or naive—to think that I would be happy on that job.
               You must improve—in typing, proofreading, and general ability—if you are to keep this position.

Hyphen

Some expressions are written as single words, as two words, or as individual words separated by a hyphen. There are no definite rules to help you decide how to type these words.
    Examples: Two words: living room
                One word: bathroom
                Hyphenated: son-in-law

If you are not sure of whether words should be hypenated, consult a good dictionary. Most dictionaries show whether expressions are written as separate words, hyphenated words, or one word. Check the instructions in the dictionary you use to make sure that you interpret its indications correctly. If an expression does not appear in the dictionary, you can safely assume that it is written as separate words.

Rule 1. The hyphen is used in some expressions which are compound words.
    Examples: son-in-law   self-reliant

NOTE: All compound words starting with "self" are hyphenated.

Rule 2. The hyphen is used at the end of a line when it is necessary to break up a word between syllables. Of course, a one-syllable word may not be hyphenated. In words of more than one syllable, use a dictionary if you are not positive of where one syllable ends and the next one begins.

Typists usually find it faster to use the margin release instead of syllabicating, and this is considered good practice unless the right margin becomes very uneven as a result of not dividing words. When dividing words by using the hyphen, it is considered poor practice to have hyphens end more than two consecutive lines or to divide the last word on a page.

Listed below are some hints for dividing words:

a. A one-syllable word may not be divided.
    Examples: the   chart   please

b. A one-letter syllable at the beginning or the end of a word should not be separated from the rest of the word.
    Examples: Do not separate **a-bout**
                Do not separate **ide-a**

c. Contractions should not be divided.
    Examples: wouldn't   doesn't   shouldn't

   d. Divide a hyphenated word only where the hyphen appears.
      Examples: sister-in-law (NOT sis-ter-in-law)   self-contained (NOT self-con-
            tained)

Rule 3. There are expressions which are hyphenated in some sentences and not in others. This depends upon the construction of the sentence. These expressions are called **compound adjectives.** As you know, adjectives modify or describe nouns or pronouns.
   When compound adjectives such as: **out of date, up to the minute, well known, first class,** etc., come immediately before the noun they describe, they are hyphenated.
      Examples: The apartment is in first-class condition.
            I see the up-to-the-minute news on TV each night.
            The well-known author will speak at our meeting.

   However, if the compound adjectives do not come immediately before the noun, they are not hyphenated but are written as separate words.
      Examples: I will travel first class.
            The news is up to the minute.
            The author is well known for his novels and short stories.
            Some letter styles are out of date.

Exclamation Mark

Rule 1. The exclamation mark is used for an expression of strong feeling or emotion. The typist leaves two spaces after an exclamation mark.
      Examples: Congratulations!   You have won first prize.
            Oh!   I am so happy.

Parentheses

Rule 1. Parentheses are used to set off that part of a sentence that is not absolutely necessary to the completeness of the sentence.
      Example: I saw my friend, Charles Dickens, (not the author, of course) at the office
            yesterday.

Rule 2. Parentheses are also used to enclose figures and dates.
      Example: Abraham Lincoln (1809-1865) was the Civil War President.

Rule 3. Parentheses are used with items which are listings in outline form.
      Examples: We think you should:
            (1) try harder,
            (2) do better,
            (3) and be happier.

Examples: We think you should:
> 1) try harder,
> 2) do better,
> 3) and be happier.

NOTE: Letters (a) or (A) may be used as well as numbers.

Rule 4. Parentheses may be used to enclose numbers or letters which are not in outline form but are part of the material in paragraph form. The examples listed in Rule 3 above could also be typed:

Example: We think you should (1) try harder, (2) do better, (3) and be happier.

Rule 5. In some legal correspondence, amounts are enclosed in parentheses after they have been typed in words.

Example: The cost of the property is Ten Thousand Dollars ($10,000).

Period

Rule 1. The period is used at the end of a sentence that makes a statement or expresses a command. The typist leaves two spaces after end-of-sentence punctuation.

Examples: I shall check my work.
Check your work carefully.

Rule 2. The period is used after an abbreviation. One space is left after the period.

Examples: Mr. Brown   Mrs. Smith   Ms. Lee   Dr. Colb

Rule 3. Sometimes there is a question in the form of a command, but it is phrased so that it is called a **polite request**. If it is a polite request which does not require a definite answer, use a period instead of a question mark.

Examples: Will you please write me by next Tuesday.
Would you please do this later.

Rule 4. The period is used as a decimal point.

Examples: 1.3% $47.23

Rule 5. Periods may be used instead of parentheses when items are listings in outline form.

Examples: We think you should:
> 1. try harder,
> 2. do better,
> 3. and be happier.

Examples: We think you should:
> a. try harder,
> b. do better,
> c. and be happier.

Question Mark

Rule 1. A question mark is used at the end of a direct question. The typist leaves two spaces after the question mark.

> *Examples*: Are you able to type without errors?   I hope so.
> Will you be in Chicago next Tuesday?   I hope to see you then.

NOTE: A period is used with a polite request rather than a question mark. (*See* Rule 3 for the Period.)

Quotation Marks

Rule 1. Quotation marks are used to enclose a direct quotation.
> *Example*: "You should check your work more carefully," Harvey said.

Rule 2. Quotation marks are used to enclose a title.
> *Example*: "Hamlet" is taught in most English courses.

NOTE: There are a number of acceptable ways of typing titles of literary or artistic works. You may use quotation marks, underscores, solid capital letters, or initial capital letters. Each of the following is acceptable:
> *Example*: My favorite opera is Aida.
> I read A Tale of Two Cities last year.
> I read the first chapter of his book, EFFECTIVE PROOFREADING.
> "Get Me to the Church on Time" is one of the hit songs of My Fair Lady.

NOTE: Placing other punctuation marks with quotation marks sometimes causes problems to the typist. Here are some simple rules:
a. Periods and commas are always placed inside quotation marks.
> *Examples*: "I am sure that he will be here soon," Martha said.
> Martha said, "I am sure that he will be here soon."

b. Colons and semicolons are always placed outside quotation marks.
> *Examples*: I will need the following tools for his so-called "Garden of Eden": a rake, a spade, and a shovel.
> Yesterday, the lawyer said, "The contracts will be ready tomorrow"; however, they are still not ready, and it is past 5 o'clock.

c. Question marks and exclamation marks go outside a closing quotation mark when they apply to the whole sentence.
> *Examples*: When did Jack say, "The contracts will be ready tomorrow"?
> Congratulations on "a perfect score"!

d. Question marks and exclamation marks go inside a closing quotation mark when they apply only to the quoted material.
> *Examples*: Sheila asked, "Is the letter ready?"
> William always says "Hurry!"

e. Apostrophes are used when there is a quotation within a quotation.
> *Example*: He said, "I believe that 'perfect' is the wrong word to use in this instance."

DIRECTIONS: Insert correctly all the necessary punctuation marks. In checking the answers, note that there may be more than one correct answer. If your answer differs, check with the rules again to see whether or not your answer is also acceptable. Note, too, that all commas have been placed correctly because the rules for commas have not yet been reviewed.

1. I shall buy the following items in the store broccoli and celery

2. The initials GWG YOI represents the dictators initials and your own initials.

3. Dear Mr Smith   I am happy to hear from you   Very truly yours represents a very brief one sentence letter

4. I hope you will be ready on time I know that I will

5. Mr Thomas had two ideas for improving productivity namely, good attendance and good punctuality

6. Mr Jacobs, our sales representative, will be away from the office for a while but Mr Powell will be able to see you

7. I was stunned need I say by your position

8. Help I am drowning

9. George Washington 1732-1799 was our very first president he became president in 1789

10. If you have self control, you will have very few problems

12. I believe that it is the best tasting coffee on the market

13. When you have recovered and are in first class condition, I will make more definite plans for us

14. David Jones a worthy opponent won the tennis match from Alberto Perez

15. Do you think that Robert will be able to travel first class to Chicago

16. Please let me know what the cost is, Pat said, and I will pay you

17. Would you please help me with all the merchandise

18. He asked will you help me with all the merchandise

19. When did Richard say come here at 2 o'clock

20. The amount of the sale is Five Thousand Dollars $5,000

21. The doctor said in my opinion, the medical situation is a very difficult one I would recommend that there be another opinion immediately

22. When I went to the hardware store, I bought the following a new brush and paint

23. Ms Jenkins possessed two office skills namely, accurate typing and good spelling ability

24. Tomorrow is my birthday next Sunday is my fathers birthday

25. Mrs Edith Stern my sister in law lives in New Jersey her children, however, live in California

26. The teacher was on time however, most of the pupils were delayed by the storm

27. You are foolish or unwise to think that you can follow this course of action

28. Was he self conscious about his weight Raymond asked

29. Good luck I hope you win the contest

30. Robert Frost the famous poet wrote about New England

31. Dr Carver, Mr Frede, and Ms Jablon will be my guests on Friday I hope you can be at my home then

32. I believe he said I think that there are many ways of punctuating these sentences

33. I wonder if he will be at the baseball game was he planning to attend

34. Hurry You will be late

35. Jennifer said to me I think that never is the wrong word to use at this time

1. I shall buy the following items in the store: broccoli and celery.

2. The initials "GWG:YOI" represents the dictator's initials and your own initials.

3. "Dear Mr. Smith: I am happy to hear from you. Very truly yours," represents a very brief one-sentence letter.

4. I hope you will be ready on time; I know that I will.

5. Mr. Thomas had two ideas for improving productivity; namely, good attendance and good punctuality.

6. Mr. Jacobs, our sales representative, will be away from the office for a while; but Mr. Powell will be able to see you.

7. I was stunned—need I say—by your position.

8. Help! I am drowning!

9. George Washington (1732-1799) was our very first president; he became president in 1789.

10. If you have self-control, you will have very few problems.

12. I believe that it is the best-tasting coffee on the market.

13. When you have recovered and are in first-class condition, I will make more definite plans for us.

14. David Jones—a worthy opponent—won the tennis match from Alberto Perez.

15. Do you think that Robert will be able to travel first class to Chicago?

16. "Please let me know what the cost is," Pat said, "and I will pay you."

17. Would you please help me with all the merchandise.

18. He asked, "Will you help me with all the merchandise?"

19. When did Richard say, "Come here at 2 o'clock"?

20. The amount of the sale is Five Thousand Dollars($5,000).

21. The doctor said: "In my opinion, the medical situation is a very difficult one. I would recommend that there be another opinion immediately."

22. When I went to the hardware store, I bought the following: a new brush and paint.

23. Ms. Jenkins possessed two office skills; namely, accurate typing and good spelling ability.

24. Tomorrow is my birthday; next Sunday is my father's birthday.

25. Mrs. Edith Stern (my sister-in-law) lives in New Jersey; her children, however, live in California.

26. The teacher was on time; however, most of the pupils were delayed by the storm.

27. You are foolish—or unwise—to think that you can follow this course of action.

28. "Was he self-conscious about his weight?" Raymond asked.

29. Good luck! I hope you win the contest.

30. Robert Frost (the famous poet) wrote about New England.

31. Dr. Carver, Mr. Frede, and Ms. Jablon will be my guests on Friday; I hope you can be at my home then.

32. I believe he said, "I think that there are many ways of punctuating these sentences."

33. I wonder if he will be at the baseball game. Was he planning to attend?

34. Hurry! You will be late!

35. Jennifer said to me, "I think that 'never' is the wrong word to use at this time."

Word List—Letters 31–40

The words on this list occur for the first time in Letters 31-40. Following the suggestions for learning how to spell words, study the spelling of these words before correcting the letters. When correcting the letters, refer to this list and to the Master Spelling List (p.24). If you are not sure of the spelling of a word, be sure to consult your dictionary immediately. The starred (*) words are repeated in the Words Often Confused section of this list. Brief definitions are given, and the part of speech is indicated in parentheses.

Some dictionaries give alternate spellings for the words indicated with a plus sign (+). These alternate spellings are shown on this page. However, when these words are given in the letters, use the spelling on the list since this is the preferred spelling.

account	balance	convenience	preferred	they're
address	bankruptcy	December	procedure	thorough
although	benefited+		proceed	transferred
analysis	bookkeeper	excellent		
analyze	brochure		responsibility	unnecessary
anxious	bureau	financial		
apologize	business	formally*	Saturday	vacuum
apparent		formerly*	several	valuable
appearance			strictly	volume
attendance	cancellation		succeed	
attorneys	commercial	improvement	success	you're*
available	conscious	institute	suggest	your*
	contract	October	superintendent	

Words Often Confused

formally (adv.)—in a formal manner
formerly (adv.)—some time ago

you're—contraction for <u>you are</u>
your (pron. adj.)—possessive case of the pronoun <u>you</u>

Alternate Spellings

Preferred	*Acceptable*
benefited	benefitted

1

2   Febuary 14 19--

3   Green Food Products, Inc.

4   1427 Springfeild Avenue

5   Chicargo, IL   60631

6   Attention: Mr Frank H Green

7   Dear Mr Greene;

8   I am please to no that you which to renew you advetising contrack.

9   Iam sure that any changes you Legal Department iwshes to maek in the

10   contact wil be satisfacroy to us.

11   You acount has been a real challenge as I had never handle a food

12   acount before. My gratest professional thrill came in Octobr when

13   that months layout of your product one for me the advetising award of

14   of the month.

15   As Mr. Richards told you, i have done considerable thinking about

16   about teh the best way to present you product this year. I think I

17   have serveral ideas that will intrest you. I shall be in Chicargo

18   on Febrary 28; may I see you than?

19   Yours very truely,

20   MADISON ADVETISING AGENCY

21   JM:YOI   John Monroe

22   Acount Executive

23

24

25

26

1

2   Mau 21, 19--

3   MR Robert Jones

4   675 Nineth Avenue

5   New Youk   NY   10032

6   Dear Sir

7   The payment book showing the balence you still have to pay on

8   you're recent purchase is enclose. The book allso discribes our

9   proceedures for payment. You will note that the terms of you new

10   contrack are paymments of $10 a week, and you are entitle to a discount

11   if you deside to pay you acount withing six month.

12   Its plesent ot have old freinds reopen they acconts with us. It

13   makes us even more concious of our responsability to the people who by

14   from us. we will do our part to keep our busines relations you with

15   as plesant as they have bin in the passed.

16   You're name has been place on our mailing list to recieve announ-

17   cements of all sales that we will conduct in the futre. These announ-

18   cements will reach you a weak or ten days befor we advertize the sales

19   the the public.

20   Cordially yours,

21   SOMERS DEPARTMENT STORE

22   YOI   Credit Depatment

23   Inclosure

24

25

26

1

2   Augest 30, 19--

3   Mr. j. B. Peters

4   370 North Caralina Street

5   Durhamm, NC   27733

6   Dear Mr Peterson

7   SUBJECT: NEW EDITION OF BULLITIN

8   Thankyou very mcuh for send us serveral pages of the new addition

9   of the bullitin you wrote to years ago. Weve read it with great in-

10   intrest because we think you hav done a good job. However, thsi new

11   bullitin do not seem to be suffishently diferent from you're first

12   book to make a new edition necessary.

13   Let me suggests the following; come to our offiec next Wwndsay

14   so that you can show us some more editions that you are planing to

15   make to the text. At that time, well meet with representives of our

16   our editorial board and make a final desision

17   Very truely your,

18   JAMES PUBLISHERS, INC.

19   JWQ:YOI   Thomas W. Quigley

20

21

22

23

24

25

26

1

2   Octobre 3, 19--

3   Bell Investment Coproration

4   322 Oklohoma Street

5   Oklohoma City, OC   73134

6   Attention of Mr. Jeremy Bell, Treasurer

7   Dear Mr. Bell:

8   We have had our attorinies analize the anual statement of

9   Brown & Company in order to fine out wheather of not it would be wise

10   to insitute bankrupcy procedings.

11   They're analisis of the situation seems to indicate that the comp-

12   any will be abel to pull thru this finantial emergency. Our attornies

13   said the following; "The volumn of busines has been increasing stead-

14   ily, an altho it is not yet aparent that the firm will be able to make

15   a profit thsi year, ther is a good possbility that it wil suceed in

16   doin so".

17   We sugest that a final desision not be made untill after the the

18   anual records are avalable. These shoud be ready by Febuary 28 of next

19   year. Do you beleive, as we do, its in the best intrests of all conc-

20   erned to do sew. Please chekc to see that the attornies and acountants

21   for you frim are agreeable to this proceedure.

22   Sincerely yours,

23   GENERAL INDUSTRIES, INC.

24   HT:YOI   Harry Thayer, treasurer

25

26

1

2   Januayr 12, 19--

3   Middleton Advertiseing Agency

4   Attention: Mr. Gregory Middleton

5   29 Iowwa Street

6   De Moine, IA   50335

7   Dear Mr. Middleton:

8   We are ankshus about the progress you are making with our adv-

9   ertising campaign for the vacum cleaners we manufacture. As you un-

10   doubtly are aware, we transfered the acount to you agency because we

11   belived that the agency we formally used was having littel sucess in

12   stimulating the sales of these appliances

13   Wehn you discribed what you would do, you mention that you were

14   planing to issue a great broshure which would be mail to all purchasers

15   of our sanding machines and carpet sweekers. Altho we set a dead line

16   for seeing these broshures, we are disapointed that the deadline has

17   past and we have not seenthem. We thought that once we transfered out

18   acount to you, it would be nunessary to worry about the lack of progr-

19   ess. Our volumn of sales has fallen off, and we need fats action.

20   We are, therfore, letting you no formerly that unless we here form

21   you in serveral days, we shall speak to our atorneys conserning the

22   posibility of the cancelation of our contrack with you.

23   Your very truely,

24   MIDWEST MANUFACTORERS, INC.

25   JG   John Garrison, Secetary

26

Desember 14, 19--

Ms. Margaret White

349 New Youk Avenue

Seracuse, NY.   13236

Dear Mrs. White,

I apoligize for not writing to you sooner about the letter you objected to recieving conserning an unpayed bill ofr $137.29. I was away from the office for allmost to weeks with a severe cold, and I have jus return. I check you acount with our asistant bookeeper, and I am happy to say that you are correct. You dont owe us any money

The error was caused because we have anoter customer wohse name is Margaret White. She ilves at 439 NewyOrk Avenue so you can see how a error like this could have occured. We are changing our records to show a credit to you of $137.28.

We no that it was unplesent for you have this occur, but we are certin that it willnot be nesessary for us to have any furthur correspondance about this matter

                          Sincerly yours,

                          MAXWELL DEPARTMENT STORE

JPM:YOI   Jane R. Martin,

                          Credit Manager

1

2   Febuary 1 19--

3 Mister Wilbert N. Jenkins

4 348 Kanses Street

5 Topeeka; KA   66637

6 Dear Mr Jenkin

7   We have check on why you haev been gettin poor service in you

8 building. You probable did'nt no that the superintendant of the build-

9 ing, Thomas Adams, was accidently hit by a automobile on Wensday, Dece-

10 mber 2. He was unconcious and had to be taken to the hospital. Whil

11 he was hospitalized, his wife attempt to keep strickly to the schedule

12 that had been set up, but she was not completly sucessful.

13   Now that Mr. Adam has recover and has once again assume his reg-

14 ula duties, you can rely on the following promise; "The appearence of

15 the building will go back to what it formally was". Mr Adams will see

16 that his adsistent vacums the halls daily, a prosedure which was allw-

17 ays followed hear.

18   We apoligize for the inconvience you and the other tenants had;

19 but you now no that it wsa a unusal and unavoidable situation.

20   Your truely,

21 HR:YOI   Henry R. Rice

22   Building Managerr

23

24

25

26

1

2   Octobr 14, 19--

3   Miss Bernice Frish, Employment Counselor

4   Commerical High School

5   439 Arazona Drive

6   Tuscon, AZ   85738

7   Dear Mrs. Frisch:

8   As you sugested, our personal department has made a through study

9   of the attendence records of the 15 pupils from your school who are wo-

10   rking as typists and bookeepers in our special cooperative program.

11   The results of the study are listed on the attach sheet.

12   Altho serveral of the students have been absent more then we woud

13   like tehm to be--as many as 15 days-, the rest of them have excellant

14   records. We are verymuch please that this has occured this year. App-

15   arantly the stress taht you placed on the need for good attendence

16   payed off. However, I woud sugest that you speak to the too pupils w-

17   ith the worst records and tell them that altho an analisis of there

18   records by there supervisors shows that theyre doing satisfactory work,

19   we shll be force to replace them unless theeir's a drastic improvment

20   in theirr atendence records by Desember 15.

21   The regular employees in the departments' in which your students'

22   work has been very favorable impress with the personnel appearance of

23   the pupils. The up to date personality training coarse which you are

24   now offering at your school evidently is meeting with great sucess.

25   Before we proced with our plans for next year, I belive we shoud

26   get together to discuss wheather you think it would be posible to sent

27 us 20 pupils instead of the 16 we now have. Attornies our in Legal

28 Department woud be benefited if more filing help was provided. The

29 head of that department, Mr. Ted Klitz, said that in the passed he

30 prefered regularly employed file clerks but for next year he would be

31 please to have three students in the mrning and three differen student

32 in the afternoon. It would be unecessary for these students to had have

33 a special course in filing because are files are set up a bit difrently

34 from thoes in other organzations.

35   Prepahs it would be of assitance if we could set up a meeting wit

36 Mr. Klottz within teh nest month or to. He could tell your exactly

37 what he has in mine, and you could start to chekc the records of you

38 students to see which ones might be availible for this type of work.

39   If youre agreable to increasing the number of pupils you will send

40 hear, please let me no so that we can make arrangments for a apointment

41 wit Mr. Klotz. At the sametime I would appriciate it if you woud look

42 at the special broshure we are in the process of preparing. Thsi wil

43 be use when we visit classes in schools to recruit employees.

44   As allways, I sertainly appriciate your find spirit of cooperati-

45 on.

46   Your Sincerely,

47   INDEPENDANCE INSURANCE COMPANY

48 MLT:YOI   Marie Louise Turnball

49   Vice Presiden

50

51

52

1

2   April 10 19--

3   Dr. Fred Clarke

4   Superintendant of Schools

5   Maconn, GA   31239

6   Dear Mr Clark

7   SUBJECT: Convention on Octobre 15

8   The Bureaw of Busines Education sincerly hopes that your sche-

9   dule will allow you to be avalable to adress the Georgai Commerical

10 Education Association on Saterday, October 16, at the Holiday Hotel in

11 Savana. As you undoubtably no, this organisation has annuel convent-

12 ions each fall at which educational matters of intrest to teahcers,

13 assistent principles and principles are discuss. Those who of atended

14 the panels in the passed have allways benefitted from what they have

15 herd.

16   Please let me no as soon as posible what you woud like to dis-

17 cuss. The general theme of the convention is "The Improvment of

18 Instruction in Bussiness Courses in the High Schools". It is sugested

19 that each speaker talk for about thrity minutes.

20   I hop you be will abel to except this invitation and that Ill

21 here from you shortly.

22   Very cordialy yours,

23 NT:YOI   Norman Thompson, Directro

24   Bureaw of Bsiness Edcation

25

26

1

2   Arpil 5 19--

3   Miss Kathleen Sweeney

4   34-89 Texes Boulevard

5   Beaumount, TX   77740

6   Dear Mrs. Sweeny

7   Do you fine that youre ankshus after a ahrd day at home or in teh

8   office. Do you have aches and pains in your back? Do yu have troubel

9   sleeping? Are you nervous over extended periods of time.

10   If you have positive ansers to any of the questions asked above,

11 we belive that you will benifit greatly from our monthly bullitin wich

12 is avalable for the anual rate of only $6.

13   The Januery and Febuery bulletins discribe how tension can cause

14 back aches, lack of sleep, and general nervousness. Famous authors

15 give som methods of over coming these difficulties in language wich is

16 easily under stood. The articals have ben written by docters who hav

17 had many valueable ;years of experience in treating patients all over

18 the country with great sucess.

19   Take avantage of the bargin rate of $7 now. Of cause, if you

20 see that youre not completely satisfy with the bullitins, your usuall

21 cancelation priveledges will apply.

22   Very truely your,

23   HEALTH HINTS

24 JAK:YOI   June Klemons

25   Circulation Manager

26

RULES FOR COMMAS—Part 1

All of the punctuation marks have been covered with the exception of the comma. The comma has been left for last because it is the mark of punctuation which causes the most difficulty for the typist. Just as the rules for other marks of punctuation are sometimes indefinite, the rules for commas have also been changing. The rules given below cover situations in which commas are used. If their use is *optional,* you may use a comma, or you may omit it. Because there are so many rules for commas, we are separating them in this book. This section covers the first four rules. Later sections will cover the rest of the rules.

Up until this time, all commas have been placed correctly in the letters and exercises. However, beginning with Letter 41, you will have to insert commas correctly.

After you have studied the first four rules for commas, do the exercises which contain sentences requiring commas. After you have done the exercises, check with the answers. Note that there are alternate uses of the comma. If you find that you have made errors, study the rules again, and do the exercises once again.

When you are ready to start correcting the letters, remember that you now have to insert commas. Since the rules allow for optional commas, there may be more than one correct way to punctuate. If, when checking your letters, you see that you have made errors in placing commas, study the rules again, and do the exercises once more.

Rule 1. A comma is used to separate words or phrases in a series. The comma before **and** is optional.

> *Examples*: We took Bill, Ed, John, and Paul on a tour of the office.
> or
> We took Bill, Ed, John and Paul on a tour of the office.

NOTE: The abbreviation **etc.** (and so forth) sometimes ends a series. A comma is placed before **etc.** but not after it.

> *Example*: The refrigerator was filled with meats, cheeses, vegetables, etc. for tonight's meal.

Rule 2. A pair of commas is used when someone is **directly addressed** or **spoken to.** (The technical term for this is **direct address.**)

> *Examples*: I believe, Mr. Hadley, that this letter is correct in all details.
> I know, Miss Smith, that you are doing your best.

Rule 3. A pair of commas is used when an expression explains or describes a preceding word, usually a noun or a pronoun. (The technical term for this is **when a term is in apposition.**)

117

Examples: Mr. Brown, our office manager, will be in charge of the new campaign for greater efficiency.

The area's principal shopping street, Fourth Street, will be closed to automobiles every Saturday this spring.

Rule 4. A comma or a pair of commas is used to set off words that could just as easily be placed in parentheses and are unnecessary to the sense of the sentence. These words really interrupt the thought of the sentence. (The technical term for this is **parenthetical word or expression.**) Some of these words are: **however, indeed, for example, therefore, too, for instance, on the other hand.**

NOTE: Sometimes it is unnecessary to set off these words or expressions if they do not interrupt the thought or the smoothness of the sentence.

Examples: We know, therefore, that you will be a very capable employee. (Comma is necessary.)

We therefore know that you will be a very capable employee. (Comma is optional.)

NOTE: Always use commas with **however** and **too** (when it means **also**).

Examples: However, I shall be happy to work on Thursday.

They knew, however, that it would be impossible to finish the job by then.

You, too, should be pleased with the success of the job.

I think that you should be ready for work, too.

DIRECTIONS: Insert correctly all necessary commas. Note that other marks of punctuation have been omitted, and they must be inserted. In checking the answers, note that there may be more than one correct answer. If your answer differs, check with the rules again to see whether or not your answer is also acceptable.

1. I shall visit Pittsburgh in February, April, June, and September.

2. Please buy the following supplies for me: carbon paper, erasers, pencils, bond paper, and file folders.

3. "I know, Mr Nielsen, that you will be here in May," he said.

4. "I know, Mr Nielsen, will be here in May," he said.

5. Do you know if Ms. Ferguson, our general manager, will be in Cincinnati next week?

6. Would you please ask Miss Combes, our purchasing agent, to give us the figures on that purchase order.

7. However, I shall be at the meeting at 2 p.m.

8. "I believe, too, that Tillie will make an excellent officer for our club," Ms. Reid said.

9. It is my opinion, however, that you should attend this meeting, too.

10. I expect that the officers of the club will be chosen from the following: Ted, Ed, Fred, Lester, and Martin.

11. I know, Mr Gray, that you will be happy with the results of the election.

12. Congratulations, Mr Haley, on winning such an exciting game.

13. Do you believe, Mr Friend that the expression, "honesty is the best policy," is always true?

14. I believe, for instance, that what she says is so.

15. Shelley says, on the other hand, that Ms Carruthers is correct.

16. However, I know that, that information is up to date.

17. Ted Lusk, the second in command, will take over when, Dr. Rios retires.

18. California, Oregon, and Washington are the three states, I want to visit.

next summer this summer I have to stay home

19. I am glad to see you,Mr Ferretti ,and hope that you are glad to see me ,too .

20. Therefore,Mr Smythe,I shall not be able to subscribe to your magazine,ELECTRONIC AGE this year.

21. Tomorrow, May 13,falls on a Saturday ;the 15th,therefore, is on Monday

22. Have you seen Ms Collins our new secretary

23. Pleasant news travels fast Captain Slocum and I know that you probably have heard of your promotion the Commanding Officer said

24. Do you think that you can make the following purchases for me Martha sugar coffee cereal and butter

25. The out of date information is useless to me Ms Foley and I have to discard it

1. I shall visit Pittsburgh in February, April, June and September.

2. Please buy the following supplies for me: carbon paper, erasers, pencils, bond paper, and file folders.

3. "I know, Mr. Nielsen, that you will be here in May," he said.

4. "I know Mr. Nielsen will be here in May," he said.

5. Do you know if Ms. Ferguson, our general manager, will be in Cincinnati next week?

6. Would you please ask Miss Combes, our purchasing agent, to give us the figures on that purchase order.

7. However, I shall be at the meeting at 2 p.m.

8. "I believe, too, that Tillie will make an excellent officer for our club," Ms. Reid said.

9. It is my opinion, however, that you should attend this meeting, too.

10. I expect that the officers of the club will be chosen from the following: Ted, Ed, Fred, Lester and Martin.

11. I know, Mr. Gray, that you will be happy with the results of the election.

12. Congratulations, Mr. Haley, on winning such an exciting game!

13. Do you believe, Mr. Friend, that the expression, "Honesty is the best policy," is always true?

14. I believe, for instance, that what she says is so.

15. Shelley says, on the other hand, that Ms. Carruthers is correct.

16. However, I know that that information is up to date.

17. Ted Lusk, the second in command, will take over when Dr. Rios retires.

18. California, Oregon, and Washington are the three states I want to visit

next summer; this summer I have to stay home.

19. I am glad to see you, Mr. Ferretti, and hope that you are glad to see me, too.

20. Therefore, Mr. Smythe, I shall not be able to subscribe to your magazine, ELECTRONIC AGE, this year.

21. Tomorrow, May 13, falls on a Saturday; the 15th, therefore, is on Monday.

22. Have you seen Ms. Collins, our new secretary?

23. "Pleasant news travels fast, Captain Slocum, and I know that you probably have heard of your promotion," the Commanding Officer said.

24. Do you think that you can make the following purchases for me, Martha: sugar, coffee, cereal, and butter?

25. The out-of-date information is useless to me, Ms. Foley, and I have to discard it.

Word List—Letters 41–50

The words on this list occur for the first time in Letters 41-50. Following the suggestions for learning how to spell words, study the spelling of these words before correcting the letters. When correcting the letters, refer to this list and to the Master Spelling List (p. 24). If you are not sure of the spelling of a word, be sure to consult your dictionary immediately.

among	inasmuch as	opinion	realize	shipment
August	incidentally		recognize	shipping
	investigate	pamphlet	repetition	somewhat
congratulations		prejudice	response	sponsored
	Messrs.	proof	restaurant	
efficiently		prove		withhold
	November		secretary	
Gentlemen	occurrence	questionnaire	separate	

1

2   December 2, 19--

3   Mr Edward Reilly

4   459 Nineth Avenue

5   Worchester, MA   01641

6   My Dear Mr. Reilley

7   Congradulations! I am very happy to tell you Mr. Reilly that you

8   son, George, has one a scholarship to our university. Pleas except

9   my best wishes.

10   Wehn you and he has a chance to come to our shcool, I hope oyu

11 will take avantage of the oportunity to do, so inasmuchas we like to

12 maek the personnel acquaintance of all of our award winners.

13   It will be a pleasure and a priviledge Mr Reilley to meet with

14 you and George. Incidently, when you come hear, we shall make it a

15 festive occassion and have lunch together.

16   I hope to heare form you soon.

17   Sincerely Yours,

18   MASSACHUSETTES INSITUTE

19 YOI   Admissions Directer

20

21

22

23

24

25

26

1

2   Febuary 3, 19--

3   Mister Theodore Jenson

4   410 Cincinatti Driveway

5   Clevland, OH   44142

6   Dear Mister Jensen

7   Last Saterday we send you a announcement about a meeting wich wil

8   take palce on Wensday March 17. We hop that you will taek avantage fo

9   the offer which was enclose in the phamphlet we mail to you than.

10   Their are many occassions when a reccommendation is nesessary to

11   attend such an converence. However in this case we espect to have

12   sufficent room to acommodate all of the person we have invite.

13   In the pamflet, there is a questionaire which you should complete.

14   We hope that you will answer it as soonas posible so that we can set

15   up teh meeting efficently easily and promply.

16   We are looking foward to seeing you than

17   Yours very Sincerely,

18   HJ:YOI   Herman Huggins

19   Publicity Director

20

21

22

23

24

25

26

1

2   Januery 5 19--

3   Messrs James & Burrell

4   4598 Missoure Avenue

5   Saint Louis, MO   63143

6   Attention: Jason Burrel

7   Gentelmen,

8   Last Saterday, I send you severil copy of our new phamphlet

9   LOOKING FOWARD TO A NEW WORLD. By this time, prehaps you have recived

10   it and had a oportunity to look at it closely/

11   After you have examine it, I belive some of the members of you

12   corporation should be tole about it. I belive that they wil be very

13   very much interest in founding out about waht our society will be like

14   within the next few year

15   After you have gotten there reaction, get in touhc with me. Ill

16   be gald to discuss it furthur with you so that we can make plans for

17   for the changes belive we will be nessessary.

18   As allways, I value you opinon.

19   Yous truely,

20   AMERICAN FUTURES, INC.

21   HRL:YOI   Harry Loomis

22   president

23

24

25

26

1

2   Mach 4 19--

3   Ms. Karen Polanski

4   243 New Mexaco Boulevard

5   Albequerque, NM   87144

6   Dear Miss Polansky

7   I was somewat suprised to learn that youwere dissatisfy wit the

8   service you recived at our Nineth Avenue restarant last Saterday. I

9   belive Ms Polanski that the difficulty was caused by the the fack that

10 the members of you party requested seperate checks after the waiters

11 had allready prepare one check for the entir party. In as much as

12 a great deal of extra work had be to done by the waters at the last

13 minite, you were undoubtdly delaied. Usully a request like thsi is

14 made before lunchon is served, an the staff of the restarant is allways

15 abel to prepair seperate checks iwth a miminum of time an effort.

16   However we do'nt want this occurence to predjice you against our

17 chain of restarants. We are, therfore enclosing a discount form with

18 this letter which will make it posible for you to have lunch or dinner

19 at any of our restuarants at a 20 percent discout. This form expires

20 in won year. I hop you will take advantige of this oportunity to let

21 us proove to you that the many years of excallent service you receive

22 in the passed were no acident.

23   Yours Very Truely

24   ALL-AMERICAN RESTARANTS

25 NW:YOI   Nathan W. Winers, General Manager

26

1

2   Octobe 16 19--

3   Miss Charlotte Ameling

4   1440 Ohhio Street

5   Ackron, OH   44345

6   Dear Miss Charlotte

7   Congradulations on your sucess in wknning one of the prizes in

8   the essay contest sponsored by our organzation   Frankly, we was some

9   what suprised at the large number fo entries we receved from secetaries

10   from all parts of the country. This is prooof that many secetaries

11   reconize the impotance of the statement; "Carefullness in proofrea-

12   ding letters is nesessary.

13   The enclosed phamphelt lists the choices you hav in selecting the

14   the prize to which youre entitle. Jus maek a notation (in the space

15   provided(of waht you would like us to sent you Ms. Ameling and we

16   we shall male it to you assoon as posible.

17   At the same time you send us you choice of prize, we shoud app-

18   reciate it if you would fill out the information aksed for on the

19   questionaire. Youre answers to these questions will be of great

20   assistants to us.

21   Cordilly Yours,

22   AMERICAN SECETARIES CLUB

23   HAM:YOI   Helene Melnick

24   Contest Editre

25

26

1

2   March 4, 19--

3   Messers. Grant and Hill

4   10 San Francisko Avenue

5   Berkley, CA   94746

6   Attention of Leonard Grant

7   Dear Mr. Grant

8   Why are you witholding payment of our onvoice of November 30

9   for $4,173.29. Wen you place the order, we told Mr. Howard your pr-

10   oduction manager that ew could make a shippnent of about ninty cartons

11   of stationary in Novembre and the rest of the cartoons on the order by

12   the middle of December. Inasmuch as the last cartons were shiped on

13   the nineth of Decembr, you shoud have recieve all that you order well

14   before the date promised.

15   We assume that all the stationary received was satisfactory be-

16   because we have not herd from you to the contrary. Incidently, you

17   you never owed us so much inthe passed, and we are somewat suprised

18   by you failure to pay this rather large bill of $4,172.29.

19   Your credit with us is good, and Im sure youwant it to stay that

20   weigh. Will you therfore, please foward you check to us as early as

21   as possibel.

22   Your very truely,

23   CALAFORNIA STATIONARY SUPPLIERS

24   HB:YOI   Harry Buckley,

25   Credit Manger

26

1

2   Decembr 2, 19--

3   Mr. Leonard Kaufman

4   Bridgeport Gas Company

5   53 Conneticut Avenue

6   Bridgport, CT. 06647

7   Gentlemen:

8   Thankyou for you acceptence of our invitation to speak at the Town

9   Hall Meeting sponsored by our organisation the Air Cpntrol Committee.

10 We have just had to change the date of the meeting from Tuesdy Januery

11 3 to Wensday Januery 4. I would appresiate it if you could have you

12 secetary telephone me to confirm the fact that you will be abel to

13 speak on the forth instead of on teh third.

14   At this meeting, we hope to have a minium of formel speeches and a

15 maximum of time aloud for questions and answeres. Will you, therefor

16 please limit your adress to about 20 minutes. Reconizing your skill

17 as a speaker Mr Kaufmann I am sure that you can get you're points ac-

18 cross in that short period of time? Than, any futher points you would

19 like to make can be aded in responce to questions.

20   Incidently, we are looking foward to having a large crowd again,

21 and we, theirfore expect a repitition of the lively program we had wen

22 you made an appearence last year at a similiar meeting

23   Yours Sincerely,

24   AIR CONTROL COMITTEE

25 JC:YOI   Jennifer Corwin

26   Program Chairperson

1

2   Agust 4   19--

3   Messers. Burton and Barr

4   1 Winston Salem Place

5   Ashville, NC   28848

6   Gentleman:

7   Congradulations on winning the cancelation of the bankrupcy pro-

8   cedings las t week in court. That you one against such high odds wsa

9   amazing but not suprizing because your attornies are amoung the best in

10 the State of North Caralina. One of the features of the case prooved

11 very intresting to me, and I would like to discuss it with yuo with a

12 minimumm of publicity.

13   I should like to meeet you for lunch at one of my favorite res-

14 tarants, the Ashville Inn one day convient to you. I realise that you

15 must be somewat busy inasmuchas their is still a great deal of work

16 that must be done in connection with with the cancelation of the bank-

17 rupcy, but I beleive you will reconize the importance of having a meeti-

18 ng early after we have gone over the feature wich still puzzle me.

19   Incidently, I woud prefer that we make arrangments for this ap-

20 ointment by your calling me at home rather then at my office.

21   Cordilly yourS,

22   EDWARDS & EDWARDS

23 EWE:YOI   Amy Beth Edwards

24

25

26

1

2   Decembr 29, 19--

3   Deluth Paper Company

4   414 Minnisota Avenue

5   Deluth, MN   55849

6   Attention of Mr. Dana Brill, Vice President

7   Dear Mr. Brill

8   We are somewaht suprised and dissappointed by the fact that we

9   have not yet recived the shippment of stationary whih we order more then

10   to months ago, on Octobre 17. Before we place the order, we told you

11   the following, "We need this stationary inorder to complete a big

12   printing order we have for pamplets and broshures for won of our

13   costumers". If we donot haev the order completed on time, it will

14   certinly effect the relationship that we have with this improtant cus-

15   tomar, and we are very ankshus about the entire situation

16   We feel that we gave you adquate notice of our requirments. When

17   you representive Mr Joliet spoke to me, he said taht the shiping date

18   would be no latter then Decembre 15. I relize that sometimes delays

19   are caused buy unexpected events, but aparently this is not sew in this

20   instance. Wehn ever I have telephone, I hav been assure that ours is

21   amoung the first orders yet to be filled, but sofar we have neither

22   neither recieved the stationary nor have we been given a deffinate date

23   for shippment. We are allways ready make to alowances, however in

24   this case it is extremely difficult to do sew.

25   If we had know taht their would have been such a long delay, we

26   would have try to get sum assistance from one or more of our other

1

2   Octobr 1   19--

3   Ms. Lois Medner

4   2333 Nibraska Street

5   Omoha, NE   68150

6   Dear Ms. Mender:

7   We are enclsoing the results of a questionaire wich we resently

8   send to a somewat large group of representives of various organsations

9   dealing with travel. Their very intresting because they give the

10 opinons of people who recugnize the need for excellant service at a

11 minumum expence.

12   After you have look thru this material, I no that you wil want

13 to use our services when ever you travell again. You were won of our

14 earliest clients, and the fack that you still make you arrangments

15 thru us is prooof that we give outstanding assistence to all of our

16 freinds

17   Under seeperate cover, we are sending you the latest adds that we

18 we have prepare for trips to Europe next spring. Look them over Miss

19 Medner and fine out whic trip will meet your requirments. Than, co-

20 mmunicate with me personnelly, and I will be happy to give you the

21 the benifit of my advise.

22   Cordilly yours,

23   NIBRASKA TRAVEL AGENCY

24 BAC:YOI   Beverly Chazon

25 Inclosure   Presidentt

26

27 suppliers. Often we can order seperately and by some paper from one

28 company and the rest fromm another. This time we did not do this be-

29 cuse we were assure by your salesman Mr. Joliet that it would be be

30 unecessary to do sew.

31   I would appriciate it if you wod personnelly investigate this ent-

32 ire transaction. An analisys of all the facks will prooove to you that

33 all my statements are acurate.

34   Unless I here from you by next Wesnesday, I shall take up this

35 this matter with may attornies to see what theirr opinon is. In the

36 passed when this has occured with other suppliers, they have recomended

37 complete cancelation of a order. We should hate to have to insitute

38 a lawsuit for the damages we will have sufferred if the stationary is

39 not ready for us allmost immediatly, but that will be a desision Ill

40 have to make based on the judgement and advise of my attornies.

41   Very Truly Yours,

42   WESTERN PUBLISHERS, INC.

43 JBE:YOI   Jeffrey B. Ely, Sr.

44   Presidennt

45

46

47

48

49

50

51

52

RULES FOR COMMAS—Part 2

The first four rules for commas and exercises were given before the Word List for Letters 41-50. The next four rules for commas are given below.

After you have studied these rules, do the exercises which contain sentences requiring commas. After you have done the exercises, check with the answers. Note that there are alternate uses of the comma. If you find that you have made errors, study the rules again, and do the exercises once again.

When you are ready to start the letters, remember that you have to insert commas. Since the rules allow for optional commas, there may be more than one correct way to punctuate. If, when checking your letters, you see that you have made errors in placing commas, study the rules again, and do the exercises once more.

Rule 5. A comma may be used after a complimentary close in a business letter. This is an optional use. If no comma appears, do not consider that an error.

    Examples: Sincerely yours,   Sincerely yours

Rule 6. A comma is used to separate parts of dates or addresses.

    Examples: Saturday, May 2, 19—, is the date of the meeting.

                    Cleveland, OH 44101 (Note: There is no comma between the state and the ZIP Code.)

Rule 7. A comma is used to separate an introductory dependent clause from the main or independent clause. **Introductory** means **beginning,** and a **dependent clause** is a group of words with a subject and verb that is not a complete sentence because it starts with words like: **after, although, as, because, before, if, provided, since, unless, when, while.** A **main** or **independent** clause can stand by itself as a complete sentence.

    Examples: Since I arrived at the office too late to see Mr. Johnson, I made another appointment.

                    If you are not sure of the correct spelling of a word, you should use a dictionary.

                    After I had studied some of the suggestions on punctuation, I was not at all confused.

NOTE: When the dependent clause does not introduce the sentence, a comma is not used to separate the independent or main clause from the dependent clause. The dependent clause is not introductory.

    Examples: I made another appointment because I arrived at the office too late to see Mr. Johnson.

You should use a dictionary if you are not sure of the correct spelling of a word.

I was not at all confused after I had studied some of the suggestions on punctuation.

Rule 8. An introductory phrase starting with a preposition (**at, between, by, from, in, of, on, to, with,** etc.) usually is followed by a comma if the phrase is long. Some authorities say that a comma should be used only if the phrase has more than five words. If the phrase has five words or fewer, the comma is optional.

    Examples: In his decision in that case, the judge was lenient. (Comma needed)

In his decision the judge was lenient. (Comma optional)

At this time of his life, the author still hopes for a great deal of success. (Comma needed)

At this time the author still hopes for a great deal of success. (Comma optional)

DIRECTIONS: Insert correctly all necessary commas. Note that other marks of punctuation have been omitted, and they must be inserted. In checking the answers, note that there may be more than one correct answer. If your answer differs, check with the rules again to see whether or not your answer is also acceptable.

1. I hope to be in Philadelphia on Friday May 25

2. He lives at 425 Fourth Avenue Chicago IL   60603

3. On Sunday July 4 1976 there were many Bicentennial celebrations all over the country

4. After a very long journey to New York George Washington was inaugurated on April 30 1789

5. For the first time in many years Jack decided that he would be self reliant and not dependent on others

6. At the time of the floods in New York State Charles was in Buffalo

7. In case of a fire in the building be sure to follow all the instruc tions

8. Between the time of the first and last meeting many important changes took place

9. At the time of Johns birth February 23 1962 Johns father was 33

10. On Thursday June 5 I shall move to my new address 609 Ninth Avenue Rochester NY   14203

11. After studying the rules above insert the necessary commas in each sentence

12. Insert the necessary commas after studying the rules above

13. The Board of Directors can make no decision until the survey has been completed

14. Until I receive word from you I shall take no further action

15. I shall take no further action until I receive word from you

16. Unless the survey is finished soon it will be too late to act

17. While I had planned to go to school next week I might stay home

18. When I have completed this course I hope to get a good job

19. I should be able to get a good job after I have been graduated

20. When he calls me this afternoon I shall ask him for an explanation

21. I shall ask him for an application when I go to that office

22. Because of her skill she received a promotion last week

23. If you are late to class you will miss the important work of the day

24. Help me as much as you can if you want me to help you

25. If you want me to help you help me as much as you can

26. Although you were weak in the use of commas I hope you are stronger now

27. Should blue material be available I will buy it for a dress

28. Since I agreed to go with him I shall keep my word

29. Because the children were there we had a very good time

30. We did not have a good time because there were few friends there

31. I can see you tomorrow since I shall be at my office then

32. If you really mean what you say we can take a trip together soon

33. We can take a trip soon if you really mean what you say

34. As you were on the team you should have spoken to the captain

35. Whenever I see her in my classes I am happy that she is there

36. Although times have changed there are still many things that have remained constant

37. Tom Joe and Ted are happy when they see Don in their classes

38. I may stay home even though I want to go to the movies

39. While she is living at home she should ask her parents if they would like her to contribute part of her salary

1. I hope to be in Philadelphia on Friday, May 25.

2. He lives at 425 Fourth Avenue, Chicago, IL   60603.

3. On Sunday, July 4, 1976, there were many Bicentennial celebrations all over the country.

4. After a very long journey to New York, George Washington was inaugurated on April 30, 1789.

5. For the first time in many years, Jack decided that he would be self-reliant and not dependent on others.

6. At the time of the floods in New York State, Charles was in Buffalo.

7. In case of a fire in the building, be sure to follow all the instructions.

8. Between the time of the first and last meeting, many important changes took place.

9. At the time of John's birth, February 23, 1962, John's father was 33.

10. On Thursday, June 5, I shall move to my new address, 609 Ninth Avenue, Rochester, NY   14203.

11. After studying the rules above, insert the necessary commas in each sentence.

12. Insert the necessary commas after studying the rules above.

13. The Board of Directors can make no decision until the survey has been completed.

14. Until I receive word from you, I shall take no further action.

15. I shall take no further action until I receive word from you.

16. Unless the survey is finished soon, it will be too late to act.

17. While I had planned to go to school next week, I might stay home.

18. When I have completed this course, I hope to get a good job.

19. I should be able to get a good job after I have been graduated.

20. When he calls me this afternoon, I shall ask him for an explanation.

21. I shall ask him for an application when I go to that office.

22. Because of her skill, she received a promotion last week.

23. If you are late to class, you will miss the important work of the day.

24. Help me as much as you can if you want me to help you.

25. If you want me to help you, help me as much as you can.

26. Although you were weak in the use of commas, I hope you are stronger now.

27. Should blue material be available, I will buy it for a dress.

28. Since I agreed to go with him, I shall keep my word.

29. Because the children were there, we had a very good time.

30. We did not have a good time because there were few friends there.

31. I can see you tomorrow since I shall be at my office then.

32. If you really mean what you say, we can take a trip together soon.

33. We can take a trip soon if you really mean what you say.

34. As you were on the team, you should have spoken to the captain.

35. Whenever I see her in my classes, I am happy that she is there.

36. Although times have changed, there are still many things that have remained constant.

37. Tom, Joe, and Ted are happy when they see Don in their classes.

38. I may stay home even though I want to go to the movies.

39. While she is living at home, she should ask her parents if they would like her to contribute part of her salary.

Word List—Letters 51–60

The words on this list occur for the first time in Letters 51-60. Following the suggestions for learning how to spell words, study the spelling of these words before correcting the letters. When correcting the letters, refer to this list and to the Master Spelling List (p.24). If you are not sure of the spelling of a word, be sure to consult your dictionary immediately. The starred (*) words are repeated in the Words Often Confused section of this list. Brief definitions are given, and the part of speech is indicated in parentheses.

Some dictionaries give alternate spellings for the words indicated with the plus sign (+). These alternate spellings are shown on this page. However, when these words are given in the letters, use the spelling on the list since this is the preferred spelling.

advertisements	chose	criticism	development	preference
all right+	column	criticize		previous
allotted	coming		encourage	
aloud	confident	defendant	essential	regret
altogether	controversy	deferred		remove
attempt		dependent	fair*	
	courteous	description		September
calendar	courtesy	develop	magazines	
			preceding	

Words Often Confused

fair (adj.)—according to rules; just; beautiful
fare (n.)—the sum charged or paid for when riding in a vehicle

Alternate Spellings

Preferred	*Acceptable*
all right	alright

1

2   Juyl 1 19--

3   Mr. Herman Held

4   207 Mew Jersy Avenue

5   Patterson, NJ   07551

6   Dear Mr Held

7   Of cause, I was very gald to write a letter of recommendation

8   for yo u when I recieved a request for infromation form the New Jersy

9   Insurence Company. I am confidant that my discription of your activ-

10 ities while you work for our organzation will be helpfull to you.

11   As I tole you when you choose to leave our firm and retrun to

12 college I woud be happy to higher you again. The high quality of

13 you're work and your curteous manner alwways impressed me and our

14 costumers.

15   I regreat that you desided to stay in New Jersy and therfore,

16 can not work for us now that you hve receive your college degree.

17 However I no that you will be comming home to visit you family soon,

18 and I hop you will stopp in to see me. I belive you will be very

19 much intrested in the new developements that have occured in our

20 company.

21   Good luck on you new job!

22   Sincerly yours,

23   HAMILTON EQUIPTMENT COMPANY

24 RHA:YOI   Roy A. Hamilton

25   President

26

1

2   Marhc 15, 19--

3   Mr. David Duval

4   976 Calafornia Street

5   Saccramento, CA   95852

6   Dear Mr. Duvall:

7   I hope that you had a good trip back to Saccremento last Frid-

8   ay March 9. The whether hear since than has been find, and we are

9   looking fward to a pleasatn spring.

10   Im sorry that we coud not have aloud suffcent time to discus more

11   fully the contraversy that has develope in our industry. As you no

12   I am dependant upon your advise wehn a situation like this arises.

13   However we simply didnt have enough time go to over all of the apsects

14   of the critisisms that have been raise

15   I wonder if you coud check your calender to see wheather the

16   second week of April would be convient for you to spend some time wiht

17   me? I shall be in San Fransisco on the nineth of the month, and I can

18   fly to Sacremento the next day. Since I reelly dont think that a de-

19   sision on the contraversy can be defered mubh beyond that tiem I would

20   like the benifit of you advise and thinking on the subject.

21   Yours very Sincerely,

22   MS:YOI   Maurice Stempler

23

24

25

26

May 25 19--

Mr. Gregory Fallon

1233 Buffallo Avenue

Siracuse, NY   13253

Dear Mr. Falon

    Our company has attemped to incourage the developement of the
arts by having mony alloted for advertisments in many newspaper an
magizines thruout the country. A disciption of the soms we have aloted
is goin to be publish in a bullitin wich we are planint to issue within the next month or to.

    We are doing thsi becuse their has been som critisism by a number
of are stockholders about the fact that we are spending this money.
We will therefore, communicate with all our stockholders to fine out
weather they agree with those who critisize our policy.

    After you have read the discription of how hte money is being
spend we are confidant that you willbe amoung the stock holders who
will be of assistants to us wen this matter is discuss at comittee
meetings and at the meeting of the stockholders on Wensday July 1st.
Because of you long association with us I wouldd appriciate you advise after you have anilyzed what we are planing to place in the
bullitin.

                          Very Truly Yours,

                          MEADOW COMPANY

AW:YOI   Alex West

                          Public Affairs Manager

1

2   Septembre 17, 19--

3   Ms. Charlotte Schwarz

4   909 Skenectidy Avenue

5   Rochestar, NY   14654

6   Dear Miss Swarz:

7   Do you speak allowed to yourself while you are working at home

8   Do you have anxus feelings about your goals in life. Do you feel that

9   the months on the calender are comming and going to quickly. Do you

10   feel disatisfked with how you are occupying your time. Are you con-

11   cious that tension is allways present.

12   If you beleive that the qestions we have aksed above give a good

13   good discription of your feelings we have the answrs to some of you

14   prolbems. Just fill out the enclosed questionaire, and we will put you

15   on our mailing list to recieve copies of the pamphlets we prepair each

16   month. After you have subscribe to these pamflets for twwo or three

17   months we belive that the advise you will recieve from our columnss

18   will make the comming year a much ahappier one you for then teh last

19   won has been.

20   Wehn you return the enclosed questionaire send us only 9$ the

21   low anuel rate, and you will get the first pamflet before the begin-

22   ing of the year.

23   Your sincerely,

24   MODERN HEALTH PUBLICATIONS

25   VM:YOI   Victor Madden, Editro

26   Inclosure

1

2   Nivember 20, 19--

3   Miss Carrie Hope

4   271 Indianna Avenue

5   Indiannapolis, IN   46255

6   Dear Ms. Hope:

7   Are you alltgether sure taht you are using all of yur skills and

8   personnel assets in your present career. Have you spend a number of

9   years on a job where each day is a repitition of the preceeding one.

10   Are you confident you that coud secure another position easily if for

11   some reason uoyr position is effected by a change in company policy

12   Our agency is begining a series of small meetings each Wensday

13   evning at 7 p.m. at the too addreses shown above on our letterhead. We

14   belive we can be of asistance to you. We shall go over the Want Adds

15   stress how skills can be improve allmost immediatly and how courtecy

16   can be used to make the day pass buy more plesently. Because we no the

17   benifits to you wil be substancial we urge you to attend the rirst

18   session whic will be on Wensday December 3. Of cause, their is know

19   fee for these meeting. If you would like to bring a freind, do sew.

20   Incidently, we chose Wensday nights becase we belived a night in

21   the middle of the weak woud be most conveinent. However if you have a

22   preferrence for another night we can attempt to change our sessions two

23   a night of your choise.

24   Sincerly yours,

25   ROBERTS EMPLOYMENT AGENCY

26   GF:YOI   Gloria Feit, Personel Director

1

2   Janery 19, 19--

3   Dr. Gary Clatworth

4   202 Michagan Avenu

5   Detriot, MI. 48256

6   Dear Mr. Clattworth:

7   I appriciate your efforts in behalf of the defendent I am

8   respresenting Glenn Johannes. As a result of the medical atention

9   you gave him he is much omre at ease then he had been previsly. As

10 you know before ou saw him he was dependant on drugs to lessen the

11 ankshus feels he had. However after you treated him twice he became

12 mcuh more independentt. Now is he able to go thru each day without

13 resorting to durgs or other medication.

14   I no that you said that you would allwo him to withold paymennt

15 untill he is better able to affort the costs of treatment. As won

16 of his attornies I am doing the same thing.

17   In my judgement Mr. Hohanes is innocent, and I hope to proove

18 this at the trail whihc will start at teh begining of next weak.

19   Sincerely yours,

20   ROMANO AND JARVIS

21 TR:YOI   Tony Romano

22

23

24

25

26

1
2   March 1   19--

3 Mr. Jerome Heller

4 207 Massachusettes Avenue

5 Washington, DC   20057

6 Dear Mr. Heler:

7   Now that the cold whether is on it's way out are you planing im-

8 provments around the house. If you are we are confidant that the

9 short discription of our servises listed below ill be of great

10 asistance toyou.

11   Hav you been disatisfied with you kitchen and not know what to

12 do about ti. As you probable no, we have remodeled kitchens for to

13 of you neighbors, and they were very mcuh please wit teh results. We

14 can remoove all of your present appliances to make room for more comp-

15 act appliences and cabinets. A knew floor covering would allso make

16 a substancial diference in the way you kitchen look.

17   Are you dependant on you playroom for peace and relaxation.

18 If you are look at it closely. Anilize weather or not it is adaquete

19 for you needs now that you family is larger than it wsa wen you bought

20 the house.

21   Wen you come up to your hosue are you prowd of it's appearence.

22 Is the paint fresh. Do you still fine it convient to put the storm

23 windows on each fall and remoove them in the spring, or wouldd you

24 like to maek life easier and simpler by having the combinationwindows

25 we sell and install.

26   Now look at the garden Mr. Heller. In the spring and the summer

27 will you be anxios about the lawn flowers trees and shrubs. Will you

28 loook at the calender in April and think that you should have done some-

29 thin about the garden. In Aprill it will be to late. Now is the time

30 to be planing for a beautifull and gracious garden

31   Now is time to fill in the enclosed card and mail it to us. Our

32 representive will than get in touch with you so that you can make a

33 apoitntment to discuss you requirments.

34   Full payment can be defered with the balence to be paid in

35 low, monthly instalments. If it is more convient for you to pay in

36 full of cause, we shall give you a substantil discoutn. We allso

37 except major credit cards.

38   Won of our curteous salesman will call on you in responce to you

39 postcard. Put it in the mail today March 1

40   Very truly Yours,

41   GOLD CONTRACTORS, INC.

42 GG   GIlbert Gold

43 Encl:

44

45

46

47

48

49

50

51

52

1

2   Novembr 13, 19--

3   Mister Arnold Kapp, Manager

4   Happy Hours Bookstore

5   57 Kentuky Street

6   Louieville, KY   40258

7   Dear Mr. Kap:

8   In responce to you request of October 20 we have alotted the

9   some of $40,000 for the repairs and modernization fo you store. We

10   no that the fire caused a great deal of damege to the store. Altho

11   the insurence company has loud us only $20,000 we belive that it is

12   essencial that we spend aditional money in order to rebuild the store

13   Pleas sent me a full decription of what basic changes you woud

14   liek to make in teh store, but remember that you must keep the st-

15   ructural changes to a minium becuse repair costs has becomme so high.

16   I am not alltogether please with the advise I have receive from

17   the contractors I have spoken to hear in Cinncinnati. I should ap-

18   priciate it if you would attemt to secure assistence form to or threee

19   local contractors before we sign a contrack to have the work done.

20   Since Im going to be in Louiville shortly we can than discus

21   the situation more fully.

22   Cordilly yours,

23   HAPPY HOURS BOOKSTORES

24   QT:YOI   Quentin Tracy, Presiden

25

26

1

2   July 14 19--

3   Ms. Pamela Peterson

4   309 Wisconsan Street

5   Milwalkee, WI   53259

6   Dear Mrs. Petersen,

7   I have defered writing to you becuse I didnt want to critisize you

8   unfarely before I had all the facts, and I am gald taht I did so. New

9   developements show that you was alltogether correct in claiming that

10   that you had met the deadline for submitting the manuscrip for the

11   artical. I was disagreeably suprised to learn that your arangements

12   with Mr Thompson were not communicated ot me. Iwas therfore, under teh

13   the impression atht you and Mr. Thompsen had allso agreeed on May 1st,

14   but now he has told me that the deadline was changed to Agust 1st.

15   I apoligize for the inconvience caused you. Now I am confidantly

16   looking foward to seeing the manuscript by Agust 1.

17   Cordilly your,

18   JEFFERSON PUBLISHERS, INC.

19   Harold Grover

20   Editor

21

22

23

24

25

26

Novembre 1, 19--

Mr. Leon Loeb

557 Ocean Parkwya

Honollulu, HA   96860

Dear Mister Loeb,

Their are many columms in the wekly magizines which attemt to give you knoeledge of what is happening in the world, however no magazie has the number and quality of columnists we that we have. Wen you have look at the sample copy that shoud be ariving at you house soon you will be aggreeably suppprised at our superior coverage of the up to the minute news of teh world. You wil want to read some some of the columnss allowed to you family becuase of the new developements in the capitals of the world.

It is all right to say that you do'nt think that you need another magizine comming into your house, but it really is not all right not to read carefully the copie we are senting.

We are confidant that after you have red this issue you wil want want to us send the subscription blank for a six month trial subscription.

Yours truely,

CURTIS PUBLICTIONS

DE:YOI

Davis B. Ellsworth

Enclosure

Circulation Manager

RULES FOR COMMAS—Part 3

The first four rules for commas were given before you had to correct Letters 41–50, and the next four rules were given before you had to correct Letters 50–60. The rest of the comma rules are given below.

After you have studied these rules, do the exercises which contain sentences requiring commas. After you have done the exercises, check with the answers. Note that there are alternate uses of the comma. If you find that you have made errors, study the rules again, and do the exercises once again.

When you are ready to start the letters, remember that you have to insert commas and all other necessary marks of punctuation. Since the rules allow for optional commas, there may be more than one correct way to punctuate. If, when checking your letters, you see that you have made errors in placing commas and other necessary marks of punctuation, study the rules again, and do the exercises once more.

Rule 9. A comma is required if two complete sentences are separated by the conjunctions **and, or, but,** or **for.** This rule means that two independent or main clauses must have a comma before a conjunction that separates them. A clause must have a subject and a verb.

> *Examples*: Tillie said that she was correct, but the office manager disagreed with her. (Comma needed)
>
> I know that Ira will be punctual, and I think that you should be there on time. (Comma needed)
>
> I bought the books for you but did not deliver them on time. (Comma not needed because the second part of the sentence is not a clause since it does not have a subject.)
>
> Joan told me that she would be there at 2 o'clock but did not show up until 3 o'clock. (Comma not needed because the second part of the sentence is not a clause since it does not have a subject.)

NOTE: Some authorities recommend omitting the comma if either clause has five words or fewer. However a comma is never wrong; its use is optional if either clause is short.

> *Example*: I know a little but he knows less.
>
> or
>
> I know a little, but he knows less.

Rule 10. A comma is used after the main clause if the following dependent clause is not necessary and can be omitted without altering the meaning of the sentence. (The technical term for this is **nonrestrictive** or **nonessential.**)

Examples: Gwen Janeway left our employ to work for Barton & Bell, which is one of Detroit's largest law firms. (The clause beginning with **which** merely adds information about the firm, and a comma is therefore needed.)

Write me on Monday, on which day I will be ready. (The clause beginning with **on** merely adds information and does not alter the meaning of the sentence, and a comma is therefore needed.)

Our organization, which is just beginning, hopes to be successful soon. (The clause beginning with **which** merely adds information and does not alter the meaning of the sentence. The sentence would make just as much sense if the clause were omitted, and the sentence read: *Our organization hopes to be successful soon.*)

NOTE: In the same kind of construction, a comma is not used after the main clause if a dependent clause is necessary and cannot be omitted without altering the meaning of the sentence. (The technical term for this is **restrictive** or **essential**.)

Examples: The secretary who works in our office is being transferred. (If commas were included after **secretary** and **office,** the sentence would give incomplete information because it would be just as though it meant, *The secretary is being transferred.* This would not describe sufficiently which secretary is being transferred.)

Snow that is two days old is dirty. (If commas were placed after **snow** and **old,** the sentence would mean: *Snow is dirty.*)

The plans that your employee made can be changed. (If commas were placed after **plans** and **made,** the sentence would mean: *The plans can be changed.* This would not give sufficient information because it would not indicate who made the plans.)

Rule 11. When two or more consecutive adjectives describe or modify the same noun or pronoun, separate the adjectives by commas, but do not place a comma after the final adjective.

Examples: He wore a handsome, stylish suit.

He was a capable, conscientious employee.

Rule 12. Insert a comma in a number of more than three digits to separate the thousands from the hundreds, the millions from the hundred thousands, etc.

Examples: 1,432   12,629   198,098   1,375,096

Rule 13. Insert a comma when a given name and a surname are reversed.

Examples: Smith, Jean   Blake, Marylou

Rule 14. Insert a comma when there is a title or a personal-name suffix.

Examples: John Smith, Office Manager   Ted Blake, Jr.

Robert Nelson, Esq.   Henry Louis, III

DIRECTIONS: Insert correctly all necessary punctuation. In checking the
answers, note that there may be more than one correct answer.
If your answer differs, check with the rules once again to
see whether or not your answer is also acceptable.

1. Gerald Okin, the purchasing agent left for Chicago, which is the first
   city on his extended trip.

2. I do not know, if our company which has offices only in San Francisco,
   is larger than Belton and Bowman.

3. Mr Lloyd Rice, the treasurer of the firm, was assigned to New York,
   which is the financial capital of the country.

4. All the financial costs which you agreed on are too high, and you
   will have to revise your estimates by Thursday, January 29.

5. All the clerks who came late were fired

6. We have $1,437,293 in our account at the present time.

7. The chief architect of the firm is James Chambers, Sr.

8. The head of the law firm is Anthony Thompson, Esq.

9. William Davis became the president of his college class on
   Saturday, April, 14, and he will serve until next April.

10. Margaret was a dedicated, conscientious worker before she retired

11. The population of that city has grown from 47,433 to 498,766 in the
    past ten years, and it is now the third-largest city in the state.

12. Edward Smith, III, was born on July 2, 1890, and is the oldest alumnus
    of that college.

13. As the teacher took attendance by calling the surname first she asked
    are Seff Philip and Stallings Joan here today

14. The error that he made can be corrected easily

15. The error like all errors can be corrected easily

16. Our college which is the oldest in the state was founded on May 2 1833

17. The employee who meets all of Mr Todds needs will never be found

18. The Empire State Building at 350 Fifth Avenue New York NY   10016
    is no longer the worlds tallest building but it is still   one of
    New Yorks greatest tourist attractions

19. All the letters which were mailed Friday should arrive there to
    morrow but the letters mailed today will not arrive on time

20. Although I thought I was on time for the party I missed him

21. Mr Thompson arrived in Boston early but Tom had already left for Rome

22. I shall go to Springfield Massachusetts if you will go there too

23. When I saw him at his fathers house I was surprised at how tall he was.

24. I am going to the theater and hope to see you there tonight

25. Please make an appointment with me if you can

26. I arrived at the school early but my pupils were not there

27. I expect to go to Chicago and may see some friends at that time

28. When I go to Chicago next month I hope to see my friends

29. I shall be in Chicago soon and I shall make an appointment to see you

30. If you would like me to visit your office let me know

31. Let me know if you would like me to visit your office

32. Please carry the typewriter here or Tom will not be able to do his
    work.

33. James and I are happy with our gifts and will send notes about them.

34. Although I expected to stay home I have decided to go to the meeting.

35. I will go to the meeting and should see you there if I come early.

36. George and Jack planned to check their work but forgot to do so and
    I think that they are sorry now

37. I hope to see you soon because I have a lot to tell you

38. The teacher said I hope that you will be in this class and I expect
    to see you soon.

39. We were going to the game but he may not be able to go with us

40. Is this the time to save money and gather possessions Toms father asked

41. I will have to be late to the meeting or I may not be able to go at all Robin said

42. I may be late to the meeting or may not be able to go at all.

43. He said that he was sorry and that he hoped it wouldnt happen again

44. Do not listen to what he says or you will be sorry Joans sister said

45. Did the boy and his sister visit us yesterday

46. Help is needed at this time and you should offer it to them

47. I know that you will be here and that John will not

48. I know that you will be here and John will not be here

49. I think that many of you will be glad to learn and I am here to help

50. She said that the time has come for you to make up your mind but you have not yet done so

51. Help Sue study her spelling words and she will be a source of pride to you

52. I may see you later this week and I know that Bob will want to see you too

53. Bill came late to the stadium and was unable to see the entire game

54. Bill came late to the stadium and was able to see only part of the game.

55. Bill came late to the stadium and he was able to see only part of the game.

56. The instructor said I hope you have put in all of the commas and have not put in any unnecessary ones.

57. Julia Haley the office manager was present at all of our meetings

1. Gerald Okin, the purchasing agent, left for Chicago, which is the first city on his extended trip.

2. I do not know if our company, which has offices only in San Francisco, is larger than Belton and Bowman.

3. Mr. Lloyd Rice, the treasurer of the firm, was assigned to New York, which is the financial capital of the country.

4. All the financial costs which you agreed on are too high; and you will have to revise your estimates by Thursday, January 29.

5. All the clerks who came late were fired.

6. We have $1,437,293 in our account at the present time.

7. The chief architect of the firm is James Chambers, Sr.

8. The head of the law firm is Anthony Thompson, Esq.

9. William Davis became the president of his college class on Saturday, April 14, and he will serve until next April.

10. Margaret was a dedicated, conscientious worker before she retired.

11. The population of that city has grown from 47,433 to 498,766 in the past ten years; and it is now the third-largest city in the state.

12. Edward Smith, III, was born on July 2, 1890, and is the oldest alumnus of that college.

13. As the teacher took attendance by calling the surname first, she asked, "Are Seff, Philip and Stallings, Joan here today?"

14. The error that he made can be corrected easily.

15. The error, like all errors, can be corrected easily.

16. Our college, which is the oldest in the state, was founded on May 2, 1833

17. The employee who meets all of Mr. Todd's needs will never be found.

18. The Empire State Building at 350 Fifth Avenue, New York, NY 10016, is no longer the world's tallest building; but it is still one of New York's greatest tourist attractions.

19. All the letters which were mailed Friday should arrive there to-morrow, but the letters mailed today will not arrive on time.

20. Although I thought I was on time for the party, I missed him.

21. Mr. Thompson arrived in Boston early, but Tom had already left for Rome.

22. I shall go to Springfield, Massachusetts, if you will go there, too.

23. When I saw him at his father's house, I was surprised at how tall he was.

24. I am going to the theater and hope to see you there tonight.

25. Please make an appointment with me if you can.

26. I arrived at the school early, but my pupils were not there.

27. I expect to go to Chicago and may see some friends at that time.

28. When I go to Chicago next month, I hope to see my friends.

29. I shall be in Chicago soon, and I shall make an appointment to see you.

30. If you would like me to visit your office, let me know.

31. Let me know if you would like me to visit your office.

32. Please carry the typewriter here, or Tom will not be able to do his work.

33. James and I are happy with our gifts and will send notes about them.

34. Although I expected to stay home, I have decided to go to the meeting.

35. I will go to the meeting and should see you there if I come early.

36. George and Jack planned to check their work but forgot to do so, and I think that they are sorry now.

37. I hope to see you soon because I have a lot to tell you.

38. The teacher said, "I hope that you will be in this class, and I expect to see you soon."

39. We were going to the game, but he may not be able to go with us.

40. "Is this the time to save money and gather possessions?" Tom's father asked.

41. "I will have to be late to the meeting, or I may not be able to go at all," Robin said.

42. I may be late to the meeting or may not be able to go at all.

43. He said that he was sorry and that he hoped it wouldn't happen again.

44. "Do not listen to what he says, or you will be sorry," Joan's sister said.

45. Did the boy and his sister visit us yesterday?

46. Help is needed at this time, and you should offer it to them.

47. I know that you will be here and that John will not.

48. I know that you will be here, and John will not be here.

49. I think that many of you will be glad to learn, and I am here to help.

50. She said that the time has come for you to make up your mind, but you have not yet done so.

51. Help Sue study her spelling words, and she will be a source of pride to you.

52. I may see you later this week, and I know that Bob will want to see you, too.

53. Bill came late to the stadium and was unable to see the entire game.

54. Bill came late to the stadium and was able to see only part of the game.

55. Bill came late to the stadium, and he was able to see only part of the game.

56. The instructor said, "I hope you have put in all of the commas and have not put in any unnecessary ones."

57. Julia Haley, the office manager, was present at all of our meetings.

Word List—Letters 61–70

The words on this list occur for the first time in Letters 61-70. Following the suggestions for learning how to spell words, study the spelling of these words before correcting the letters. When correcting the letters, refer to this list and to the Master Spelling List (p.24). If you are not sure of the spelling of a word, be sure to consult your dictionary immediately. The starred (*) words are repeated in the Words Often Confused section of this list. Brief definitions are given, and the part of speech is indicated in parentheses.

devise*	eliminate	noticeable	partial	price list
die*	embarrass	occurring	permanent	pursue
discrepancy	emphasize	offered	persuade	referred
dye*	extension	original	possession	remittance
eligible	incurred	overdue	practical	yield

Words Often Confused

devise (v.)—to invent
device (n.)—an invention

die (v.)—to suffer death; expire
dye (v.)—to take or give color

<pre>
1
2   March 14 19--
3   Thomas Stationary Company
4   235 Tenesee Street
5   Memfis, TN   38161
6   ATTENTION: Mr Harvey Weiss
7   Gentleman:
8   Than you for sending you're remittence for $473.29 which is
9   in parshul payment of your acount. Wen are bookeeper recieve your
10   check, she noted that their seemed to be a discrpency, between what
11   was fowarded, and the ammount on our books. She refered the matter
12   to me and my invesigation shows tht what probabley happened is that
13   you didnot use our current pricelist. If you look at the pricelist
14   in your posession you will see weather or not it is the spring list
15   or the fall list. You shoud be using the won that is dated "October".
16   Insted of sending us $873.29, you should of snt $523,29. We
17   woul apreciate it if you could male us the balanse due within ten
18   ten days which will help you take avantage of the discount offerred
19   for promt payment.
20   Your very truely,
21   GENERAL SUPPLY COMPANY
22   RH:YOI   Richard Herbers
23   Colection Manager
24
25
26
</pre>

1

2   Decembr 17, 19--

3   Mr. Michael Greco, Credit Manger

4   Independance Plumbing Company

5   375 Pensylvania Avenue

6   Harrisburgh, PA   17162

7   Dear Mr Michael,

8   SUBJECT: OVERDUE ACOUNT OF ROY MARTIN

9   In anser to you inquirey of Decembr 4 I am writing to let you no

10 that I have had practicly know sucess in trying to pursuade Mr Martin

11 to take care of his overdo accont.

12   I regreat that I think we wil have to persue legal action becuse

13 Mister Martin is unwilling to acknowlege the fack that he must pay for

14 for that part of the goods, which were damaged in shippment from Har-

15 risburgh to Cincinnatti. He refuses to except full responsability

16 for the damages, altho this was clearlly one of the terms of teh sale

17   He says that while he woud pay for half of the goods that were

18 damage that is as far as he wil go.

19   I refered to the term terms of the orignal contrack but he says

20 says that the damag was caused by poor packaging. Pleas let me no if

21 you wouldd like me to comtinue my eforts with Mr. Mortin, or weather

22 you would now like to trun the matter over toyour attornies.

23   Very truley your,

24 JAD:YOI   John Davis

25   Colection Specialist

26

1

2   Septembr 14 19--

3 Ms. Jane Milton

4 203 New Jersy Street

5 Jersy City, NJ   07363

6 Dear Mrs. Milton

7   Now that you are leaveing Jersy City permenently to settle In

8 Italy have you any posessions that you would like to sell. Our shop

9 is noted for the high prices it pays to estates and indivduals for

10 valueables including orignal oil panitings silver and china

11   If you are intrest in selling any of these items our representive

12 will comme to you home ta a time that will suit your convience. He

13 will be able to assume all responsability for desicions he makes in

14 seting prices for waht he purchasses.

15   Of cause, I regreat that you are leaving Jesrey City after so many

16 years but I am confidentt that you wil be very happy in you new home in

17 in Rome.

18   Sincerey your,

19   JERSEY ANTIQUE SHOP

20 BL:YOI   Bertha Losey

21 Enclosure

22

23

24

25

26

1

2   July 7   19--

3   Mr. James Messer Vice Presideent

4   Linclon Federal Savings Bank and Loan Association

5   4987 Nobraska Street

6   Linclon, NE   68564

7   Dear Mister Messor:

8   RE: Branch Bank at Linclon Shoping Center

9   You have been witholding $500 on this project sinse early las

10   Desember for work that had not yte been completed.

11   We now belive that wll work has been completed and we are in

12   possesion of documents to this affect.

13   Please send us this balanse promply so that we can close cacounts

14   our on this developement. We regreat any inconvience that this delay

15   delay may have caused byou but untill now our efforts to pursuade the

16   electricials to complete the work was not sucessfull. They have finaly

17   met there responsabilities and everything shoud be in good shape now.

18   Ver Truly yours,

19   TUCKER CONSTRUCKTION COMPANY

20   RT,YOI   Robert Tucker

21   Tresurer

22

23

24

25

26

1

2   Arpil 24 19--

3   Ms. Joan Zeller

4   Wells and Raymond

5   Post Office Box 750

6   Hardford, Ct   06165

7   Dear Mrs. Zellar:

8   RE: Conneticut Bank and Trust Company Balance

9   In responce to your letter of the nineth of this month to

10   Mr. Fred Gomez I am inclosing photocopies)front and back) of our

11   checks numbered 1027 and 1079 dated Septembre 13 and 20 respectively.

12   We hope that now you will be abel to correct what ever error exist

13   exist so that the balanse do will aggree wiht our figurres.

14   As I wrote you previsly I refered you letter to our boookkeeper.

15   He check his records with extream care and is certin the responsability

16   for the error is not his. He beleives that the error occured becuse

17   these to checks werent posted properly on you records

18   If you have any furthere inquireys about this matter please

19   referr it to Mr Gerald Zak our bokeeper because I will be on vaction

20   for for the nex monthe.

21   Yours Sincerely

22   SUTTER COMPANY

23   AS:YOI   Arnold Tatum

24   Enclosure   Acounting Department

25

26

1

2   Januery 22, 19--

3   Arthur Hill, Esq.

4   French & Thomas

5   980 Louisianna Street

6   Baton Roug, LA   70866

7   Dear Mr. Hill,

8   RE: KILLEWARE INDUSTRIAL PARK

9   In acordance with you request for a statement on the above

10   construction loan as of Januery 26 please be adviced as follows;

11   Princi;le $300000.00

12   Intrest Due   2135.41

13   TOTAL $302135.42

14   The above figures represent the ammount nesessary to make repaym-

15   ent of the loan assuming credit is recieved (via transfer thru the

16   Federal Reserve Bank of New York.

17   In teh event that credit is not recieved by Januery 26 a intrest

18   charge of $85,42 per day will be incured untill repayment is affected.

19   Pleas note that if payment is made by check intrest will accrue untill

20   the check is recieved by us and subsequently cleared throug banking

21   channels. We are inclosing the folowing documents to be held by you

22   you in escrow pending the payment of the loan in full;

23   1) Assignment of Morgage from First Natinal State Bank to Metro-

24   politaan Insurance Company, dated Januery 22.

25   2. Income Loan Note from the Borrower to the Bank, dated

26   Decembre 22.

27   3) Construction Morgage Note from the Borrowers to the Bank, dated

28   Novembr 13, in the amount of $170000.00.

29   4) Construcktion Morgage from the Borrowers to the Bank, dated

30   November 13, in the ammount of $170000.00

31   5) Modification and Extention Aggreement between Killeware Ind-

32   ustrial Park and First National state Bank, dated May 15.

33   6) Financial Statment and Acknowledgement filed in the Secetary

34   of States Office on Agust 7, File No. 1373.

35   7) Standard Fire Insurance Policy of Commerical Insurance Company,

36   No. 3WT-023-596.

37   9) Hazard Insurance Policy of Independance Insurence Company,

38   No. FF4-51-68-93.

39   The Construction Morgage, Modification and Extention Aggreement

40   been have endorsed for cancelation, the Construcktiin note has been

41   stamped "Paid", and we have executed the termination statments on teh

42   the finnancial statment.

43   Pleas acknoledge reciet and exceptence of the above by signing an

44   returning the enclosed copy of tihs letter.

45   Very truely yours,

46   WC:YOI   William M. Clark

47   Assistent Cashier

48

49

50

51

52

1

2   Juen 4 19--

3   Ms Rita Hunter

4   1046 Ohhio Boulevad

5   Tolledo, OH   43667

6   Dear Ms. Hunter:

7   You are in posession of this letter. This placess you in the

8   the middle of a exciting mystery Miss Hunt.

9   First, there is to be the mistery of the valueable package that

10   the Tolledo mailman is soon to deliver to you at 1045 Ohio Boulevard.

11   Than their is the mystery of teh money, and weather you will win the

12   $50000 grand prize.

13   We hav an mystery gift all wrapped and ready to deliver to you as

14   as soon as you return you shiping lable. This gif is yours free, wehn

15   you order from our catolog. You must order merchandize of at lease

16   5$. In edition, we have issue a $50000 prize entry ticket in you name.

17   We can not emphazize two much hoew very much pleasure the pruchase

18   of our producks will yeild to you. Just loook at all of the originel

19   and practicel products we offer and you will not have to be pursuaded

20   to purchas som of them write now.

21   Dont forget to send your remittence for at least 5$ and you will

22   be elligible for the grand prize. Act today?

23   Very truly your,

24   MA:YOI   Mary Ann Spence

25

26

1

2   Janurary 9; 19--

3   Miss Harriet Kaplan

4   598 Tennesee Lane

5   Chattanoogga, TN   37468

6   Dear Ms. Kaplane,

7   We hav deviced a new system which we use to die shoes. Never

8   agin will you die you shoes and be embarassed because the die has run

9   run on your feet or on you stockings. The diffrence between are system

10 and those systemms used in the passed is that we elliminate the removal

11 of the orignal color. You just apply our polish and the job is done

12 quickly efficently and smoothely. We except resplnsibility if you

13 arent satisfy with the results. Your shoes will have a attractive

14 permanant finish and, off course, it will not be noiticable that you

15 used a die to change the collar.

16   We are enclosin our lastest pricelist. Please note that we dont

17 ecept parshul payments. Please sent us a remitance in full.

18   We no that you you will not regreat taking avantage of this op-

19 potunity to have "new shoes' at little cost.

20   Very sincerly yours,

21   CHATANOOGA POLISH COMPANY

22 YOI   Sales Maneger

23

24

25

26

1

2   Septembr 2, 19--

3   Mr. Kenneth B. Marlin

4   208 Arizonna Avenue

5   Tuscon, AZ   85769

6   Dear Mr Martin

7   Thankyou for you inquirey about Savings Bank Life Insurence

8   (SBLI.) Hear are some of the facts on low cost SBLI:

9   1) SBLI is low in cost becuse you by it direckt form the bank.

10   By not having a outside sales force we are abel to keep our costs and

11   and over head to a minium.

12   2) SBIL has trained salaried personal who have past the same

13   state examination as anyone selling insurence in this state. They hav

14   the time and the knowlege to analize yourneeds and make reccommenda-

15   tions. Their is no obligation and no pressure to by.

16   4) SBLI has a variety of plans; which are avalable in ammounts up

17   to $30000. The low cost plans include straight life term limited pay-

18   ment morgage and others. All plans pay dividends begining the first

19   year.

20   If you are interest in bying substancial ammounts of protection

21   at a low cost, it is not nesassry for you to make a inquirey about it

22   at the bank. Just mail the enclosed card and furthur infromation wil

23   be in you posession by retrun mail/

24   Yours truely

25   ARIZONNA STATE BANK

26   RY:YOI   Ray Terrasi, Customer Service

1

2   Mach 4. 19--

3   Mr Randolph Webb

4   2037 Nebrasska Stree

5   Lincon, NE   68570

6   Dear Mr. Web,

7   If you were to dye tommorrow would your family regreat that you

8   did'nt take the resopnsibility of providing enough funds for them after

9   you have dyed. We can not emphasise to strongly, that you shoud not

10 have to be pursuaded to to carry enough lifte insurence to elliminate

11 finantial embarassment to your survivors.

12   The enclosed broshure contains a parcial listing of the types fo

13 policies we offer. As you can see you are elligible for some types fo

14 insurence up the to age of 70. Chose won that is pratical for your

15 needs and then you shoud telephone us so that we can make an apoint-

16 ment wit one of our experienced expert and courteous representives

17 for you. He will tell you whihc policy yeilds the most benifts for

18 a person in you sircumstances.

19   We hop to here from you shortly. If you have an imediate in-

20 quirey which you would like anser by telephone just call me at the

21 number listed above/

22   Yours Very truly,

23   NEBRAKSA INSURENCE COMPANY

24 AR   Albert Rossiter

25   Districk Maneger

26

Word List—Letters 71–100

The words on this list occur for the first time in Letters 71-80. This is the last word list because there are no new spelling words in Letters 81-100.

Following the suggestions for learning how to spell words, study the spelling of these words before correcting the letters. When correcting the letters, refer to this list and to the Master Spelling List (p.24). If you are not sure of the spelling of a word, be sure to consult your dictionary immediately. The starred (*) words are repeated in the Words Often Confused section of this list. Brief definitions are given, and the part of speech is indicated in parentheses.

all ready	except	fourth	maintenance	sew
device	exercise	freight		stationary
	existence		omission	
		genuine	omitted	who's
envelope*	fare			
equipped	forfeit	indebtedness		
exceed	forty	indispensable	reference	

Words Often Confused

envelop (v.)—to enclose; to wrap
envelope (n.)—a paper case or wrapper

1

2   Agust 3 19--

3   Mr. Eugene Hellers

4   10 Illinoise Street

5   Chicargo IL.   60671

6   Dear Mr. Heller:

7   In anser to your inquirey about Individual Retirement Acounts

8   (IRA(I am happy to send you a pamhplet wich gives all the nesessary

9   infromation about IRA.

10   If you are elligble for a IRA plan stop in at any of this banks

11   branches. If it is more convient for you to do sew mail the enclosed

12   forms to us in the envelop wich we are sending with this correspondents

13   and we will take car of the rest.

14   Pleas note your that contrkbutions can not excede $1500 anually.

15   You may chose to have you funds earn the same high dividend rates

16   payed by the bank on other savings acounts or you may build even

17   larger RIA funds by using one of the many higher-yeilding time deposit

18   acounts vailablbe at our bank.

19   If you have any further questions please dont hesitate to com-

20   unicate with m.e

21   Yours truely

22   ILLINOISE NATIONAL BANK

23   JB   John Berry Cashier

24

25

26

1

2   Agust 5, 19--

3   Mr. Leslie Caban

4   390 Florada Highway

5   Miama, FL. 33172

6   Dear Mr Kaban:

7   In anser to you inquirey of July 25 I am happy to give you in-

8   fromation about the bus fairs in this city. The present fair of fourty

9   cents has been in existance since last Febuery. In Febuery, the bus

10   company had an indebtness which made it nessassary to raise the fair

11   for the forth time to in years. The bus company made know garantee

12   that the fairs would not be raised again soon but tehy hope to be abel

13   to excercise good management caution and economy. May be the present

14   fair will stay in affect for quit some time but it maybe that it wil

15   will have be to increased once agin.

16   As you no bus transportion is indispensible in our community. All

17   the equipement is well-equiped and well-serviced. All lines accept

18   the Forth Avenue Line run untill midngiht and an extention of service

19   on that line is being cnsider.

20   I hope that this information will be helpfull to you in prepairing

21   the broshure you are writing

22   Cordial yours,

23   CHAMBER OF COMMERCE

24   BM:YOI   Brian Murray, Director

25

26

1

2   Aprli   9, 19--

3   Mr. James C Amara Jr.

4   Real Estate and Contsruction Division

5   Amara Equippment Company

6   606 Alibama Avenue

7   Mobile,, AL   36673

8   Gentelemen:

9   I appriciate your keeping me up-to-date on your office relocation

10   project. We certinly would like to have you as a tenaant in our new

11   building. I am confidant that we coud work out the frieght and loading

12   arrangments to meet you requirments.

13   We can not garantee that the traffic situation will have clear

14   up by the summer. the Parkway Authority is building a extention of

15   the State Parkway and I blieve that this will work be completed buy

16   early summer.

17   Thank you very much for the curtesies you extended to me and to

18   to Mr Fuller on our last visit. We if can provied you with any furthur

19   assistence please d'ont hesitate to call on me.

20   Sincery Yours,

21   CHASE CONSTRUCTION COMPANY

22   JL:YOI   Joseph Localio Vice President

23   Real Estate Developement

24

25

26

1

2   Agust 18, 19--

3   Armstrong Frieght Conpany

4   27 Minnisota Avenue

5   Minneapilis, MN   55474

6   ATT: Mr Fred Burk Assistent Vice Prisident

7   Genttelmen:

8   This is the forth time I have had to write you about your in-

9   debtness of $14327.29 to our organzation. It is urgent that you make

10   payment by Agust 29 in as much as at that time we are planing to turn

11   the acount over to our attornies.

12   I am sure taht you are concious of the fact that we are as de-

13   pendant upon collecting money owed us, as you are. We want to ellimi

14   nate finantial embarasment when ever it is posible to do sow and the

15   decicion to turn the matter over for leagal procedings is the last

16   resort. Our business existense is effected by not reciving remittancs

17   promply and we do'nt want to be finantially inconvienienced because of

18   very high Acounts Recivable.

19   I am enclosing a stamped, selfadressed envelop with this letter.

20   I genuinly hope that we shall not be force to communicate with our

21   our attornies. You can prevent this by mailing us a check in full for

22   you debts which you have incured $14327.29

23   Very truly yourS,

24   JENKINS BOX CONPANY

25   YOI   Assistent Treasurer

26

1

2   Octobre 8 19--

3   Ms. Ina Clarke

4   43 Niagra Falls Avenue

5   Buffallo, Ny   14275

6   Dear Mrs Clark

7   In referrence to you inquirey about a stationery model of a soing

8   machine to replace you porrtable won I am genuinly sorry to tell you

9   taht we no longer are the manufactures of these larger units. In as

10 muchas the demand for this type fo soing machine has allmost entirly

11 disappear, it was know longer profitable to manufactor them.

12   Wehn our company came in to existance about fourty years ago

13 we manufacture only the stationery model. Within the last few years

14 we analized our sales figures and made the desision that it wiuld be

15 foolish to continue manufacuring the stationery model, since we were

16 loosing money on it. We have had excellant reports from upurchasers

17 about our new model the D-147 with it's many new devises.

18   We are enclosing with this letter copies of our lastest advertis-

19 ments, calatogs and pricelists. In edition if you would like to stop

20 in at won of our local stores one of our curteous and helpfull salesman

21 will be already for you. He will show you that owning our Model D-146

22 will make it plesent easy and efficent for you to make you own clothes.

23   Coridally yours,

24 YOI:MO   Manuel Ortiz

25

26

1

2   Arpil 4, 19--

3   Mr. Gerald Koppel

4   437 Indianna Avenue

5   Indianipolis, IN   46276

6   Gentlemen:

7   Whos ready for a drive in the country?" is a question that is of-

8   fen ask at this time of year. However if your car is not equiped with

9   a efficint air-conditioning system you regret may that drive in the

10   country, if the weater turns very hot, as it is likly to do. While a

11   air-conditioner may not be indispensible now by the time July and Agust

12   roll around you will be consience of the fact that air-conditioning

13   ads to you convience and confort while you are riding troughout the

14   countryside.

15   Investagate the newest develoopments in air-cpnditioning for you

16   car. We are enclossing broshures and our pricelist. In edition look

17   at the adds which will be place in the Sunday papers for the nex to

18   weeks.

19   Remember if you are driving the Forth of July you will not have a

20   happy Independance Day if you are badly effected by the breezes heat

21   and humidity. Make a defanite decison now and you will be gratful for

22   this advise, as you drive this summer. Our curteous mechanics will

23   do the work efficently and all work is throughly garanteed

24   Sincerly yours,

25   INDIANNAPOLIS AIR-CONDIONING, INC.

26   APF:YOI   Art Forrest, Assistent Manager

1

2   Marrch 14   19--

3   Miss Mae Lovett

4   2964 Bridgport Road

5   Waterberry, CT   06771

6   Dear Mrs. Lovitt

7   Does the ommission of daily exersize bother you. Do you loook at

8   the calender and think of what you wil look liek in you bathing outfit

9   this summer. Will every one in you group accept you look slim and attr-

10 active. Will you be embarassed because your weight excedes you best

11 wait? Are you looking fro a improvment in you self image.

12   If your ansers to all of the questions listed above are "Yes", I

13 reccommend very strongly that you make a apointment with us in the ver

14 near futrue. Ta our gyms you will fine many men and woman who are doin

15 something to garantee that they will have a summer fill with fun excit-

16 ment and pleasure. In our judgement nothing has been ommitted to meet

17 you requirments. In edition to the equipmennt there are experts who

18 advice you about self improvment.

19   We maek it a principal to keep our fees so moderate that they will

20 not excede the limits of your bugdet. If you are disatisfied in any

21 way after your first visit, you donot forfiet your deposit. It will be

22 be refund to you promply and cheerfuly.

23   Cordially your,

24   EASTERN GYMS, INC.

25 JE:YOI   June W. Esposito, Manager

26

1

2   Jully 14, 19--

3   Fried and Gross

4   437 New haven Avenue

5   Hardford, CT   06178

6   Attention: Maynard Fried

7   Dear Mr. Freid:

8   Milton Spieler sugested that I call you in refarance to office

9   office space you need hear in New Jersy.

10   We are owners anddeveloppers of industrial commerical and office

11 buildings throuout New Jersy and we would certinly like to be helpfull

12 to you in satissfying you office requirments.

13   At present we have space availalbe in our Davis Metropark Building

14 which is located at the Garden State Parkway Extention and the Metrop-

15 ark Rail Station. This afords direct train access into New Youk

16 Philidelphia and Washington as well as excellant and convient highway

17 connections. In edition train and bus connections are more then ada-

18 quate and the fairs are resonable. We are hopping that the building

19 will defanately be avalbe in Novmber of this year. In this buidling

20 we will have some very desirable office suites on the third and forth

21 floors.

22   In Springfeild New Jersy which is in the Morristown districk, we

23 have nearly completed the construckion of a fourty story building wich

24 is all ready being talk about as won of the outstanding structures in

25 the entire state. It is located at teh intersection of Route 10 and

26 Root 287. This allso provides good access thruout the metropolitan

27 are. Thiss building is schedule for bompletion buy the first ofnext

28 year.

29   Im encolsing floor plans of these twoo buidlings. Inasmuchas so

30 much space has allready been rented I urge you to look at these floor

31 palns immediatly, if you think that you might be intrested in setting

32 up offices in this part of New Jersy. In case you are not familar wiht

33 with this section of the state, I am enclsing a map wich indicates th

34 locations of these to buildings.

35   I am allso enclosing a coppie of our companys brocchure which list

36 the buildings we manage. This bochure discribe our principle buildings.

37 Theyre practicly all rented at the present time but it is posible that

38 there will be vacancies soon, becase some senants have express a

39 prefference for larger quaters. We shll try to meet there requirments

40 in our too new buildings.

41   In edition to reading our literature you'r welcome to visit me at

42 any time which is mutually convient. May be a Saterday in Agust would

43 proove to be the best time that we can get together hear. It iwll be

44 unecessary for you to make a papointment more then a few days in adv-

45 ance, becuse that month is the won in wich I am least busy.

46   If you belive our organzation can be of assistence to you please

47 dont hesitate to get in touch with me

48   Sincerely Yours,

49   DAVIS CONSTRUCTION COMPANY

50 JA:YOI   Joseph T. Albertson

51 Inclosures   Assistent Managger

52

1

2   Janurary 16, 199

3   Mr. Roy Potter

4   241 Milwaulkee Avenue

5   Racien, Wi   53479

6   Dear Mr. Potters:

7   I am retruning you check for this months rent, becase you ommitted

8   you signature. I am enlosing a envelop adressed to me so that after you

9   have sign the check you can return it to me promply

10   Accept for three or four tenants everyone else has renewed his le-

11   ase. Im incourage by this fack, because everone seems to realise that

12   the maintainance probelms that we had while the superintendant was ill

13   were not permenent. In our tenants opinon efficency has return to its'

14   formally high state. As soon as the frieght elevator has been equiped

15   with new doors the building should be back to it's orignal condition

16   Las year you said you would be intrested in mooving to a smaller

17   apartment, and that this move wold be dependant on its' location.

18   Amoung the tenants who are apparrently not renewing theirr leases are

19   too with apartments on the forth floor. These apartments shoul be

20   avaiilable in the near futur. I sugest therefore, htat you speak to

21   the superintendant immediatly, to see whether or not these apartment

22   woul meet you requirments.

23   Sincerly yours,

24   INDEPNDANCE MANAGEMENT CO.

25   FB   Foster Bailey

26

1

2   NOvember 2, 19--

3   Mrs. Joan Alexander

4   271 Fourtieth Street

5   Garry, In   46480

6   Dear Ms. Alexander,

7   The new American Sowing Machines are already for you on the forth

8   floor of our store, Each machine is equiped with about fourty features

9   which will be indispensible to you in making clothing curtains and

10 decorative items for each room in you hous. The manufactures have om-

11 mitted nothing wich will addd to you convience in operating this mac-

12 hine. Its our genuinne opinon that their is no other sowing machine in

13 existance which does it's work as well as the American

14   Once you have seen the machine you willnot have to be perswaded

15 that its a practicel edition to your sewing room. The machine maybe

16 bought for cash with a credit card or by means of a parcial payment.

17   Dont loose any time in coming to our store to look at the various

18 modls we have on display. In asmuch as we are having our anuel No-

19 vembr sale you will be ablel to by a machine at about half of wat you

20 formally would have had to pay. Our curteous efficent and well trained

21 sales force will be gald to be of assistants to you.

22   Cprdially yours,

23   MORTON DEPARTMMENT STORE

24 TT:YOI   Tina Throck Sewing Department

25

26

1

2   Octobr 4 19--

3   Cinncinati Equipement Company

4   4090 Clevland Road

5   Ackron Oh   44381

6   Attention of Mr. Herbert Lewes, Treasurer

7   Dear Mr. Lewis:

8   The maintainance of of a good credit rating is indispensible to

9   any responsable businessman. Wehn you indebtness excedes your usull

10   credit limit your'e in danger of loosing the credit benifits receive

11   in the passed.

12   I am genuinnely sorry to hvae to writ this letter tu you but i

13   have defered writting it as long as posible. I have anilized our

14   our records, and fine that we have aloud your indetness of $17423,67

15   to last much to long. We have send you the usul collection letters

16   but we have had know responce form you. As we wroet you in our lett-

17   er of Septembr 17 even a parcial payment for the overdo acount would

18   have been a incouraging development. However even this parshal paym-

19   ent has been witheld.

20   As you have been won of our costumers all most since our organi-

21   sation has been in existance we regreat very much thta we can wait

22   wait no longer. If If you had been won of our resent costumers we

23   would have insituted legal procedings many months ago. We did'nt do

24   this, because we are concious of the fack that we have had a long an

25   pleasent association.

26   I am now force to right that unless we get a imediate responce

27 form you with at lease a partiall payement of what is ode us we shall

28 hve to turn the acont over to a collection agency. This is a very

29 disaggreable action to have to take but Im certin that you will aggree

30 that we have been more than fare and patient

31   Dont make us take htis step. INStead use the enclosed self

32 addressed envelop and foward your check to us buy retrun mail. Once

33 we have receive a parsial payment we can give a extention of about

34 ninty days for paying teh balense. However untill you have payed us

35 sum of the some owing we wo'nt attemt to discuss the payment of the

36 balence.

37   At the risk of endless repitition I am once again sayint that its

38 essencial that you mail us a check imediately. Otherwise the acount

39 will bee in the hands of the collection ajency and you will here form

40 them or from their attornies rather then from me

41   Very Truley yours,

42   OHIO STATIONARY COMPANY

43 AAA:YOI   Amos Andrews

44   Comptroller

45

46

47

48

49

50

51

52

1

2   AUgust 11   19--

3   Mr Bruce Raymond

4   205 Minnisota Avenue

5   Saint Paul, Mn   55182

6   Gentlemen:

7   Under seperate cover we are senting you the six invitations to

8   to the luncheon will which be held on Saterday, Novemmber 12 at the

9   Mineapolis Restarant at noon. The principle speaker at the lunchon

10   will the be the Superintendant of Schools Dr. Benjamain Marlowe

11   Mister Marlow is honoring a group of teachers assistent principles

12   principles and liberians who have retire or transfered to other school

13   districks. Sence you no that many of them have given valueable servi-

14   ces and have been responsable for theimprovement of learning and tea-

15   ching, I no that you and sum of the members of you organzation will

16   want to attend. Of cause, you will be our guests becuse you have help

17   to sponser so many joint activites wit us in the pass.

18   I woud be very gratful if you woud sent me the names of those who

19   will attend so that our program canbe prepared promply efficently and

20   acurately. Incidently we regreat that we cannote send more then six

21   invitation. As you undoubtably no, our buget has to be strickly ad-

22   hered to.

23   Sincerly yours,

24   JP   Joseph Paxton

25

26

1

2   Octobr 14 19--

3   Pennsyllvania Stationary Store

4   489 Pittsburg Avenue

5   Philidelphia, PA   19183

6   Gentleman

7   An analisis of our recordds by our head bookeeper shows that you

8   have not yet payed your overdo acount, inspite of the letters we have

9   have send and the telphone calls we made have withing the last to

10   month. If you woud like to ellimiante the embarassment of legal proc-

11   eedings we sugest that you use the enclosed stamped self adressed en-

12   velope and place your remittence of $143;29 in it

13   To you the ammount of $142.29 may not seem to be a large some.

14   Never the less we could not attemp to have suhc low prices if payments

15   were witheld for more then to months. We have deviced a through system

16   for notifying our costomers when they have unpayed ballances in there

17   acounts we and we gone thru all these steps in this system with you

18   Aparently the only solution we have is too turn turn over to our

19   attornies copies of our corespondence with you and they will take teh

20   necessery steps to see that the debt you have incured is payed promply.

21   We are hopping that we will recieve your check in the male by the

22   beginnig of next week so that we do'nt have to take the step discribe

23   above.

24   Yours Very Truly

25   YOI   Miriam Paine

26   Colection Manager

1

2   June 4, 19--

3   Coolidge Vacumn Cleaners, Inc

4   4596 San Fransisco Street

5   Berkley, Ca   94784

6   Attention: Mr. Wilson Forbes

7   Dear Mr Forbes,

8   We are ver unhappy with the shiping company youre using in ship-

9   ing the vcumn cleaners we by from you. As a responsable manufactorer

10 you no that "the custommer is allways right" In this case we beleive

11 thatt we are entirly right.

12   Wehn we remooved the vacumn cleaners from the cartons for the

13 the las two shipments we receive we found that too of the vacumn

14 cleanders were damage. Since this occurrance took palce on to seprate

15 occassions we belive that the time and expence involve for you and fro

16 us is to valueble to have to spend on unecessay damage. We sugest,

17 therefor that you consider changing to another frieght agency whihc

18 will be more careful efficient and satisfactroy.

19   Enclosed are the orignal and duplicate shiping cocuments. Theyre

20 complete and corect. After you have red them, you undoutably will tell

21 us wat to do wit the damage vacum cleaners. Of cause we woudl like you

22 to invesigatethrourhgly the causes of the damage so that you can palce

23 the responsability for these occurrances.

24   Yours truely,

25   CALAFORNIA MERCHANDIZE COMPANY

26 YOI:TE   Ted Elkins, Manager

1

2   MarcH 4 19--

3   Miss. Mary Lou Parton

4   498 Seracuse Avenue

5   Rochestar, Ny   14685

6   Dear Miss Partonn:

7   Please beginn to make arangements for the end-of year lunchon for

8   our volunteers. The principle purpose of this affair is to show our

9   apreciation to the voluntears for the ecellent quality of their baluable

10 services throughowt the year. The last to affairs whcih you planed

11 yeilded many benifits and messages of congradulations resulted. I no

12 you will excercise the same good judgement that you have use in the past

13   In as much as I no that you allways do such a efficeint job I am

14 greatful that I dont have to spend unecessary time trying to pursuade

15 you to except this aditional chore.

16   Alltogether the some of $1000 has been alotted to this function.

17 We can expect about 75 aceptances so that there should be sufficent

18 funds. It maybe that we will excede our budjet but we can allways

19 find funds to make up the diffarance.

20   Please see me witin the next two of three days so that we can

21 discus possibel dates. If we wait untill the whether becommes much

22 milder many of the restarants with outdoor facilities will allready

23 have been booked.

24   Sincerly yours

25 YOI:LAP   Lillie Popp, Administrator

26

1

2   Decemmber 7 19--

3   Mr. George Margo,

4   1253 Washinngton Avenue

5   Seatle, WA   98186

6   Dear Mister Marggo,

7   We genuinly beleive that our bank offers indispensible service to

8   its' custommers. We have been in existance for more then fourty years

9   and we are the forth largest bank in the entire state. Our deposits

10   excead more than $4500000000 and we offer more kinds of services tehn

11   any other bank in in this city.

12   Alltogether we have eight difrent kinds of savings accouns. We

13   have to kinds of interest paying club acounts and offer many general

14   general services

15   As a spcial offer at this time, we offer free safe deposit boxes

16   in every branch accept the Calafornia Highway branch. The only re-

17   quirment is the maintainance of a ninimum balence of at least $5000,

18   while you have the safe deposit box.

19   For you convience, we are enclossing a free clendar and a specia;

20   bullitin which lists sum of our services.

21   Sincerly yours,

22   SEATTLE TRUST COMPANY

23   JA:YOI   John A. Anderson Vice President

24

25

26

1

2   Octobar 5,, 19--

3   Mrs. Adrienne Danforth

4   98 Nineth Avenue

5   Louiville, KY   40287

6   Dear Miss Danforth

7   What are you doing to incourage your childrens food prefarances

8   so that your'e certin that theyr're getting all the essencial nutrition

9   to develope strong healthy bodies. Doyou fine that you have to remoove

10   the so called junk" foods from your shoping lists so that you're child-

11   ren dont become dependant upon snacks insted of ofood wich will bring

12   improvment to they're health

13   We sugest that you check the special colums ni our magizine

14   which are devoted to simple snacks which yeild exceptionally find

15   benifits. We alsew think that you should sent for copies of our

16   phamphlets which contain sugestions which have been sucessful in pre-

17   previous years.

18   Send $1 and a self address envelop and we will rush to fo our

19   pamphlats to you by retrun mail.

20   Very truly your,

21   GOOD HOMEMAKING

22   JAM:YOI   Jane Martinson, Food Editr

23

24

25

26

1

2   Febuary 27, 19--

3   Mrs. Janet Deborah Collings

4   9701 Misouri Parkway

5   Saint LOuis, MO   63188

6   Dear Ms. Collins

7   Do yuo have the feeling that the redecoratting of you home is

8   is long overdo, Do you loook at advertisments in the newspaers and

9   magizines and akse yourself if your prefferances and tastse of 10 or

10   15 years ago have change. Do you have the feeling that whatyou thougt

11   of as perminent when you bought it has outlive its usefullness? Are

12   you embarassed when freinds and neighbors drop in. Do you critisize

13   waht you see in your livingroom silently or allowed?

14   If you have ansered these questions with a "Yes', you reely shoud

15   not have to be pursuaded to stop in our at stocre. As you no our

16   sales force is noted for its' curtesy patience and knowledge. One of

17   our salesmen will help you chose furnishings and accessories which will

18   will be practicle beautiful and up-to-date.

19   We hope to see you sooon.

20   Coridally yours,

21   MISOURI FURNITURE S:ORE

22   RXH:YOI   Rex Harris Manager

23

24

25

26

1

2   May 4, 19--

3   Dr Edward Samson

4   5987 Nasheville Avenue

5   Chatanooga, TN   37489

6   Dear Dr. Sampson:

7   Are you allready for the fare and warm whether that has been pred-

8   icted for this spring and summer. Is your backyard equiped with ever-

9   ything you will need to make outdoor living pleasent easy and comfor-

10 table.

11   I sugest that you after have refered to our pricelist and ctalog

12 you will have to excercise restraint to by only what you require. In

13 the passed, we have offerred to take back any merchandize witin twwo

14 weeks and that same offer still applies

15   Sence you hav been won of our costomers for many years a deposit

16 or a parcial remittence will be aceptable to us for purchases up to

17 $500. Any charges incured above that ammont can be payed for with any

18 reconized credit card.

19   It is essencial that you shop now, while the weatther is still

20 cool. Undoubtably, as soon as it turns warmer our costomers will rush

21 to the store. If you wait to long you may regreat the fact that what

22 what you want has all ready been sold.

23   yours very truly,

24   TENESEE OUTDOOR FURNISHINGS

25 TD:YOI   Thomas e. Drake Manager

26

1

2   Septembr 16   19--

3   Shreaveport Equipement Company

4   49 Louisanna Street

5   New Orleens, La   70190

6   Dear Sir:

7   We were gennuinely suprised when you write to us on Agost 30

8   that their is still a indedtedness of $170 on our acount. We had made

9   parshal payments of $85 for twwo sucessive weeks in Agust and we were

10 certin that the ccount had been cleered up in its' entirety.

11   Has your bookeeper omited to record these checks in his books

12 Undoubtably the error is in your books, because we have check and

13 double checked our records and fine that the're absolutely acurate.

14   As you say in you letter we do no that the maintainance of a good

15 good credit record is indispensible. We have allways attemted to keep

16 this principal in mind, because we don"t want to forefiet our excellant

17 credit rating.

18   Pleas check you records agin and let me knwo what your findings

19 are.

20   Very Truly yous,

21   LOUISIANNA STATIONARY COMPANY

22 JGMYOI   John Joseph Miller

23   Acconuting Departemnt

24

25

26

1

2   Mrach 3 19--

3   Mr. Arthur Maxwell

4   1248 Govenment Square

5   Washinggton, DC.   20091

6   Dear Mister Maxxwell

7   Tho you are probabley a sucess in the govenment bureaw in wich

8   you are employed have made you any noticable improvment in you standardo

9   of living, Is their a discrepency between waht you would liek to be

10 earning and the ammount you carrry home each month. Do you recent the

11 fact that som of you freinds are doing alright finansially, while youre

12 finding it difficult to make ends meet?

13   Whos going to say to you, "Stay on your job untill you retire or

14 dye?' Who's resources should you use.

15   We beleive you should make a apointment wih won of our counselors

16 as soonas posible to discuss thees important matters. May be sum of

17 your fellow workers may have prefered to do nothing in the passed and

18 they have not benifitted from the assistence and advise that you can

19 secure. We belive you should persue this matter before it is to late.

20   Jusst fill in the enclosed from and mail it in the stamped self=

21 address envelop. Onne of our representives will telephone to make and

22 appoinment at a itme mutually convient.

23   Yours very Truly,

24   WaSHINGTON EMPLOYMENT AGENCY

25 RJ:YOI   Ruth A. Jacoby

26 Inclosure   Presiden

1

2   Junne 3, 19--

3   Ms. Harriet Shipmann

4   249 Phenix Street

5   Tuscon, AZ   85792

6   Deer Ms. Shipman

7   Do you no that as a govenment employee you are elligible for

8   misellaneous allowences and benifits on the insurence policies ofered

9   by our oragnization.   Theyr'e all explain in the phamphlet whihc Im

10   enclosing.

11   Do you want to elliminate the concern about unpayed or late

12   premiuns/ See page 19 of the phamphlet.

13   Have fintial dificulties been occuring which make it dificult

14   for you to meet all of you expences and obligations. See page 21.

15   Do you relize that the policies you orignally choose five oar ten

16   years ago may be unsiutable for your present needs. Prehaps a examinat-

17   ion of your policies once again is long over due. See page 26.

18   I sugest that you read thru the pamphlat throughly. A analisys

19   of the infromation wil convince you that you should fill out the the

20   questionaire which is on page 35. Retrun it to me immediateley. I

21   will be already to come to see yyou with prove that you will benifit

22   form one fo our insurence programs.

23   Very sincrely Yours,

24   INDEPENDANCE INSURENCE ASSOCIATION

25   YOI   Districk Office Maneger

26   Inclosure

January 14 19--

Mr. Clark Gateson

5698 Ohhio Avenue

Cincinnatti OH 45293

Dear Mister Gatesen

At the sugestion of the atornies for you sister Lillian Wise I
have made a through analisis of the to volumns of testimony in the case
in whihc she was the defendent las year in Clevland. I agre with them
that their were many omisions in Judge Smiths statement which served to
predujice the jury against her. Sum of the proceedures in the trial
it'self were questionable and i do not dissagree with her attornies
that furthur action be taken as soon as all areas hav been invesigated.

I belive that the best coarse we can take is to reach a desision
soon as to wheather or not to bring aditional attornies in to the picture. Its my opinon that the orignal set of atorneys which you sister
choose did a excellant job considering all the circumstances. Never
the less it maybe wise to meet with them and with the atorneys to whom
I refered you las month. It is essencial that we be fare to the prev-
previous attornys, but we must allso try to avoid a repition of waht
took place in Clevleand.

If anything developes call me at once. In the mean time think
about what your prefferences woud be about changing atorneys.

Cordialy your,

JA:YOI   John D. Adams

1

2   Octobre 19 19--

3   Mister Irwin Grill

4   109 Kantucky Avene

5   Luisville KY   40294

6   Dear Mister Grille

7   Has it been occuring to you that prices are finally begining to

8   get more resonable. Are you loosing the feeling that you can not aff-

9   ord to by the merchandize you want and need.

10   If the answrs to these questions is in the affirmative, we re-

11 guard it as a real achievment that our adds in the colums of our local

12 papers may have brought these feelings about.

13   Lets talk about our Book Depatment and our Stationary Department.

14 Our Book department was formally under the direction of Miss Amy Coe.

15 However she has been transfered to the stationary Deparrment. Before

16 she left she arrange for a specail purchase of first additions of the

17 classics and our advertisments this week emphazise the fact that you

18 can make editions to your home libary at reasonalbe prices.

19   Stop in to see Mrs. Coe and say, "Hello.' She is throughly

20 familar with both the personel and commerical stationary and you will

21 allso recieve a courteos welcomme form her.

22   Sincerely Your,

23   LOUIEVILLE DEPARTMENT SOTRE

24 RB:YOI   Rose Barrett, Manager

25   Second Floor Departments

26

1

2   Juen 25, 19--

3   Messers. Harrison & Cooper

4   1398 Conneticut Avenue

5   Waterberry, Ct   06795

6   Gentleman:

7   RE: Building at 137 Fourth Street in Springfeild

8   In the bsence of any commmunications form you, I am going ahead

9   with my planns to remoove the lose shingles from our building at

10   137 Forth Street. This is in acordance with my letter of June 15th

11   which was sent to you formerly by registered mail. The return reciept

12   we recieved was signed by "John Parker".

13   Frankly I dont think that we should be in a possition to have ot

14   apoligize for the apearance of our property. Yet this has been neces-

15   sarie becuse of the way in which the shingles were replace. We thought

16   that with all the expences we incured in the modernization of teh

17   property the improvment would be noticable. In som instances it was

18   but the shinkles which you attach aded no improvment to the aperance

19   of the prprty, becase they were not attach strickly acording to the

20   specifications of our contrack with you.

21   Assoon as the shingles have been remooved and replaced, we shall

22   send you the bill which result form this work.

23   Very truly your,

24   MORGAN GENERAL STORE

25   TM:YOI   Thomas A Morgan

26   Proprietor

1

2   Mya 4th, 19--

3   Mr. Lester Barrow,

4   475 Massachusettes Avenue

5   Worchester   MA   01696

6   Dear Mr Barow,

7   If you are intrested in bying commerical property we sugest thta

8   you see won of our representives. Our organzation handles property

9   accross the entire state accept for the Cape Cod area.

10   We blieve that this maybe the write time for you to see us bec-

11   ause during the comming months we expect to be handling some property

12   for frims whihc have jus gone into bankrupcy. Its' our opinon that

13   these propertiees will hav be to sold at very resonable prices. If

14   their are any special sections of Massachusettes in wich you are

15   particularly intrested one of our efficent curteous and helpfull

16   salesman will persue the matter wit you.

17   If your'e intrested in low prices dont forfiet your chance to sec-

18   ure property at these bargin prices. Its essencial that you get in

19   touch with us imediately, because these opportunitie's are temporary

20   one's not permenent one's.

21   We have one our reputation farely because of the excellance of the

22   service we have offerred for over ninty yers. Let us be of assistants.

23   Very trulyyours,

24   RELIABLE REALTY CORPORATION

25   PW:YOI   Paul Walters Maneger

26

1

2   Septeber 4 91--

3   Mrs. Harreit Rosenborg

4   4954 North Caralina Avenue

5   Winstonsalem NC 27197

6   Dear Ms. Rosenberg

7   Congradulations. It is a priviledge for us to let you knwo that

8   you have been sponsered by Mr. Seymour White 432 Sixth Avenue Spring-

9   feild Massachusettes 01103 for membership in the American Libary

10 Society. He has payed the one year membership feee for you. You maybe

11 sure that membership in our oganization will enable you to secure

12 posessions which ad will to the joys of life.

13   The folowing are sum of the advantiges of you membership;

14   1) Each month you will recieve the LIBERY BULLETIN a publication

15 which reviews the up to the minute books being published buy leading

16 publishers raound the country.

17   2(All books listed in the LIBERY BULLETTIN maybe purchase at

18 resonable prices. Proceedures for ordering books is given on Page 17

19 of the BULLITIN each month

20   3) In edition to the curent books each months issue of the LIBARY

21 BULLETINN list new addtions of some favorite books form the passed.

22 These boooks are attractivly bound in leather and are limited ad-

23 ditions. Proceedures for ordering thees books is also given on

24 page 17.

25   4. Attendence at lectures iw won of the benifits you will recieve.

26 Twice a year leading writers adress our mebership meetings. The

1

2   Febuary 4 19--

3   Ackron Filing Company, Inc

4   296 Tolledo Avenue

5   Cincinnatti OH   45298

6   Gentllemen

7   Tehre has been a great deal of contraversy and critisism about the

8   sumes of money alloted to the Beureau of Files in out organzation.

9   Amoung the complaints is the frequent won that the filles hav been so

10   poorly kep that it is allmost imposible to find corresponence which has

11   been transfered. Misellaneous govenment papers which are so essencial

12   to the efficent running of our insitute offen can not be found. Its a

13   frequent occurence for one of the file clerks to say, "I just cant

14   find what you are looking for.

15   Sinse you firm sold us most of our filling equipement during the

16   passed to of three years it has been suggest that won of your represe-

17   ntives visit our filing department. He can incourage our personal

18   where necessery and critsize wher necesssary. Both our commerical

19   and goverment files are in need of improvment and we beleive that only

20   a expert will suceed in bein of assistence

21   Please call me so taht we can make and appoinment to go over

22   this matter throughly.

23   very truly Yours,

24   OHHIO INSITUTE OF EDUCATION

25   JE:YOI   Jan Edwards Ofice Manager

26

27 arangements for there personnel apperances are made well in advance and

28 publicity is given ahead of time. The Juyl meeting is alwasy held at a

29 vacation spot. You can, therfore combine a vacation with a stimulating

30 meeting. Each member is aloud one guest at these lectures and their

31 is no charge for the guest or for the membre.

32   4) The annuel dinner is held in a restarant in one of the exclusi-

33 ve hotels in Washinton. Last years dinner was a grate sucess. Not

34 only was the food esceptional but our speekers were too writers who had

35 just one important literary awards. Altho many of the guest's dress

36 formerly it is unecessary to do so, since dress is "Optional". As

37 your'e know doubt familar with the costs of similiar dinners Im sure

38 you realize that the cost of $20 for this dinner are extremly resonabl.

39 This year we hop to have the winer of the Bancroft Award julia Morse.

40   5) The maintainance of you membership doesnt depend upon the numb-

41 er of books you by. Instead you mearly have to spend $50 anuelly and

42 your membership will stay in affect   If you spend more then $100

43 annuelly you will be elligible for sum of the special dividends which

44 are listed monthly in the BULLITIN. Wehn you look at the BULLITIN you

45 will see that the plan we have deviced for dividend allowences is fare

46 and simple.

47   After you hav been a member, we shoud apprecaite recieving sug-

48 estions, or critisisms for helping us improove our services.

49   Sincerly yous,

50   AMERICAN LIBRERY SOCIETY

51 JAB:YOI   Janet Baker

52

1

2   Octobr 19 19--

3   Mr. Glenn Johansen, President

4   Johansen Electrical Components Company

5   986 Pensylvania Turnpike

6   Wilkesbarre, Pa   18799

7   Dear Mr. Johanson:

8   Have bankrupcies been occuring with regularity in you insustry?

9   Is it noticable that they are incresing each year. Is their somewon in

10 you orrganization who is responsable for the analysys of unpayed debts

11 and over due acounts. Have you resently incured lossses which you

12 didnot anticipate.

13   We can not emphazize to strongly that though strick precautions

14 are offen taken things sometings accidently 'go wrong". If you look

15 at som of the columens in the magizines in your industry, you probaly

16 realise that their are many things taht "go wrong' even in the largest

17 firms. Prooof of this can be easily seen on Page 95 of this months

18 issue of MODERN ELECTRONICS

19   We d'ont mean to criticise you present policies. Never the less

20 they should be check throughly. Fill in the enclosed questionaire and

21 return it to me immediateley in the stamped self=addressed envelop. I

22 will than get in tuch with you to discuss proceedures we would recomend.

23   Very truly your,

24   ELECTRONICS FINTIAL ADVISORS

25 MA:YOI   Mark Austin, Anilyst

26

1

2   Agost 4, 19--

3   Illinoise Button Company

4   495 Chicargo Drive,

5   Springfeild, IL   62701

6   Gentleman:

7   SUBJECT: Prefered Devises for Door Locks

8   This letter is in refarance to the letter you rote to our firm

9   on Juyl 14

10   In anser to you inquires, I can assure you that we are the

11   manufactures of devises wich have suceeded more then any others at

12   present the on market. Prove of this can be found in the phamphlet we

13   are enclosin wiht this letter.

14   Your desision on installing new locks can not be delaied unlesss

15   you want to wait untill your offices is robbed. We can not emphzise

16   to strongly that the ommision of adaquate protection wil result in

17   disaster.

18   Form your letter Ibelive that you are in need of our assistence

19   imediately. Telephone me at 896-0933 so that we can set up a apointm-

20   ent.

21   Yours very truely,

22   ILLINOISE LOCK COMPANY

23   KI   Karl Irwinson

24   Sales Manager

25

26

NOW THAT YOU HAVE REACHED THIS POINT

By the time you have reached this page, you should have torn out the 100 "terrible transcripts," made corrections in them, checked with the 100 corrected letters and re-typed the letters correctly. What is left intact in your copy of *Letter-Perfect* should be very helpful to you because it gives a full review of spelling, punctuation, letter styles, and proofreading techniques. In addition, the corrected letters can give you excellent typing practice of rough-draft material.

If you are not sure of correct letter styles, there are samples of the three most-frequently used styles of business letters.

Refer to the section on spelling for hints on how to avoid spelling errors.

Use *Letter-Perfect* as your own personal reference guide. The Master Spelling List contains most of the words which are frequently misspelled in business correspondence. The correct spelling of cities and states (with their two-letter abbreviations) will save you time when you type letters. The word lists not only repeat the words on the Master Spelling List, but they also give you examples of words which may be spelled in different ways and definitions of words commonly confused.

Proofreading and copy editing are skills which are invaluable to the secretary and the typist. The proofreading checklist gives many suggestions for checking your work and that of others.

Before the review of punctuation marks, there are rules for the correct use of verb endings and apostrophes. The rules for punctuation are simply stated, and they are followed by examples and exercises.

What follows this page are the 100 corrected letters. It is hoped that you had fun and enjoyment as you learned how to make all the letters *Letter-Perfect*.

Corrected Letters 1-100

1

February
2   ~~Fobuery~~ 8, 19--

3   Mr. Fred Kelley

         Illinois
4   439 ~~Illinoise~~ Avenue

    Chicago,
5   ~~Chicargo,~~ IL   60601

       dear   Kelley:
6   My ~~Dear~~ Mr. ~~Kelly:~~

            think   problems
7   Do you ~~thing~~ it might be a good idea to solve the ~~prolbems~~ of

                          the next   organization.
8   ~~of~~ the world? If so, come to ~~toh nest~~ meeting of our ~~organazation.~~

        would   privilege   friend.   know
9   We ~~woud~~ consider it a ~~priviledge~~ if you would bring a ~~freind.~~ We ~~no~~

                                         also
10 that you will both have a good time, and we ~~allso~~ think that our ~~mem~~

            always   something.
11 members ~~allways~~ learn ~~someting.~~

                    advice   find that
12   We sometimes give ~~advise~~ where it is needed, and we ~~fine thta~~

                     resent   hear   the
13 our members do not ~~recent~~ the words of wisdom which they ~~here~~ at ~~toh~~

                         course,   promptly,
14 monthly meetings. Of ~~cause,~~ if you cannot be there ~~promply,~~ try to

          whenever
15 come ~~when ever~~ you are able to do so. We look forward to seeing you

                      that   hear
16 often, and we hope ~~taht~~ we will ~~here~~ from you telling us that you are

                    the   gathering.
17 going to be ~~the~~ at next ~~gatherin.~~
                       ^

                        truly,
18   Yours ~~truely,~~
                        PROBLEMS,
19   WORLD ~~PROLBEMS,~~ INC.

    ADE:
20 ~~AE:YOI~~   Albert D. Evans

21

22

23

24

25

26

1

2   February ~~Febuary~~ 18, 19--

3   Miss Judith Brown

4   1492 Niagara ~~Niagra~~ Falls Avenue

5   Buffalo, ~~Buffallo,~~ NY   14202

6   Dear Miss Brown: ~~Miss. Browne:~~

7   It would ~~woud~~ be very fortunate and helpful ~~helpfull~~ if you could work for us

8   during the Christmas season. We usually ~~asully~~ have a sale then, ~~than,~~ and we need as

9   ~~as~~ much help as we can get. On some occasions, ~~occassions,~~ we call on retired men

10   and women, ~~woman,~~ but this year we have decided ~~desided~~ to look for younger persons.

11   We are, therefore, ~~threfore,~~ writing to you to ask if you would ~~woud~~ be willing to

12   ~~to~~ be at our store on Thursday ~~thursday~~ nights during the month ~~months~~ of December.

13   There ~~Their~~ are many benefits ~~bonifits~~ to be gained from being there, ~~their,~~ and we hope

14   ~~hope~~ you will take advantage ~~avantage~~ of all of them. For example, you can buy

15   many of our products ~~produets~~ at a fine ~~find~~ discount. Of course, ~~cause,~~ you can choose ~~chose~~

16   them after you have looked at all our merchandise. ~~merchandize.~~

17   Sincerely yours, ~~Sincerly Yours,~~

18   MARTIN'S DEPARTMENT STORE

19   JM:YOI   Jack Mason,
                                          Personnel
20   ~~Personal~~ Department

21

22

23

24

25

26

February
~~Fobuary~~ 9, 19--

Miss Joan Flowers

454 ~~Nineth~~ Ninth Avenue

Los ~~Angeles,~~ Angeles, CA   90003

Dear ~~Mrs.~~ Miss Flowers:

I ~~no~~ know that you will ~~fine~~ find it a pleasure and a ~~priviledge~~ privilege to shop

at our store ~~becuse~~ because we have many ~~bargins.~~ bargains. We have a ~~find~~ fine selection

of clocks and ~~watchs,~~ watches, and I ~~belive~~ believe you will want to pick up one or

~~to~~ two the ~~nex~~ next time you are in ~~in~~ our store.

Whenever you come in, you will be ~~mor~~ more ~~then~~ than welcome ~~becuase~~ because our

~~salesman~~ salesmen treat ~~there costumers~~ their customers very well. We ~~thing~~ think you will ~~apprecite~~ appreciate

what we have to offer since we try very hard to stock a line of ~~mer-~~

~~chandize~~ merchandise which is attractive in every way.

Come in promptly and give ~~yourselves~~ yourself a treat. We ~~beleive taht~~ believe that

you will want to take our ~~advise~~ advice and buy a watch or clock.

~~Sincerly your,~~ Sincerdy yours,

ROTH JEWELRY STORE

~~JR:~~ JAR:YOI

James A. Roth

~~Pressident~~ President

1

2 ~~Febuary~~ February 3, 19--

3 Mr. John Brown

4 14 ~~Minnisota~~ Minnesota Avenue

5 ~~Mineapolis,~~ Minneapolis, MN 55404

6 Dear ~~Dr. Browne:~~ Mr. Brown:

7   We are ~~veyr~~ very sorry that ~~resently~~ recently you were ~~disatisfied~~ dissatisfied with

8 ~~with~~ the treatment you ~~recieved~~ received at our ~~Mineapolis~~ Minneapolis store.

9   In the ~~passed~~ past we have ~~alwasy~~ always considered it a ~~privelege~~ privilege to serve

10 you ~~becusase~~ because we honestly ~~beloive~~ believe that we have the ~~findest~~ finest ~~merchandize~~ merchandise

11 available in this ~~sity.~~ city. We ~~no that~~ know that you agree with us because we have

12 checked our records and note that you have ~~usualy~~ usually taken ~~avantage~~ advantage of our

13 special ~~bargin~~ bargain days in the months of ~~Febuery~~ February and March. Of ~~cause,~~ course, we

14 hope that you will continue to do so. We now have a new selection of

15 ~~of find~~ fine clothing on sale ~~begining nest~~ beginning next Monday, ~~Febuary~~ February 10.

16   We shall ~~investi gate~~ investigate the rudeness of one of ~~are salesman.~~ our salesmen. Since

17 our ~~Personal Deaprtment~~ Personnel Department gives full training to our salesmen on how to

18 treat ~~costumers,~~ customers, we are upset that ~~she~~ he treated you ~~roudely.~~ rudely.

19   As soon as we have completed our investigation, you shall ~~here~~ hear

20 from us. In the meantime, we are ~~enclosin~~ enclosing a special listing of ~~sum~~ some

21 of the ~~itmes~~ items which will be on sale.

22   Yours ~~Truely,~~ truly,

23   ADAMS DEPARTMENT STORES

24 JA:~~JB:~~YOI   James Adams
Enclosure

25   ~~Customer~~ Customer Service

26

1
2   February
   ~~Febuary~~ 6, 19--

3 Mrs.
   ~~Mrs~~ Kay Welles

4   Connecticut Avenue
   245 ~~Connecticutt Avenu~~

5 Hartford,
   ~~Hardfort,~~ CT   06105

6 Dear ~~Miss Wells,~~ Mrs. Welles:

7   There is an expression that you can always depend upon your
   ~~Their~~   ~~espression~~   ~~allways~~

8 friends for good advice.
   ~~freinds~~   ~~advise.~~

9   I believe that you have been shopping at my store for so long
     ~~bleieve~~   ~~shoping~~

10 long that you consider me a friend. I know that I feel that way about
   ~~long~~   ~~freind.~~   ~~no~~

11 you. I am, therefore, giving advice to you now.
          ~~therfore,~~   ~~advise too~~

12   If you shop at the store before the end of February, you will be
                          ~~befor~~   ~~Febuery,~~

13 able to choose many table linens at bargain prices. During this season
       ~~chose~~   ~~bargin~~

14 of the year, there are many occasions which you like to celebrate by
       ~~car, their~~   ~~occassion~~

15 having a small dinner party for two or three friends. We have new
                          ~~to~~   ~~freinds.~~

16 cloths with matching napkins in various colors and sizes. The patterns
                                          ~~adn size.~~   ~~patter-~~

17 ns are even more attractive than those we have carried in stock in the
                                          ~~tsook~~   ~~teh~~

18 recent past.
   ~~recent passed.~~

19   I would advise you to visit the store promptly so that you can
     ~~woud advice~~

20 choose what you need while we have a complete stock. Even if you
   ~~can chose~~   ~~cojplete~~

21 decide that you do not want to buy anything at this time, please stop
   ~~deside~~   ~~thsi~~

22 in to visit me. We will have a friendly chat.
                          ~~freindly~~

23   Sincerely yours,
                                       ~~your,~~

24 VD: DAVIS LINEN SHOP

25 ~~VAD:YOI~~   Vera Davis

26

1

2   February
                                                  ~~Febuery~~ 1, 19--

3   Mrs. Alice Sharp
                      Wisconsin
4   2345 ~~Wisconcin~~ Avenue
      Racine,
5   ~~Raseen,~~ WI   53406
              Mrs. Sharp:
6   Dear ~~Miss Sharpe:~~

7   We have ~~jus~~ just received ~~recieved~~ a letter from ~~Mr~~ Mr. Herbert Black, advising ~~advicing~~ us

8   that you have recently ~~resently~~ purchased a house in Milwaukee ~~Milwakee~~ and will be moving ~~movi-~~

9   ~~ng~~ to our city within ~~withing~~ the next two ~~neet too~~ months. ~~monthes.~~ Of course, ~~cause,~~ we wish to

10   to welcome ~~welcom~~ you and to wish you many years ~~hears~~ of happiness ~~happyness~~ in your home.

11   As Mr. Black ~~Blake~~ may have told ~~tole~~ you, we are the oldest bank in the

12   city, and we invite you to become a depositor as soon as possible.

13   You will find ~~fine~~ that there ~~their~~ are many benefits ~~benifits~~ to be gained by doing your ~~you~~

14   banking business with us. ~~you.~~ You can choose ~~chose~~ from many different types of

15   accounts. We have a special savings account which gives you interest

16   from the first of the ~~teh~~ month if you deposit your ~~you~~ money by the ninth ~~ninoth.~~ We

17   have two ~~too~~ different kinds of personal ~~personnel~~ checking ~~checkin~~ accounts that are real

18   bargains, too. ~~bargins, to.~~

19   Our entire organization ~~organzation~~ will always ~~allways~~ be in a position ~~possession~~ to offer

20   ~~offer~~ you friendly advice. ~~freindly advise.~~ All our personnel ~~personal~~ in every department will

21   be helpful, ~~helpfull,~~ and we hope that you will decide ~~deside~~ to take advantage ~~advantige~~ of

22   their ~~there~~ expert opinions after you have moved into your ~~you~~ new home.

                                        Sincerely yours,
23   ~~Sincerly your,~~

24   FIRST FEDERAL BANK

      TAS:
25   ~~TS:~~YOI   Thomas A. Smith, President

26

1

2   May ~~Mya~~ 6, 19--

3   Mr. Robert Nelson

              Nebraska
4   4725 ~~Nerbraska~~ Avenue

    Lincoln,
5   ~~Lincoln,~~ NE   68507

              Mr.
6   Dear ~~Dr.~~ Nelson:

                            this opportunity
7   I should like to take ~~tihs~~ ~~oportunity~~ to invite you to become

                          benefit   which   Monday,
8   a sponsor of our annual ~~benifit~~ concert ~~wich~~ will be held on ~~Munday,~~

    February   concert
9   ~~February~~ 12, at the Municipal Opera House. Details of the ~~consert~~

10 are enclosed with this letter.

              believe   receive
11   I sincerely ~~beleive~~ that you will ~~recieve~~ great pleasure on this

         occasion   the committee decided
12 ~~this~~ ~~occassion.~~ After ~~teh~~ ~~comitee~~ ~~desided~~ to have a concert to raise

                                  was   choose
13 funds for cultural activities, it ~~wuz~~ difficult to ~~chose~~ the artists

             perform. Therefore,   committee   advice
14 who would ~~preform.~~ ~~Thorfore,~~ the ~~comittee~~ asked the ~~advise~~ of the

                                              organization
15 National Opera Society, the largest such ~~organixation~~ in this area.

        personnel   their   Friendly   usual,   consulting
16   The ~~personal~~ in ~~there~~ offices, ~~froindly~~ as ~~usul,~~ helped by ~~cons-~~

              some   their   advised
17 ~~ulting~~ the schedules of ~~sum~~ of ~~there~~ famous artists. They ~~adviced~~

                                                            course,
18 us of the availability of John Thomas and Ella Browning. Of ~~cause,~~ we

        promptly   touch   their
19 ~~we~~ ~~promply~~ got in ~~tuch~~ with ~~there~~ agents, and contracts for this joint

           have   privilege   hear   two
20 recital ~~hav~~ been signed. It will be a ~~priviledge~~ to ~~here~~ these ~~too~~

    Fine   because
21 ~~find~~ artists ~~becusase~~ they have never appeared together in this city.

              Find   advantages
22   You will ~~fine~~ that the ~~advantiges~~ of being a sponsor are many.

                                  entitled   two   orchestra.
23 In the first place, you will be ~~intitled~~ to ~~too~~ tickets in the ~~ore-~~

           also   for your   Friends
24 ~~hestra.~~ You can ~~alloo~~ secure tickets ~~fro~~ ~~you~~ family and ~~froinds~~

           the   the   receive
25 before ~~teh~~ sale of tickets ~~the~~ to general public. You will ~~recieve~~

                                              dissatisfied
26 the ticket locations well in advance, and if you are ~~disatisfied~~ in

228   **Corrected Letter 7**

27   any way, ~~tthe~~ the tickets can be exchanged for seats in another section of

28   the Opera House. Secondly, sponsors are invited to the ~~suppr~~ supper ~~whitch~~ which

29   will follow ~~teh~~ the concert.

30   Please let us ~~here~~ hear from you promptly so that we can be sure to

31   include ~~you~~ your name on ~~teh~~ the printed program.

32   I ~~no~~ know that you will want to join the many other outstanding ~~citis-~~ citizens

33   ~~ons~~ of the city who are ~~allways~~ always willing to do more ~~then~~ than their share in

34   supporting the cultural activities ~~wich~~ which we think ~~truely~~ truly make this a

35   ~~a~~ wonderful city in which to live.

36   I hope you will take ~~advantige~~ advantage of this special ~~oportunity~~ opportunity to

37   render service to our city.

38   Yours ~~Sincerly,~~ sincerely,

39   ~~LINGLON~~ LINCOLN CULTURAL ~~COMITTEE~~ COMMITTEE

40   ~~MJ~~ MAJ:yol

41   Enclosure   Mary A. Johnstone

                                       Chairperson

42

43

44

45

46

47

48

49

50

51

52

1

2   February
                                        ~~February~~ 1, 19--

3   Mrs. Helen Morse
                 Connecticut
4   398 ~~Connectieutt~~ Avenue
     Waterbury,
5   ~~Waterberry,~~ CT   06708
              Mrs.
6   Dear ~~Mr.~~ Morse:
                               resent   advice
7   People rarely ~~recent~~ ~~advise~~ about how to save money, and that is
                      taking   to
8   why I am ~~takin~~ the liberty of writing ~~too~~ you. Our records show that
                                                two   before
9   you have not shopped at our store for almost ~~to~~ years although ~~befor~~
                                                      departments.
10   that time you shopped often in many of our ~~department.~~
                therefore,   take   advice
11   I am, ~~therefor,~~ writing to you to urge you to ~~tak~~ the ~~advise~~ of
                                                                            says
12   the manager of our Fancy Food Department, Mrs. Gladys Smith. She ~~say~~
                                       are   than   before.
13   that the items in that department ~~is~~ better ~~then~~ ever ~~befor.~~ You will
                  find   always   there.
14   be able to ~~fine~~ all the famous brands ~~allways~~ carried ~~their.~~ You also
            find   there   brands,   selection
15   will ~~fine~~ that ~~their~~ are new ~~bands,~~ and you will now have a wider ~~sele-~~
         from   than   before.   advantage
16   ~~ction~~ ~~form~~ which to choose ~~then~~ ever ~~befor.~~ The ~~advantige~~ of shopping
            too   passed   benefit
17   before ~~to~~ much time has ~~past~~ is that you will ~~bonifit~~ from low prices.
     Mrs.   asked   bargain
18   ~~Miss~~ Smith ~~aksed~~ us to write you to tell you that the ~~bargin~~ prices you
         find   than
19   will ~~fine~~ will save you more money ~~then~~ you would think possible. Of
     course,   personal advice   helpful,   too.
20   ~~cause,~~ the ~~personnel~~ ~~advise~~ that she gives will be ~~helpfull,~~ ~~to.~~
         believe   no   match
21   I ~~believ~~ that ~~know~~ other Fancy Food Department can ~~mach~~ ours for
                          merchandise
22   the high quality of the ~~merchandise~~ and the low prices.
                         Yours truly,
23   ~~Your truely,~~
                                              STORE
24   WATERBURY DEPARTMENT ~~STOR~~
                                         Manager
25   EW:YOI   Edgar Waters, ~~Manger~~

26

1

2   March 8, 19--

3   ~~Mister~~ **Mr.** Richard Defranco

4   89 ~~Pensylvania~~ **Pennsylvania** Avenue

5   ~~Pittsburg,~~ **Pittsburgh,** PA   15209

6   Dear Mr. ~~De Franco:~~ **Defranco!**

7   I am writing this letter in answer to ~~you~~ **your** letter of ~~Febuary~~ **February** 27

8   concerning ~~you disatisfaction~~ **your dissatisfaction** with the ~~merchandize~~ **merchandise** you ordered from

9   the Amerigo Distributing Company. We have written to ~~taht~~ **that** company on

10   ~~on~~ many ~~occassions~~ **occasions** in the ~~passed,~~ **past,** but the company has never responded

11   to our letters. ~~Sinse there~~ **Since their** offices are not in this city, we have

12   ~~have~~ no way of taking ~~furthur~~ **further** action.

13   If you ~~decide~~ **decide** that you would like to bring this situation to ~~teh~~ **the**

14   attention of the authorities, we ~~belive~~ **believe** that the ~~bes~~ **best** way to do this is

15   to write to the Attorney General in ~~Harrisburgh.~~ **Harrisburg.** We ~~hav~~ **have** done so, and

16   he has assured us that ~~she~~ **he** is ~~doin~~ **doing** all ~~taht~~ **that** he legally can.

17   It is the ~~advise~~ **advice** of our ~~organzation~~ **organization** that consumers ~~shoud~~ **should** be more

18   careful ~~befor~~ **before** buying ~~merchandize~~ **merchandise** from a company about whom they ~~no~~ **know**

19   nothing. We ~~beleive, to,~~ **believe, too,** that it is generally ~~too~~ **to** your ~~advantige~~ **advantage** to

20   see what you are buying rather ~~then~~ **than** to depend only on literature.

21   It is ~~allways~~ **always** a ~~privelege~~ **privilege** for our ~~organzation~~ **organization** to be ~~helpfull.~~ **helpful.** I

22   am sorry that we can do little in ~~thsi~~ **this** instance.

23   Yours ~~Very Truely,~~ **very truly,**

24   FEDERAL BUSINESS BUREAU

     JM:YOI
25   ~~YOI:JM~~   Jane Milton, Legal Department

26

1

2   February ~~12th,~~ 12, 19--

3   Mr. Louis Rivera

4   876 ~~Massachusettes~~ Massachusetts Avenue

5   ~~Springfoild,~~ Springfield, MA   01110

6   Dear Mr. ~~Rivers:~~ Rivera:

7   I am very much pleased that you ~~desided~~ decided to buy your new color

8   television set at our store. I am ~~sincerly~~ sincerely happy ~~taht~~ that you ~~allways~~ always

9   ~~allways~~ choose to buy your radios and television sets ~~hear.~~ here.

10   We ~~no~~ know that ~~personnel~~ personal service is important to please our ~~freinds,~~ friends.

11   ~~Taht~~ That is why we ~~aks~~ ask you to call our Service Department promptly if you

12   are in any way ~~disatisfied~~ dissatisfied with our ~~producks.~~ products. This ~~benifits~~ benefits us ~~bee-~~ because

13   ~~ause~~ we ~~than~~ then can ~~fine~~ find the cause for the ~~unappiness~~ unhappiness and remedy it. ~~Un-~~

14   Unless we ~~here~~ hear from you ~~promply,~~ promptly, we cannot ~~no~~ know that ~~their~~ there is anything

15   wrong. We, ~~therefor,~~ therefore, ask you to ~~advice~~ advise us when ~~their~~ there is the ~~slightes-~~ slightest

16   ~~difficult wit~~ difficulty with any of ~~you pruchases,~~ your purchases.

17   It gives me great satisfaction to ~~no~~ know that you are such a regular

18   ~~costumer.~~ customer. I am enclosing ~~to~~ two copies of the service contract. As you

19   can see, there are ~~know~~ no changes in the ~~benefts~~ benefits to be gained by ~~chosing~~ choosing

20   Plan A, and it is my ~~advise~~ advice that you ~~chose~~ choose this plan rather ~~then~~ than Plan B.

21   After you have ~~desided~~ decided which plan you want, please sign one copy and

22   ~~retrun~~ return it to me ~~promply.~~ promptly. The second copy is ~~fro~~ for you.

23   Very truly ~~your,~~ yours,

24   ~~MASSACHUSETTES~~ MASSACHUSETTS RADIO SHACK

25   ~~JAB~~ JB:YO1   John Burrell, ~~Manger~~ Manager
      Enclosures

26

1

2   January
                                                          ~~January~~ 21, 19--

        Pittsburgh
3   ~~Pittsburgh~~ Paper Company

         Pennsylvania
4   62 ~~Pensylvania~~ Street

        Philadelphia,
5   ~~Philedelphia,~~ PA   19111

6   Gentlemen:

                    the   stationery.
7   We are ~~the~~ in market for some new ~~stationary.~~ Please send us a
                      latest catalog.   know   very important
8   ~~a~~ copy of your ~~lastest catolog.~~ We ~~no~~ that it is ~~vur impotant~~ to have
            equipment,   also   necessary   image
9   new ~~equiptment,~~ but we ~~allso~~ think it is ~~nesessary~~ to give a good ~~ima-~~
                              therefore,   correspondence
10   ge to the public. We, ~~therfore,~~ hope that new paper for our ~~corres-~~
                        helpful.
11   ~~pondance~~ will be ~~helpfull,~~
                                        catalog,   decide
12   After you have shipped us your ~~catolog,~~ we shall be able to ~~deside~~
        whether   products.   so)
13   ~~weather~~ or not we can use your ~~producks.~~ If we can do ~~sou,~~ we will get
            touch   immediately.   would   appreciate
14   in ~~tuch~~ with you ~~immediatly,~~ We ~~woud apreciate~~ it if you answered us
                        possible   usually   substantial amount
15   as soon as ~~posible~~ because we ~~usuelly~~ need a ~~substaneial ammount~~ of

16   paper at this time of the year, and we are dissatisfied with what we

17   ~~we~~ have on hand.

                                            sincerely
18   Very ~~Sincerely~~ yours,

19   GENERAL SUPPLY COMPANY

        JB:
20   ~~JD:~~YOI   James Brown
                                    Manager
21   ~~Manger~~

22

23

24

25

26

1

2   February 4, 19--

3   Springfield Insurance Company

4   444 Illinois Street

5   Chicago, IL   60612

6   Gentlemen:

7   I am enclosing the policy you sent me last month. I have looked

8   at it very carefully, and I find that it will not be suitable for

9   my needs. Also, the premiums are too high in my judgment.

10   What I am looking for is a policy which will give me a substantial

11   income after I have retired. The policy you sent me did not have the

12   provisions I am seeking, and I am, therefore, returning it to you at

13   this time. Please have your agent call me so that we can make an

14   appointment to discuss what I have in mind. I can see him at any time

15   that is convenient for him during the next week or two.

16   In addition, one of my partners expressed an interest in a similar

17   policy, and we can both receive the advice of your agent at the same

18   time.

19   Cordially yours,

20   WORTH & CHAMBERS

21   JBW:YOI   James B. Worth
     Enclosure

22   Treasurer

23

24

25

26

1

2   April 3,
~~Aprill 5~~, 19--

3   ~~Mister~~ Mr. Theodore Johnson

4   145 ~~Ohhio~~ Ohio Street

5   ~~Clevland,~~ Cleveland, OH   44113

6   My ~~Dear Miss Johnson:~~ dear Mr. Johnson:

7   You are ~~cordialy invite~~ cordially invited to ~~a~~ an anniversary luncheon at the ~~the~~

8   American Hotel on ~~Wensday, Febuary~~ Wednesday, February 5. This ~~lunchen~~ luncheon will be held to

9   celebrate the ~~organzation~~ organization of our club and its ~~achievments~~ achievements throughout

10   the years.

11   At ~~thsi~~ this affair, we are, of ~~cause, hopping~~ course, hoping to have a very good

12   time. I ~~no~~ know that you will be able to see ~~sum~~ some of ~~you freinds~~ your friends at that

13   time. ~~Therfore, undoubtdly~~ Therefore, undoubtedly you will want to go.

14   The price of the ticket ~~si~~ is only $15, and ~~thoi~~ this includes the meal,

15   checking, and tipping. Please reply as soon as ~~posible becuase~~ possible because we

16   expect more ~~then~~ than one hundred ~~resopnses~~ responses to ~~tihs~~ this letter. You are ~~pr-obabley~~ probably

17   ~~familar~~ familiar with the fact that ~~wen~~ when we had a ~~similiar~~ similar affair five

18   ~~year~~ years ago, we were unable to ~~acommodate~~ accommodate all who ~~want~~ wanted to come. ~~Therfore,~~ Therefore,

19   we ~~woud recoomend~~ would recommend that you answer ~~promply.~~ promptly. We will send you ~~a~~ an

20   ~~acknowldegment~~ acknowledgment and ~~you reciet~~ your receipt by return mail.

21   Yours ~~turly,~~ truly,

22   WS:
     ~~WAS:~~YOI   Walter Scott

23   ~~Pres dent~~ President

24

25

26

1

2   June
                                          ~~Juen~~ 4, 19--

3   Ms. Shirley Rogers

                    California
4   4372 ~~Galafornia~~ Lane

        Francisco,
5   San ~~Fransisco,~~ CA   94114

            Ms.
6   Dear ~~Mrs.~~ Rogers:

                                                          the   California
7   We are planning an exhibit of the works of ~~teh~~ noted ~~Galafornia~~

                            recommended   catalog
8   artist, John Fischer. He has ~~reccommend~~ you to write the ~~cataloge~~ of
    the   accept
9   ~~teh~~ exhibit, and we hope you will ~~except~~ this invitation.

            Fischer   his achievements
10   Mr. ~~Fisher~~ says that you are well aware ~~his~~ of ~~achiovments~~ and
       believes   would   best possible   this
11 ~~and beleives~~ that you ~~woudl~~ be the ~~pest possible~~ art critic to do ~~thei~~

12 work for us.

            exhibition will   Library   months
13   The ~~exibition wil~~ be in the University ~~Libary~~ during the ~~month~~
       January   February.   substantial amount   interest
14 of ~~Januely~~ and ~~Febuary.~~ We anticipate a ~~substancial~~ ~~ammount~~ of ~~int-~~
            exhibit because   judgment
15 ~~reet~~ in the ~~exhibit bocuse~~ it is the ~~judgement~~ of many gallery owners

16 that Mr. Fischer has outstanding talent.
         would appreciate   send   acceptance
17   I ~~woud appriciate~~ it if you would ~~sent~~ me a letter of ~~acceptance~~
                            possible.   receipt   from
18 or telephone me as soon as ~~posible.~~ Upon ~~receipt~~ of word ~~form~~ you,
                    an appointment almost immediately so
19 we can set up ~~a apbointment allmost immediatly sew~~ that we can fill you
                                                what   included
20 in on the details of the exhibit and ~~waht~~ we would like ~~include~~ in the
    catalog.   add   appointment   held
21 ~~cataloge.~~ I need not ~~ad~~ that this ~~apbointment~~ will be ~~hel~~ at a time
                 convenient.   hear
22 mutually ~~convient.~~ I hope to ~~here~~ from you shortly.
                                        Yours
23   ~~Your~~ sincerely,
                                        CALIFORNIA
24   ~~GALAFORNIA~~ ART STUDIOS

25 WD:YOI   William Davis

26

1

2   October 15, 19--

3   Johnson and Johnson

4   4576 ~~Indianna~~ *Indiana* Road

5   ~~Indiannapolis,~~ *Indianapolis,* IN   46215

6   ~~Dear Mr. Hojnson:~~ *Gentlemen:*

7   I am going to be working on the preparation of a new ~~addition~~ *edition* of

8   a book on styles of ~~correspondance~~ *correspondence* currently being ~~use.~~ *used.* I came ~~acros~~ *across*

9   the name of ~~you~~ *your* company in ~~a add~~ *an ad* in a recent magazine, and I am, there-

10   fore, writing you for your ~~judgement~~ *judgment* on the various kinds of ~~stationary~~ *stationery*

11   now in use.

12   In the ~~absense~~ *absence* of one outstanding style of letter form, I ~~belive~~ *believe*

13   that the book ~~shoud~~ *should* include samples of letterhead ~~papre~~ *paper* ~~wich~~ *which* can be

14   ~~use~~ *used* easily with all ~~style.~~ *styles.*

15   Since you are a ~~manufacture~~ *manufacturer* of paper which is ~~use~~ *used* for ~~cor-~~ *correspondence,*

16   ~~respondance,~~ I thought it ~~woud~~ *would* be to ~~me avantage~~ *my advantage* to communicate with

17   ~~with~~ you. I have made inquiries in the field, and I do not have to ~~ad~~ *add*

18   that you have a ~~find~~ *fine* reputation.

19   Please let me ~~no weather~~ *know whether* you would be able to make ~~a apointment~~ *an appointment*

20   to see me ~~promply.~~ *promptly.* If not, can you ~~recomend~~ *recommend* someone or some company

21   ~~wich~~ *which* in ~~you judgement~~ *your judgment* might be ~~helpfull.~~ *helpful.* Since this is a job ~~wich mus~~ *which must*

22   be completed by ~~nest January~~ *next January* or ~~Febuery,~~ *February,* I am eager not to ~~loose~~ *lose* any

23   time. I should ~~apreciate hering~~ *appreciate hearing* from you as quickly as ~~possable.~~ *possible.*

24   ~~Cordialy~~ *Cordially* yours,

25   MAF: ~~WISCONSAN~~ *WISCONSIN* PUBLISHING COMPANY

26   ~~MF:~~YOI   Martin A. Fine, Editor

1

2   January 3, 19--

3   Dr. Ted Shanley

4   604 New York Avenue

5   Schenectady, NY   12314

6   Dear Dr. Shanley:

7   I wish that we could accommodate your request that we repair your

8   camera without charge, but we are unable to do so. An examination of

9   the camera indicates that it was probably dropped accidentally.

10   In accordance with the terms of your purchase, equipment can be

11   repaired at no charge only if the fault is with the manufacturer. In

12   this case, this is evidently not so.

13   I would recommend that you have the camera shipped to us promptly.

14   Our Service Department loses no time in checking cameras quickly and

15   with accuracy. That department will be able to inform you whether the

16   camera can be repaired cheaply enough to warrant repair. If this cannot

17   be done, they will advise you of this fact, too.

18   In your letter you wrote that you no longer have your receipt. In

19   the absence of a receipt, we request that you send us a copy of your

20   check or something similar so that we will know the date of purchase.

21   We are sorry that we cannot repair this camera without charge, but

22   we must adhere to our usual policy.

23   Yours very truly,

24   TARGO CAMERA COMPANY

25   JT:YOI   James Targo, Service Department

26

1

2   February
                                                         ~~Febuery~~ 28, 19--

        Mrs.
3   ~~Mrs~~ William Crane

                Kentucky
4   1235 ~~Kantucky~~ Street

        Louisville
5   ~~Louieville,~~ KY   40217

                        Crane:
6   Dear Mrs. ~~Williams:~~

                        weather   beginning   substantial
7   Now that warmer ~~whether~~ is ~~begining~~ to cover a ~~substancial~~ section

                        probably thinking   additions   your
8   of the country, you are ~~probable~~ ~~thinkin~~ of making ~~editions~~ to ~~you~~

9   garden supplies.

                    enclosing   latest catalog   and
10   We are ~~encolsing~~ a copy of our ~~lates~~ ~~catolog~~ of garden tools ~~an~~

                        recommend   very
11   machinery. We ~~reccommend~~ that you look at it ~~veyr~~ carefully and order

                        without   losing   looked
12   whatever you need ~~with out~~ ~~loosing~~ any time. After you have ~~look~~ at

            catalog,   Add
13   ~~at the~~ ~~catolog,~~ fill out the order blank. ~~Ad~~ $1 to the total only if

                                    than   merchandise
14   the supplies ordered come to less ~~thon~~ $10. The ~~merchandize~~ will be

        shipped   able   receive
15   ~~shiped~~ so that you will be ~~albe~~ to ~~recieve~~ it intime to take care of

        planting your
16   ~~palanting~~ ~~you~~ garden early.

            accordance   usual   send
17   In ~~acordance~~ with our ~~usul~~ policy, we shall ~~sent~~ you a refund

        immediately   equipment   which   dissatisfied.
18   ~~immediatly~~ if you return any ~~equiptment~~ with ~~wich~~ you are ~~dissatisfy.~~

            know   have   sent
19   We ~~no~~ that you ~~hav~~ been pleased with the items we have ~~send~~ you in the

        past,   hoping   same   when
20   ~~passed,~~ and we are ~~hopping~~ that you will have ~~same~~ the reaction ~~wen~~ you

                        equipment.
21   order the new ~~equipoment.~~

                                        Cordially
22   ~~Cordialy~~ yours,

23   GRASSO GARDEN SUPPLY COMPANY

        TAG:
24   ~~TG:~~YOI   Thomas Alex Grasso
        enclosure
25   Sales Manager

26

1

2   July
                                          ~~Juyl~~ 5, 19--

3   Mr. Lee Kotter

4   251 ~~Misouri~~ Missouri Avenue

5   ~~Saint~~ St. Louis, MO   63118

6   Dear ~~Mr. Kottre:~~ Mr. Kotter:

7   To find out why you are ~~dissatiefy~~ dissatisfied with the ~~acuracy~~ accuracy of your watch

8   which you ~~ship~~ shipped us last week, we have ~~examine~~ examined it carefully. A ~~lose~~ loose

9   mainspring is the cause of ~~teh difficult.~~ the difficulty. In the ~~absonce~~ absence of any ~~rop-~~ re-

10 ~~ort~~ port from you, we ~~muse~~ must assume that the watch ~~were damage accidontly.~~ was damaged accidentally.

11   Although we do not ~~usualy~~ usually repair watches when the difficulty is

12 caused by ~~a~~ an accident, we shall do ~~sew~~ so in ~~you~~ your case in order to ~~accom-~~ accommodate

13 ~~odate~~ you. We are ~~doin~~ doing this because you have been such a loyal ~~cos-~~ customer

14 ~~tumer~~ for many years. The repairs should be ~~finish promply,~~ finished promptly, and you

15 ~~you shoud~~ should have the watch ~~withing~~ within a week or ~~to.~~ two.

16   ~~Wit~~ With this letter we are sending ~~a~~ you a new ~~addition~~ edition of our price

17 list which we have just ~~publish.~~ published. This gives the prices of our new

18 line of clocks and ~~watchs.~~ watches. We ~~belive~~ believe that you will ~~fine~~ find that they

19 are better ~~then~~ than ever from the point of ~~you~~ view of style and price. We

20 ~~thing~~ think it is a great ~~achievmet~~ achievement that we have been able to keep the

21 prices of ~~are~~ our watches at the same level as in ~~passed~~ past years. The

22 prices of material ~~has~~ have gone up. Labor costs have ~~allso~~ also been much

23 higher this year ~~then~~ than in the past ~~to~~ two years, but we are trying to hold

24 ~~hold~~ the line on prices ~~as~~ much as ~~possibel,~~ possible.

25   Needless to say, we ~~apreciate you~~ appreciate your patronage and hope that we

26 will continue doing business with you for many years to come.

27   As in the ~~passed,~~ past we shall offer the ~~personnel~~ personal touch ~~wich~~ which we

28 have always ~~bin~~ been able to give to you and to all our ~~costumers,~~ customers. Although

29 our ~~organzation~~ organization is large, we ~~allways~~ always try to act like the small, ~~froi~~ friendly

30 ~~ndly~~ firm that we were when we started more ~~then ninty~~ than ninety years ago.

31   Of ~~cause,~~ course, if you ~~fine~~ find that you are not happy with your watch

32 after it has been ~~return~~ returned to you, please do not hesitate to let us ~~no.~~ know.

33   ~~Allso,~~ Also, we ~~woud~~ would ~~apreciate~~ appreciate it if you would ~~examin~~ examine our new price

34 list with care. ~~Their~~ There may be some clocks or watches ~~wich~~ which would just

35 meet your needs as gift items at ~~iihs~~ this time.

36   ~~Sincerly~~ Sincerely yours,

37   JASPER WATCH COMPANY

38 ~~HAJ:~~YOI HJ: Harold Jasper

39 enclosure   ~~Pressident~~ President

40

41

42

43

44

45

46

47

48

49

50

51

52

January 5, 19--

Swanson Hardware Company

4244 Hawaii Boulevard

Honolulu, HI 96819

Attention: Mr. Robin Swanson

Gentlemen:

Of course, we appreciate the business you have given us in the recent past, and we hope it will continue to grow. However, in checking our records, we note that there is a substantial amount owing to us, $4,510.09. Our Accounts Payable Department has asked me to write to you so that you can check the accuracy of your records against ours. The amounts outstanding have never added to more than $2,000, and we are concerned by this large increase.

We know that the equipment we have shipped has always pleased you because you evidently sold it and reordered it. In addition, we have rushed shipments to you on an emergency basis whenever you have requested us to do so.

Please send us an acknowledgment of this letter and a statement of how soon you intend to settle this account of $4,510.09. Whether you can pay us immediately is unimportant. We would appreciate hearing from you promptly.

Cordially yours,

Jeffrey Hartman,

Collection Manager

JH:YOI

1

2   January 4, 19--

3   Miss Sandra Colon, Personnel Department

4   Bell Telephone System

5   623 Arizona Street

6   Phoenix, AZ   85020

7   Dear Miss Colon:

8   We certainly appreciate your willingness to accommodate a group of

9   35 pupils at your offices on Monday, April 18. I know that our pupils

10   will benefit from this visit because they will see some of the modern

11   equipment which they have heard about in class but have not seen. They

12   are particularly interested in seeing the Correspondence Department since

13   most of the 35 pupils are preparing to be typists. In addition, the

14   film you usually show them in your library will be most helpful.

15   I believe that you are familiar with the type of student we have

16   at our school because you have arranged similar trips in the past two

17   or three years. You will find that they will ask your advice about

18   the Bell Telephone System and the possibilities of job placement in your

19   offices. Their skills are good, and I feel that they will make ex-

20   cellent employees.

21   In accordance with your request, we are filling out the acknowledg-

22   ment form for this visit and are enclosing it with this letter.

23   Sincerely yours,

24   HC:YOI
     Encl.
25

26

January 2, 19--

Midwest Manufacturers, Inc.

90 Ohio Avenue

Cincinnati, OH   45221

Gentlemen:

I'm happy to accept your production manager's offer for me to visit your organization at the beginning of next month. It cannot be after the ninth of the month because I already have urgent appointments in Baton Rouge and Shreveport the second week in February. When I have more definite plans, I shall telephone your office to make the necessary arrangements to give you adequate time to be prepared for my visit.

I hope to see the new machinery which you manufacture, and I know that what I'll see will not disappoint me.

In the near Future, we are planning to open some new offices across the country, and we shall require some new machines. We hope to be able to acquire them from you because we know that you are the manufacturers of some of the finest equipment in this area.

I'm certainly looking Forward to seeing you. It will be a fine opportunity to talk Further about this matter. I shall have my assistant, Mr. Walter Burleigh, with me.

Yours truly,

HELLER TOOL COMPANY

Paul Heller, Vice-President

PH:YOI

1

2   February
                                                          ~~Febuary~~ 21, 19--

3   Miss
      ~~Miss.~~ Elsie Hellman

4   Carolina
      787 North ~~Carolinna~~ Street

5   Raleigh,
      ~~Ralleigh,~~ NC   27622

6   dear Miss
      My ~~Dear Miss.~~ Hellman:

7   Until   it   impossible
            ~~Untill~~ recent times, ~~ti~~ was ~~impossibel~~ to secure the services

8   unpaid assistant   there   and
      of ~~unpaid assistent~~ teachers, but now ~~their~~ are many young men ~~an~~

9   women among recent   whose interest
      ~~woman amoung resent~~ graduates ~~who's intrest~~ has been stimulated.

10   It's   college   students
           ~~Its~~ easy to see why ~~cologe~~ graduates and ~~studens~~ would be eager

11   their
      to help improve life in ~~there~~ communities. As a result, we think

12   will   these positions.
      that many ~~wil~~ apply for ~~thes positosn.~~

13   should appreciate   would   touch   you
         I ~~shoud apprieiate~~ it if you ~~woud~~ get in ~~tuch~~ with me when ~~your~~

14   receive   letter.   know   able   find
      ~~recieve~~ this ~~leter.~~ I ~~no~~ that you maybe ~~abel~~ to ~~fine~~ the time to

15   speak   then   arrangements
      ~~speek~~ to me soon, and we can ~~than~~ make ~~arrangemonts~~ to plan a program

16   the   future.
      the in near ~~futhure.~~
        ^

17   children's   considered,   it's   belief
      Our ~~childrens~~ needs must be ~~consider,~~ and ~~its~~ my ~~beloif~~ that

18   reasonable   their   the
      this is a ~~resonable~~ method of filling ~~there~~ needs and those of ~~teh~~

19   recent
      ~~the resent~~ graduates.

20   yours,
                                Sincerely ~~your,~~

21   Jws: Principal
      ~~JSM:~~YOI   James W. Smith, ~~Principle~~

22   ~~Enclosure~~

23

24

25

26

1

2   January
                                 ~~January~~ 4, 19--

3   Ms. Edith Mills

4   Rhode
      89 ~~Road~~ Island Street

5   Worcester,   MA
      ~~Worchester, MA.~~   01623

6   Mills:
      Dear Ms. ~~Miles:~~

7   We are ~~begining~~ a drive for new members in our ~~organzation.~~ ~~I'm~~
              beginning   organization.   I'm

8   ~~writin~~ this letter to you ~~hopping~~ that you may be ~~planing~~ to ~~joinn~~ our
      writing   hoping   planning   join

9   club at the ~~minium~~ new rate ~~fo~~ $9 a year.
                   minimum   of

10   ~~Their~~ are many ~~advantiges~~ to ~~joinin~~ this ~~organzation.~~ In the
           There   advantages   joining   organization.

11   first ~~palce,~~ you will ~~injoy~~ the company of many young people like ~~you-~~
            place,   enjoy   yourself.

12   ~~self.~~ We have ~~sum~~ discussions at ~~are~~ meetings which take place ~~allmost~~
                         some   our   almost

13   every month, and ~~youll~~ have a chance to ~~tack~~ part. Then, club members
                        you'll   take

14   ~~mmebers~~ are ~~allso~~ ~~entitle~~ to ~~discoounts~~ ~~wenover~~ they want to go to
                    also entitled   discounts   whenever

15   shows. For ~~ecample,~~ a $5 ticket ~~cost~~ only $3.50 if you ~~by~~ it ~~thru~~
                  example,   costs   buy   through

16   the club.

17   A membership blank is ~~enclose.~~ ~~Im~~ sure ~~youll~~ want to join after
                                  enclosed. I'm   you'll

18   you have ~~rod~~ ~~waht~~ we are sending you.
               read what

19   Very truly ~~your,~~
                                          yours,

20   AMERICAN LITERARY CLUB

21   GS:
      ~~GZ:YOI~~   Gerald Supp

22   Enclosure
      ~~Inclosure~~   Membership ~~Chairmon~~
                                           Chairman

23

24

25

26

1

2   February
                                                        ~~Febuery~~ 6, 19--

3   Mr. Roy Robertson, Chairman
                         ~~Chairmon~~

4   Southern States Committee
                       ~~Comittee~~

5   704 Florida Avenue
         ~~Floridda~~

6   Miami,
     ~~Miammi~~, FL   33124

7   Dear Mr. Robertson:
              ~~Robinson:~~

8   I want to take this opportunity to thank you for the work you did
                             ~~oportunity~~

9   in making my task so much easier in planning for this year's convention
                                    ~~planing~~   ~~years~~

10   which has just been concluded in Savannah.
           ~~have~~   ~~conclude~~   ~~Savanna.~~

11   I knew that when I appointed you as my assistant, I wouldn't be disappointed.
            ~~now~~   ~~apoint~~   ~~asistant,~~   ~~wouldnt~~   ~~dissap-~~

12   ~~pointed.~~ There were so many miscellaneous things that you did that I'm
         ~~Their was~~   ~~miscelaneous~~   ~~taht~~   ~~Im~~

13   unable to express my appreciation adequately. It's always rewarding to
                         ~~apreciation adequately.~~ ~~Its~~

14   know that there is someone responsible to make sure that there are no
     ~~no~~   ~~their~~   ~~responsable~~   ~~their~~

15   loose ends in planning such a convention. You made certain that all
     ~~no lose~~   ~~planing~~   ~~certin~~

16   arrangements were taken care of with a minimum of difficulty.
     ~~arrangments~~   ~~fo~~ ~~wiht~~ ~~minimumm~~ ~~fiddiculty.~~

17   It was a real pleasure to work with you on this convention, and I'm
                                                                          ~~Im~~

18   hoping that this will be the beginning of a long and pleasant relation-
                                 ~~begining~~   ~~plesent~~ ~~relations-~~

19   ship. Already I believe that I shall be glad to call on you whenever
     ~~hip.~~ ~~Allroady~~ ~~boloive~~   ~~sahll~~   ~~when-ever~~

20   there is similar work to be done. I'm grateful to you that I'm able
     ~~their~~ ~~similiar~~   ~~Im graetful~~   ~~Im abol~~

21   to have this feeling.
        ~~hav~~

22   sincerely yours,
                                   Very ~~sincerly your,~~

23   NINTH INSURANCE CO. OF SAVANNAH
                                   ~~NINEPH~~   ~~SAVANNA~~

24   PM:YOI   Patrick Moriarty

25   President
                                   ~~Presidotn~~

26

1

2   ~~January~~ January 31, 19--

3 Ms. Amy Germontt

4 202 ~~Louisianna~~ Louisiana Street

5 New ~~Orleens,~~ Orleans, LA 70125

6 Dear Ms. ~~Germont:~~ Germontt:

7   ~~May be~~ Maybe you have not yet started to think about ~~thsi~~ this ~~summers~~ summer's ~~vacat=~~ vaca-

8 ~~ion~~ tion plans. Has it ~~occured~~ occurred to you that unless you plan now and begin to

9 make all the ~~nesessary arrangments,~~ necessary arrangements, you will be ~~disappointed?~~ disappointed? Have

10 you ~~past~~ passed travel agencies in ~~passed~~ past summers and ~~aksed~~ asked yourself why you

11 were still in New ~~Orleens whne~~ Orleans when you could be in ~~Honollulu,~~ Honolulu, Los ~~Angelos,~~ Angeles,

12 or San ~~Francico?~~ Francisco?

13   Higher prices may|be in ~~affect~~ effect soon, and we ~~cant garantee~~ can't guarantee that

14 the prices quoted in the enclosed ~~bullitin~~ bulletin will remain steady. However,

15 we have ~~allways~~ always made it a ~~principal~~ principle to keep our operating costs so low

16 that even ~~tho~~ though prices do rise, the total cost to you will not be ~~gratoly~~ greatly

17 ~~effeoted.~~ affected.

18   You will be ~~suprised~~ surprised at how ~~resonable~~ reasonable a trip will be this summer.

19 Stop in at ~~won~~ one of our local ~~office.~~ offices. Our ~~represontive~~ representative will be happy to

20 ~~to~~ make all the ~~nescassary arangements fro~~ necessary arrangements for you.

21   ~~Cordiall yours,~~ Cordially yours,

22   ACE TRAVEL AGENCY

23 YOI   Manager
   enclosure

24

25

26

1

2   May 3, 19--

3   Mr. Allen Lawlor

4   209 ~~Indianna~~ Indiana Street

5   ~~Garry,~~ Gary, IN   46426

6   Dear ~~Mrs.~~ ~~Lawlor:~~ Mr. Lawlor:

7   Thank you very much ~~fro~~ for responding to our previous letter, that

8   of ~~Febuary~~ February 25, in which you ~~ansored~~ answered some of the ~~qestions~~ questions we ~~aksed~~ asked about

9   ~~waht~~ ~~occur~~ what occurred when you were ~~accidently~~ accidentally struck by a hit-and-run ~~driever~~ driver on

10   ~~Wensday,~~ ~~January~~ Wednesday, January 29.

11   We have gone ~~thru~~ through your answers very ~~carefuly,~~ carefully, and we ~~beleive~~ believe we

12   shall soon be able to make ~~defanite~~ ~~arangements~~ definite arrangements to pay for the ~~ex-~~

13   ~~penees~~ expenses which you ~~payed~~ paid as a result of ~~thee~~ ~~acident.~~ the accident.

14   However, it will be ~~neeesary~~ necessary for one of our ~~representative's,~~ representatives,

15   Miss Alberta Glenn, to confer ~~wiht~~ ~~yu~~ with you to make ~~cortin~~ certain that our records

16   ~~is~~ are complete and correct. Would it be ~~poseable~~ possible for you to stop ~~buy~~ by

17   to see ~~him~~ her at our ~~principle~~ principal office at 112 ~~Nineth~~ Ninth Street in ~~Chicargo.~~ Chicago.

18   There ~~is~~ are a few ~~miscellaneous~~ ~~items'~~ miscellaneous items which Miss ~~Glen~~ Glenn must ~~diseus~~ discuss with

19   you. We would be ~~greatful~~ grateful if you filled in the enclosed card, ~~tellin-~~ telling

20   ~~g~~ us just ~~wehn~~ ~~a~~ ~~apbointment~~ ~~woud~~ when an appointment would be ~~convient~~ convenient for you. Upon ~~reciet~~ receipt of

21   the card, ~~Mr.~~ Miss Glenn will get in touch with you.

22   Yours ~~truely,~~ truly,
                                             INDEPENDENCE INSURANCE
23   ~~INDEPENDANCE~~ ~~INSURENCE~~ COMPANY
     KW:Yol
24   ~~YOI:KW~~   Kurt Weiss, ~~Districk~~ District Manager
     enclosure

25

26

1

2   March 14, 19--

3 Metropolitan Advertising Agency

4 34 Delaware Road

5 Wilmington, DE   19827

6 Gentlemen:

7   We are planning a sales drive when we introduce some new products

8 to our line of lighting equipment. We are hoping to place these products

9 on the market the beginning of next year, and we are now writ-

10 ing to various advertising agencies to set up appointments for their

11 representatives to meet with some of our officers to see whether our

12 requirements can be met.

13   Our budget allowances for this sales campaign are not yet definite,

14 but we believe that the sum of $50,000 should be sufficient. It may be

15 that some more funds will have to be spent. Nevertheless, this is

16 our company's budget at this time.

17   If you're interested in bidding for this account, please have one of

18 your representatives get in touch with me. I'm looking forward to beginning

19 to set up appointments as early as possible so that we can see just what

20 each organization has to offer.

21   Cordially yours,

22   LEVITZ ELECTRICAL SUPPLIES, INC.

23 HL:YOI   Henry Levitz

24   Advertising Department

25

26

1

2   January
                                                         ~~January~~ 15, 19--

3   Ms. Victoria Grant

                  Tennessee Avenue
4   247 ~~Tenesee Avemue~~

     Knoxville, TN
5   ~~Noxville, TN.~~ 37928

              Ms. Grant:
6   Dear ~~Miss Grantt:~~

         Thank   month's correspondence   sent
7   ~~Thang~~ you for last ~~months~~ ~~correspondenc~~ you ~~send~~ me concerning the

     budget   Nashville.
8   ~~budgit~~ we are now discussing in ~~Nacheville.~~ As a member of the Finance

     Committee, I'll certainly   mind.   know   al-
9   ~~Comittee, Ill certinly~~ keep your thoughts in ~~mine.~~ You ~~no~~ that I ~~all-~~

                   principle
10   ways make it a ~~principal~~ to take into consideration the views of the

                district,   then   decision.
11   people in my ~~districk,~~ and only ~~than~~ do I make a ~~decision.~~

                   it's   Government's
12   This year ~~its~~ very difficult to meet all of our State ~~Governments~~

     requirements because there   than there
13   ~~requirments becuse their~~ are so many more demands on funds ~~then their~~

     have   past.   assured   committee
14   ~~has~~ been in the ~~passed.~~ However, be ~~assure~~ that our ~~comittee~~ will

         its   spent
15   try ~~it's~~ very best to see that the funds are ~~spend~~ wisely.

         I'm planning   Knoxville   future,   course,
16   ~~Im planing~~ to be in ~~Noxville~~ in the near ~~futhure,~~ and, of ~~cause,~~

     I'm   Forward   one   at-
17   ~~Im~~ looking ~~foward~~ to seeing you at ~~won~~ of the dinners which I will ~~a-~~

     tend.   through
18   ~~ttend.~~ You can make reservations to attend a dinner ~~thru~~ the regular

     district organization.
19   ~~districk organization.~~

                                           sincerely
20   Very ~~sincerly~~ yours,

     PAM:
21   ~~PM:YOI~~   Perry A. Miller

22   State Senator

23

24

25

26

1

2   March 5, 19--

3   Dr. Edward Myers
          Wilkes-Barre
4   333 ~~Wilkes-Barre~~ Highway
     Pittsburgh,
5   ~~Pittsburg,~~ PA   15229
                 Myers:
6   Dear Dr. ~~Meyers:~~
              believe   than
7   We ~~belive~~ that we have more property to show you ~~then~~ any other
                                             Pennsylvania.   Whether you
8   real estate agency in this section of ~~Pennsylvania.~~ ~~Weather~~ ~~your~~ want
                                                                    certain
9   a home in the country, in a suburb, or in the city itself, we are ~~cer-~~
                    meet your requirements.
10   ~~tani~~ we can ~~met~~ ~~you~~ ~~requirments.~~
                                                   two houses which
11   If you want to remain in Pittsburgh, we have ~~to~~ ~~house~~ ~~wich~~ are
            already   their   planning
12   not ~~allready~~ on the market, but ~~there~~ owners are ~~planint~~ to place them
               within   been
13   for sale ~~withing~~ the next two months. We have ~~ben~~ their agents in the
     past, and   offer   customers
14   ~~passed, an~~ they will ~~offered~~ the houses to our ~~costumers~~ first. Both
                 similar in   their
15   houses are ~~similiar~~ ~~tin~~ that ~~there~~ main features include good location,
                              minimum   mortgages
16   excellent structure, and a ~~minimun~~ down payment with ~~morgatgos~~ easy to
                          one   house
17   obtain. The cost of ~~won~~ house will be about $35,000. The other ~~hose~~
18   has more rooms, a larger plot, and maybe either $45,000 or $50,000. We
                   told   allowed   houses
19   have been ~~tole~~ that we will be ~~alloud~~ to see the ~~houses~~ the first of
20   May.
                           would   Pittsburgh,
21   If you think that you ~~woud~~ like to live outside of ~~Pittsburg,~~ we
     know   two   They're   district
22   ~~no~~ of ~~to~~ groups of houses being built. ~~Their~~ in this ~~districk~~ but out
                    reasonable   surprise
23   of the city. The ~~resonable~~ prices will ~~suprise~~ you. Planning for the
                          finished,
24   houses is just about ~~finish,~~ and the building should begin no later
     than   effect
25   ~~then~~ July 1. The ~~affect~~ of the economic situation should result in
                                                probably   forward
26   speedy completion of these houses, and you ~~probable~~ can look ~~foward~~

27   to moving into the house about a year ~~form~~ from July. A ~~definate~~ definite selling

28   price has not yet been ~~determine,~~ determined, but the two ~~builders~~ builders' ~~representives~~ representatives

29   of these houses have ~~inform~~ informed us that they will be in the range of

30    $55,000. Each of the houses will be ~~diffrent,~~ different, the area is a ~~plesont~~ pleasant

31   ~~won,~~ one, and the builders did assure us that these houses will be ~~especia-~~ especially

32   ~~lly~~ suitable for families ~~similiar~~ similar to yours.

33   Are you ready for a vacation home in ~~teh~~ the mountains? Has it

34   ~~occured~~ occurred to you that a second home is what you want for your ~~familys~~ family's

35   summers? If ~~sew,~~ so, I would urge you to ~~olook thru~~ look through the listings we have

36   in ~~teh~~ the special ~~bullitin~~ bulletin which we have ~~prepare.~~ prepared. ~~Wehn~~ When you look at the

37   ~~bullitin,~~ bulletin, you will see that you do not need a ~~millionaires buget~~ millionaire's budget to ~~by~~ buy

38   ~~won~~ one of the cabins in the mountains. ~~May be~~ Maybe you have not yet thought

39   ~~thought~~ seriously about such a move, but ~~thsi~~ this literature ~~wil~~ will show you

40   how ~~agreable~~ agreeable country living is and how you can look ~~foward~~ forward to many

41   vacations for a ~~sprisilngly~~ surprisingly small sum of money. The prices listed ~~wil~~ will

42   be in ~~affect~~ effect only ~~untill~~ until May 30. After that date, prices will ~~probable~~ probably

43   be much ~~hire.~~ higher.

44   Of ~~cause,~~ course, we ~~woud~~ would consider it a ~~privolege~~ privilege and a pleasure to serve

45   you by discussing the housing ~~opportunities~~ opportunities covered in ~~thiss~~ this letter.

46   May we ~~here~~ hear from you ~~shourtly~~ shortly and make ~~arrangments~~ arrangements for ~~personnel~~ personal visits

47   to ~~som~~ some of the properties.

48   Cordially ~~your,~~ yours,
                                 PENNSYLVANIA
49   ~~PENSYLVANIA~~ REAL ESTATE COMPANY

50   ~~EOB:~~ EB:YOI

                                 Eric Blandington,
                                 Pittsburgh District Manager
51   ~~Pittsburg Dietrick Managerr~~

52

1

2   January
                                                  ~~January~~ 27, 19--

3   Mrs. Wanda Goldmann

4   2368 ~~Tenesee~~ Tennessee Street

5   Nashville,
     ~~Nasheville,~~ TN   37230

6   Dear ~~Ms. Goldman:~~ Mrs. Goldmann:

7   Do you feel that time has ~~past~~ passed you ~~buy?~~ by? Can you look ~~in to~~ into your

8   ~~futhure~~ future and ~~no~~ know that you will have ~~sufficent~~ sufficient resources to enable you

9   to lead a happy life after you have ~~stop~~ stopped working? Do you ~~belive~~ believe that

10   it is very ~~improtant~~ important to be ~~planing~~ planning activities which will make life more

11   ~~intresting~~ interesting and rewarding?

12   These ~~questions~~ questions' answers ~~certinly~~ certainly are not easy ~~wons.~~ ones. However, we

13   think we have ~~something whiehh~~ something which will be of ~~assistence~~ assistance to you in making

14   ~~making arranghments~~ arrangements for a very ~~aggreeable~~ agreeable lifestyle after you have

15   ~~retiror.~~ retired.

16   We are taking this ~~oprtunity~~ opportunity to send you ~~corespondence~~ correspondence from ~~som~~ some

17   other teachers, ~~assistent principles~~ assistant principals and ~~principles discribing there~~ principals describing their

18   experiences with our ~~organisation.~~ organization. ~~There~~ Their comments indicate that ~~that~~

19   they are ~~greatful~~ grateful for the work that we do.

20   The cost of joining and ~~reciving~~ receiving our monthly ~~bullitins~~ bulletins is only

21   $10 annually. Fill out the attached membership blank and rush it ~~ot~~ to

22   us as soon as ~~posible.~~ possible. You ~~wont~~ won't be sorry!

                                              Cordially
23   ~~Cordilly~~ yours,

                                                     PERSONNEL,
24   RETIRED SCHOOL ~~PERSONAL,~~ INC.

         JM:
25   ~~JAM:~~YOI   John Marsdent, President

     Enclosures
26   ~~Enclsoure~~

1

2   February
                                                        ~~Febuary~~ 14, 19--

3   Green Food Products, Inc.

              Springfield
4   1427 ~~Springfoild~~ Avenue

     Chicago,
5   ~~Chicargo,~~ IL   60631

6   Attention: Mr. Frank H. Green

     Gentlemen:
7   ~~Dear Mr Greene;~~

            pleased   know   wish   your advertising contract.
8   I am ~~please~~ to ~~no~~ that you ~~which~~ to renew ~~you~~ ~~advetising~~ ~~contrack.~~

     I   your   wishes   make
9   ~~I~~am sure that any changes ~~you~~ Legal Department ~~iwshes~~ to ~~mack~~ in the

     contract will   satisfactory
10   ~~contact~~ ~~wil~~ be ~~satisfacroy~~ to us.

          Your account   handled
11   ~~You~~ ~~account~~ has been a real challenge as I had never ~~handle~~ a food

     account   greatest   October
12   ~~acount~~ before. My ~~gratest~~ professional thrill came in ~~Octobr~~ when

           month's   won   advertising
13   that ~~months~~ layout of your product ~~one~~ for me the ~~advertising~~ award of

     of
14   ~~of~~ the month.

                                           I
15   As Mr. Richards told you, ~~i~~ have done considerable thinking about

           the   your
16   ~~about~~ ~~teh~~ the best way to present ~~you~~ product this year. I think I

          several   interest   Chicago
17   have ~~serveral~~ ideas that will ~~intrest~~ you. I shall be in ~~Chicargo~~

     February 28. May   then?
18   on ~~Febrary 28,~~ ~~may~~ I see you ~~than?~~

                                             truly,
19   Yours very ~~truely,~~

                                   ADVERTISING
20   MADISON ~~ADVETISING~~ AGENCY

21   JM:YOI   John Monroe

                            Account
22   ~~Acount~~ Executive

23

24

25

26

1

2   ~~Mau~~ May 21, 19--

3   Mr.
      ~~MR~~ Robert Jones

4   Ninth
      675 ~~Nineth~~ Avenue

5   York,
      New ~~Youk~~ NY   10032

6   Dear Sir:

7   The payment book showing the ~~balance~~ balance you still have to pay on

8   your
      ~~you're~~ recent purchase is ~~enclose.~~ enclosed. The book ~~aliso discribes~~ also describes our

9   procedures
      ~~proceedures~~ for payment. You will note that the terms of ~~you~~ your new

10   contract   payments   entitled
      ~~contrack~~ are ~~paymments~~ of $10 a week, and you are ~~entitle~~ to a discount

11   if you decide to pay ~~you acount withing~~ your account within six ~~month.~~ months.

12   It's pleasant to   friends   their accounts
      ~~Its plesent ot~~ have old ~~freinds~~ reopen ~~they accounts~~ with us. It

13   conscious   responsibility   buy
      makes us even more ~~conoious~~ of our ~~responsability~~ to the people who ~~by~~

14   We   business   you
      from us. ~~we~~ will do our part to keep our ~~busines~~ relations ~~you~~ with

15   pleasant   been   past.
      as ~~plesent~~ as they have ~~bin~~ in the ~~passed.~~

16   Your   placed   receive announce-
      ~~You're~~ name has been ~~place~~ on our mailing list to ~~recieve announ-~~

17   ments   future.   announce-
      ~~cements~~ of all sales that we will conduct in the ~~futre.~~ These ~~announ-~~

18   ments   week   before   advertise
      ~~cements~~ will reach you a ~~weak~~ or ten days ~~befor~~ we ~~advertize~~ the sales

19   to
      ~~the~~ the public.

20   Cordially yours,

21   SOMERS DEPARTMENT STORE

22   YOI   Department
      Enclosure   Credit ~~Depatment~~
23   ~~Inclosure~~

24

25

26

1

2 ~~Augest~~ August 30, 19--

3 Mr. ~~J.~~ J. B. Peters

4 370 North ~~Caralina~~ Carolina Street

5 ~~Durhamm,~~ Durham, NC   27733

6 Dear Mr. ~~Peterson~~ Peters:

7 SUBJECT: NEW EDITION OF ~~BULLITIN~~ BULLETIN

8 Thank you very ~~much~~ much for ~~send~~ sending us ~~serveral~~ several pages of the new ~~addition~~ edition

9 of the ~~bullitin~~ bulletin you wrote ~~to~~ two years ago. ~~Weve~~ We've read it with great ~~in-~~ interest

10 ~~intrest~~ because we think you ~~hav~~ have done a good job. However, ~~thsi~~ this new

11 ~~bullitin~~ bulletin ~~do~~ does not seem to be ~~suffishently~~ sufficiently ~~diforent~~ different from ~~you're~~ your first

12 book to make a new edition necessary.

13 Let me ~~suggets~~ suggest the ~~following;~~ following: come to our ~~offiec~~ office next ~~Wwndsay~~ Wednesday

14 so that you can show us some more ~~editions~~ additions that you are ~~planing~~ planning to

15 make to the text. At that time, ~~well~~ we'll meet with ~~represenives~~ representatives of our

16 ~~our~~ editorial board and make a final ~~decision~~ decision.

17 Very ~~truely yours,~~ truly yours,

18 JAMES PUBLISHERS, INC.

19 ~~JWQ:~~ TWQ: YOI   Thomas W. Quigley

20

21

22

23

24

25

26

October 3, 19--

Bell Investment Corporation

322 Oklahoma Street

Oklahoma City, OK   73134

                Attention of Mr. Jeremy Bell, Treasurer

Gentlemen:

        We have had our attorneys analyze the annual statement of
Brown & Company in order to find out whether or not it would be wise
to institute bankruptcy proceedings.

        Their analysis of the situation seems to indicate that the company
will be able to pull through this financial emergency. Our attorneys
said the following: "The volume of business has been increasing stead-
ily; and although it is not yet apparent that the firm will be able to make
a profit this year, there is a good possibility that it will succeed in
doing so."

        We suggest that a final decision not be made until after the
annual records are available. These should be ready by February 28 of next
year. Do you believe, as we do, it's in the best interests of all concerned to do so? Please check to see that the attorneys and accountants
for your firm are agreeable to this procedure.

                                Sincerely yours,

                                GENERAL INDUSTRIES, INC.

HT:YOI   Harry Thayer, Treasurer

1

2   January
                                                   ~~Januayr~~ 12, 19--

                          Advertising
3   Middleton ~~Advertising~~ Agency

4   Attention: Mr. Gregory Middleton

          Iowa
5   29 ~~Iowwa~~ Street

     Des Moines,
6   ~~De Moine~~, IA   50335

     Gentlemen:
7   ~~Dear Mr. Middleton:~~

                  anxious   ad-
8   We are ~~ankshus~~ about the progress you are making with our ~~adv~~

     vertising   vacuum   undoubtedly
9   ~~ertising~~ campaign for the ~~vacum~~ cleaners we manufacture. As you un-

                          transferred   account   your
10   ~~doubtly~~ are aware, we ~~transfered~~ the ~~account~~ to ~~you~~ agency because we

     believed   formerly   little   success
11   ~~belived~~ that the agency we ~~formally~~ used was having ~~littel~~ ~~sucess~~ in

12   stimulating the sales of these appliances.

          when   described   mentioned
13   ~~Wehn~~ you ~~discribed~~ what you would do, you ~~mention~~ that you were

     planning   brochure   mailed
14   ~~planing~~ to issue a great ~~broshure~~ which would be ~~mail~~ to all purchasers

                                      sweepers. Although   deadline
15   of our sanding machines and carpet ~~sweepers.~~ ~~Altho~~ we set a ~~dead line~~

                      brochures,   disappointed
16   for seeing these ~~broshures,~~ we are ~~disapointed~~ that the deadline has

     passed;   transferred   our
17   ~~past~~ and we have not seen them. We thought that once we ~~transfered~~ out

     account   unnecessary   prog-
18   ~~acount~~ to you, it would be ~~nunessary~~ to worry about the lack of ~~progr~~

     ress.   volume   fast
19   ~~ess.~~ Our ~~volumn~~ of sales has fallen off, and we need ~~fate~~ action.

                  therefore,   know formally   hear from
20   We are, ~~therfore,~~ letting you ~~no formerly~~ that unless we ~~here form~~

              several)   attorneys concerning
21   you in ~~sorveral~~ days, we shall speak to our ~~atorneys~~ ~~conserning~~ the

     possibility   cancellation   contract
22   ~~posibility~~ of the ~~cancelation~~ of our ~~contrack~~ with you.

                                      Yours   truly,
23   ~~Your~~ very ~~truely,~~

                                      MANUFACTURERS,
24   MIDWEST ~~MANUFACTORERS~~, INC.

                                                    Secretary
25   JG:YoI   John Garrison, ~~Secetary~~

26

1

2 December
~~Desember~~ 14, 19--

3 Ms. Margaret White

4 349 New York ~~Youk~~ Avenue

5 Syracuse, NY ~~Seracuse, N.Y.~~ 13236

6 Dear Ms. White: ~~Mrs. White,~~

7   I apologize ~~apoligize~~ for not writing to you sooner about the letter you

8 objected to receiving ~~recieving~~ concerning ~~consorning~~ an unpaid ~~unpayed~~ bill for ~~ofr~~ $137.29. I was

9 away from the office for almost two ~~allmost to~~ weeks with a severe cold, and I

10 have just returned. ~~jus return.~~ I checked your account ~~check you acount~~ with our assistant bookkeeper, ~~asistant bookeeper,~~ and

11 I am happy to say that you are correct. You don't ~~dont~~ owe us any money.

12   The error was caused because we have another customer whose ~~anoter customer wohse~~ name

13 is Margaret White. She lives ~~ilves~~ at 439 New York ~~NewyOrk~~ Avenue so you can see

14 how an ~~a~~ error like this could have occurred. ~~occured.~~ We are changing our records

15 to show a credit to you of $137.29. ~~$137.28.~~

16   We know ~~no~~ that it was unpleasant ~~unplesent~~ for you have this occur, but we are

17 certain ~~certin~~ that it will not be necessary ~~nesessary~~ for us to have any further ~~furthur~~ cor-

18 correspondence ~~respondance~~ about this matter.

19   Sincerely ~~Sincerly~~ yours,

20   MAXWELL DEPARTMENT STORE

21 JRM: ~~JPM:YOI~~   Jane R. Martin,

22   Credit Manager

23

24

25

26

1

2 ~~Febuary~~ February 1, 19--

3 ~~Mister~~ Mr. Wilbert N. Jenkins

4 348 ~~Kanses~~ Kansas Street

5 ~~Topeeka,~~ Topeka, KA   66637

6 Dear ~~Mr. Jenkin~~ Mr. Jenkins:

7   We have ~~check~~ checked on why you ~~haev~~ have been ~~gettin~~ getting poor service in ~~you~~ your

8 building. You ~~probable~~ probably ~~did'nt~~ didn't ~~no~~ know that the ~~superintendant~~ superintendent of the build-

9 ing, Thomas Adams, was ~~accidently~~ accidentally hit by ~~a~~ an automobile on ~~Wensday, Dece-~~ Wednesday, Decem-

10 ~~mber~~ ber 2. He was ~~unconcious~~ unconscious and had to be taken to the hospital. ~~Whil~~ While

11 he was hospitalized, his wife ~~attempt~~ attempted to keep ~~strickly~~ strictly to the schedule

12 that had been set ~~up,~~ up; but she was not ~~completly successful.~~ completely successful.

13   Now that Mr. ~~Adam~~ Adams has ~~recover~~ recovered and has once again ~~asoume~~ assumed his ~~reg-~~ regular

14 ~~ula~~ duties, you can rely on the following ~~promise;~~ promise: "The ~~appoarence~~ appearance of

15 the building will go back to what it ~~formally was".~~ formerly was." ~~Mr~~ Mr. Adams will see

16 that his ~~adsistent~~ assistant ~~vacums~~ vacuums the halls daily, a ~~prosedure~~ procedure which was ~~allw-~~ always

17 ~~ays~~ followed ~~hear.~~ here.

18   We ~~apolfgize~~ apologize for the ~~inconvience~~ inconvenience you and the other tenants had,

19 but you now ~~no~~ know that it ~~wae a unusal~~ was an unusual and unavoidable situation.

20 ~~Your truoly,~~ Yours truly,

21 ~~HR:YOI~~ HRR:YOI

21   Henry R. Rice

22   Building ~~Managerr~~ Manager

23

24

25

26

1

2   October
~~Octobr~~ 14, 19--

3   Miss Bernice Frish, Employment Counselor

4   Commercial
     ~~Commerical~~ High School

5   439 Arizona
     439 ~~Arazona~~ Drive

6   Tucson,
     ~~Tuscon,~~ AZ   85738

7   Miss Frish:
     Dear ~~Mrs. Frisch:~~

8   As you suggested, ~~suggested,~~ our personnel ~~personal~~ department has made a thorough ~~through~~ study

9   of the attendance ~~attendence~~ records of the 15 pupils from your school who are ~~wo-~~

10   working
     ~~rking~~ as typists and bookkeepers ~~bookkeepers~~ in our special cooperative program.

11   The results of the study are listed on the attached ~~attach~~ sheet.

12   Although several
         ~~Altho serveral~~ of the students have been absent more than ~~then~~ we would ~~woud~~

13   like them ~~tehm~~ to be--as many as 15 days--; ~~days-;~~ the rest of them have excellent ~~excellant~~

14   records. We are very much pleased ~~please~~ that this has occurred ~~occured~~ this year. ~~App-~~

15   Apparently
     ~~arantly~~ the stress that ~~taht~~ you placed on the need for good attendance ~~attendence~~

16   paid
     ~~payed~~ off. However, I would suggest ~~woud sugest~~ that you speak to the two ~~too~~ pupils ~~w-~~

17   with
     ~~ith~~ the worst records and tell them that although ~~altho~~ an analysis ~~analisis~~ of their ~~there~~

18   records by their ~~there~~ supervisors shows that they're ~~theyre~~ doing satisfactory work,

19   we shall ~~shll~~ be forced ~~force~~ to replace them unless there's ~~theoir's~~ a drastic improvement ~~improvment~~

20   in their attendance ~~theirr atendence~~ records by December ~~Desember~~ 15.

21   The regular employees in the departments ~~departments'~~ in which your students ~~students'~~

22   have
     work ~~has~~ been very favorably ~~favorable~~ impressed ~~impress~~ with the personal ~~personnel~~ appearance of

23   the pupils. The up-to-date ~~up-to-date~~ personality training course ~~coarse~~ which you are

24   now offering at your school evidently is meeting with great success. ~~suess.~~

25   Before we proceed ~~proced~~ with our plans for next year, I believe ~~belive~~ we should ~~shoud~~

26   get together to discuss whether ~~wheather~~ you think it would be possible ~~possible~~ to send ~~sent~~

27 us 20 pupils instead of the ~~16~~ 15 we now have. ~~Attornies~~ Attorneys ~~our~~ in our Legal

28 Department ~~woud~~ would be benefited if more filing help was provided. The

29 head of that department, Mr. Ted Klitz, said that in the ~~passed~~ past he

30 ~~prefered~~ preferred regularly employed file ~~clerks~~ clerks; but for next year he would be

31 ~~please~~ pleased to have three students in the ~~mrning~~ morning and three ~~differen student~~ different students

32 in the afternoon. It would be ~~unecessary~~ unnecessary for these students to ~~had~~ have ~~have~~

33 a special course in filing because ~~are~~ our files are set up a bit ~~difrently~~ differently

34 from ~~thoes~~ those in other ~~organzations.~~ organizations.

35 ~~Prepahs~~ Perhaps it would be of ~~assitance~~ assistance if we could set up a meeting ~~wit~~ with

36 Mr. ~~Klottz~~ Klitz within ~~teh nest~~ the next month or ~~to.~~ two. He could tell ~~your~~ You exactly

37 what he has in ~~mine,~~ minds, and you could start to ~~choke~~ check the records of ~~you~~ your

38 students to see which ones might be ~~availible~~ available for this type of work.

39   If ~~youre agreable~~ you're agreable to increasing the number of pupils you will send

40 ~~hear,~~ here, please let me ~~no~~ know so that we can make ~~arrangments~~ arrangements for ~~a apointment~~ an appointment

41 ~~wit~~ with Mr. ~~Klotz.~~ Klitz. At the same time I would ~~apprioiate~~ appreciate it if you ~~woud~~ would look

42 at the special ~~broshure~~ brochure we are in the process of preparing. ~~Thsi wil~~ This will

43 be ~~use~~ used when we visit classes in schools to recruit employees.

44   As ~~allways,~~ always, I ~~sertainly~~ certainly ~~appriciate~~ appreciate your ~~find~~ Fine spirit of ~~cooperati-~~ cooperation.

45 ~~on.~~

46   Yours sincerely,
                                        ~~Your Sincerely,~~

47   INDEPENDENCE
                                        ~~INDEPENDANCE~~ INSURANCE COMPANY

48 MLT:YOI   Marie Louise Turnball
    Enclosure   Vice President

49   ~~Vice Presiden~~

50

51

52

1

2   April 10, ~~Aprill 10~~ 19--

3   Dr. Fred Clarke

4   Superintendent
    ~~Superintendant~~ of Schools

5   Macon, ~~Maconn,~~ GA   31239

6   Dear Dr. Clarke: ~~Mr Clark~~

7   SUBJECT: Convention on October ~~Octobre~~ 15

8   The ~~Bureau~~ of ~~Busines~~ Business Education ~~sincerly~~ sincerely hopes that your ~~scho-~~ schedule

9   ~~dule~~ will allow you to be ~~avalable~~ available to ~~adress~~ address the ~~Georgai~~ Georgia ~~Commerical~~ Commercial

10 Education Association on ~~Saterday,~~ Saturday, October ~~16,~~ 15, at the Holiday Hotel in

11 ~~Savana.~~ Savannah.   As you ~~undoubtably no,~~ undoubtedly know, this ~~organisation~~ organization has ~~annuel~~ annual ~~convent-~~ conven-

12 ~~ione~~ tions each fall at which educational matters of ~~intrest~~ interest to ~~teahcers,~~ teachers,

13 ~~assistant principles~~ assistant principals and ~~principles~~ principals are ~~discuss.~~ discussed. Those who ~~of atended~~ have attended

14 the panels in the ~~passed~~ past have ~~allwyas benefitted~~ always benefited from what they have

15 ~~hord.~~ heard.

16   Please let me ~~no~~ know as soon as ~~posible~~ possible what you ~~woud~~ would like to dis-

17 cuss. The general theme of the convention is "The ~~Improvment~~ Improvement of

18 Instruction in ~~Bussiness~~ Business Courses in the High ~~Schools",~~ Schools." It is ~~suggsted~~ suggested

19 that each speaker talk for about ~~thrity~~ thirty minutes.

20   I ~~hop~~ hope you ~~be~~ will be able ~~abel~~ to ~~except~~ accept this invitation and that ~~Ill~~ I'll

21 ~~hore~~ hear from you shortly.

22   Very ~~cordialy~~ cordially yours,

23 NT:YOI   Norman Thompson, ~~Directro~~ Director.

24   Bureau ~~of Bsiness Education~~ Bureau of Business Education

25

26

1

2 April 5, 19-- ~~Arpil~~

3 Miss Kathleen Sweeney

4 34-89 ~~Texes~~ Texas Boulevard

5 Beaumont, ~~Beaumount,~~ TX   77740

6 Dear ~~Mrs. Sweeny~~ Miss Sweeney:

7 Do you ~~fine~~ find that ~~youre~~ you're ~~ankshus~~ anxious after a ~~ahrd~~ hard day at home or in ~~teh~~ the

8 office? Do you have aches and pains in your back? Do ~~yu~~ you have ~~troubel~~ trouble

9 sleeping? Are you nervous over extended periods of time?

10 If you have positive ~~ansers~~ answers to any of the questions asked above,

11 we ~~belive~~ believe that you will ~~benifit~~ benefit greatly from our monthly ~~bullitin~~ bulletin ~~wich~~ which

12 is ~~avalable~~ available for the ~~anual~~ annual rate of only $6.

13 The ~~Januery~~ January and ~~Febuery~~ February bulletins ~~diseribe~~ describe how tension can cause

14 ~~back aches,~~ backaches, lack of sleep, and general nervousness. Famous authors

15 give ~~som~~ some methods of ~~over coming~~ overcoming these difficulties in language ~~wich~~ which is

16 easily ~~under stood.~~ understood. The ~~articals~~ articles have ~~ben~~ been written by ~~doctors~~ doctors who ~~hav~~ have

17 had many ~~valueable ;years~~ valuable years of experience in treating patients all over

18 the country with great ~~sucess.~~ success.

19 Take ~~avantage~~ advantage of the ~~bargin~~ bargain rate of ~~$7~~ $6 now. Of ~~cause,~~ course, if you

20 see that ~~youre~~ you're not completely ~~satisfy~~ satisfied with the ~~bullitins,~~ bulletins, your ~~usuall~~ usual

21 ~~canoelation priveledges~~ cancellation privileges will apply.

22 Very ~~truely your,~~ truly yours,

23 HEALTH HINTS

24 JK: ~~JAK+YOI~~ June Klemons

25 Circulation Manager

26

December 2, 19--

Mr.
Mr Edward Reilly

459 ~~Nineth~~ Ninth Avenue

~~Worchester,~~ Worcester, MA   01641

My ~~Dear~~ dear Mr. ~~Reilley~~ Reilly:

~~Congradulations!~~ Congratulations! I am very happy to tell you, Mr. Reilly, that ~~you~~ your

son, George, has ~~one~~ won a scholarship to our university. ~~Pleas except~~ Please accept

my best wishes.

~~Wehn~~ When you and he ~~has~~ have a chance to come to our ~~sheool,~~ school, I hope ~~oyu~~ you

will take ~~avantage~~ advantage of the ~~oportunity~~ opportunity to do so inasmuch as we like to

~~mack~~ make the ~~personnel~~ personal acquaintance of all of our award winners.

It will be a pleasure and a ~~priviledge Mr Reilley~~ privilege, Mr. Reilly, to meet with

you and George. ~~Incidently,~~ Incidentally, when you come ~~hear,~~ here, we shall make it a

festive ~~occassion~~ occasion and have lunch together.

I hope to ~~heare form~~ hear from you soon.

Sincerely ~~Yours,~~ yours,
~~MASSACHUSETTES INSTITUTE~~ MASSACHUSETTS INSTITUTE

YOI   Admissions ~~Directer~~ Director

1

2   February
                                        ~~Febuary~~ 3, 19--

        Mr.
3   ~~Mister~~ Theodore Jenson

              Cincinnati
4   410 ~~Cincinatti~~ Driveway

        Cleveland,
5   ~~Clevland,~~ OH   44142

              Mr.   Jenson:
6   Dear ~~Mister~~ ~~Jensen~~

              Saturday   sent   an   which will
7   Last ~~Saterday~~ we ~~send~~ you ~~a~~ announcement about a meeting ~~wich~~ ~~wil~~

              place Wednesday,   hope   take advantage of
8   take ~~paloe~~ on ~~Wensday~~ March 17. We ~~hop~~ that you will ~~taek~~ ~~avantage~~ ~~fo~~

                                enclosed   pamphlet   mailed   then.
9   the offer which was ~~enclose~~ in the ~~phamphlet~~ we ~~mail~~ to you ~~than.~~

        There   occasions   recommendation   necessary
10   ~~Their~~ are many ~~occassions~~ when a ~~reccommendation~~ is ~~nesessary~~ to

                    a conference.   expect
11   attend such ~~an~~ ~~converence.~~ However, in this case we ~~expect~~ to have

     sufficient   accommodate   persons   invited.
12   ~~suffieent~~ room to ~~acommodate~~ all of the ~~person~~ we have ~~invite.~~

              pamphlet,   questionnaire
13   In the ~~pamflet,~~ there is a ~~questionaire~~ which you should complete.

                                                    possible
14   We hope that you will answer it as soon as ~~posible~~ so that we can set

        the   efficiently,   promptly.
15   up ~~teh~~ meeting ~~officently~~ easily and ~~promply.~~

              forward   then.
16   We are looking ~~foward~~ to seeing you ~~than~~

                                        sincerely,
17   Yours very ~~Sincerely,~~

     HH:
18   ~~HJ:~~YOI   Herman Huggins

19   Publicity Director

20

21

22

23

24

25

26

1

2   January 5, 19--

3 Messrs. James & Burrell

4 4598 Missouri Avenue

5 St. Louis, MO   63143

6   Attention: Jason Burrell

7 Gentlemen:

8   Last Saturday, I sent you several copies of our new pamphlet,

9 LOOKING FORWARD TO A NEW WORLD. By this time, perhaps you have received

10 it and had an opportunity to look at it closely.

11   After you have examined it, I believe some of the members of your

12 corporation should be told about it. I believe that they will be

13 very much interested in finding out about what our society will be like

14 within the next few years.

15   After you have gotten their reaction, get in touch with me. I'll

16 be glad to discuss it further with you so that we can make plans for

17 for the changes believe we will be necessary.

18   As always, I value your opinion.

19   Yours truly,

20   AMERICAN FUTURES, INC.

21 HL:YOI   Harry Loomis

22   President

23

24

25

26

1

2   March 4, 19--

3   Ms. Karen Polanski

4   243 New Mexico Boulevard

5   Albuquerque, NM   87144

6   Dear Ms. Polanski:

7   I was somewhat surprised to learn that you were dissatisfied with the

8   service you received at our Ninth Avenue restaurant last Saturday. I

9   believe, Ms. Polanski, that the difficulty was caused by the the fact that

10 the members of your party requested separate checks after the waiters

11 had already prepared one check for the entire party. Inasmuch as

12 a great deal of extra work had to be done by the waiters at the last

13 minute, you were undoubtedly delayed. Usually a request like this is

14 made before luncheon is served, and the staff of the restaurant is always

15 able to prepare separate checks with a minimum of time and effort.

16   However, we don't want this occurrence to prejudice you against our

17 chain of restaurants. We are, therefore, enclosing a discount form with

18 this letter which will make it possible for you to have lunch or dinner

19 at any of our restaurants at a 20 percent discount. This form expires

20 in one year. I hope you will take advantage of this opportunity to let

21 us prove to you that the many years of excellent service you received

22 in the past were no accident.

23   Yours very truly,

24   ALL-AMERICAN RESTAURANTS

25 NWW:YOI
    enclosure   Nathan W. Winers, General Manager

26

1

2   October
                                                         ~~Octobe~~ 16, 19--

3   Miss Charlotte Ameling

4   1440 ~~Ohhio~~ Ohio Street

5   ~~Ackron,~~ Akron, OH   44345

6   Dear Miss ~~Charlotte~~ Ameling:

7   ~~Congradulations~~ Congratulations on your ~~success~~ success in ~~winning~~ winning one of the prizes in

8   the essay contest ~~sponsored~~ Sponsored by our ~~organzation~~ organization! Frankly, we ~~was~~ were some-

9   what ~~suprised~~ surprised at the large number ~~fo~~ of entries we ~~receved~~ received from ~~secetaries~~ secretaries

10   from all parts of the country. This is ~~prooof~~ proof that many ~~secetaries~~ secretaries

11   ~~recohize~~ recognize the ~~impotance~~ importance of the ~~statement;~~ statement, "~~Carefullness~~ Carefulness in ~~proofrea-~~ proofreading

12   ~~ding~~ letters is ~~nesessary.~~ necessary."

13   The enclosed ~~phamphelt~~ pamphlet lists the choices you ~~hav~~ have in selecting the

14   ~~the~~ prize to which ~~youre~~ you're ~~entitle.~~ entitled. ~~Jus mack~~ Just make a notation (in the space

15   ~~provided(~~ provided) of ~~waht~~ what you would like us to ~~sent~~ send you, ~~Ms.~~ Miss Ameling, and we

16   ~~we~~ shall ~~male~~ mail it to you as soon as ~~posible.~~ possible.

17   At the same time you send us ~~you~~ your choice of prize, we ~~shoud~~ should ~~app-~~ ap-

18   ~~reciate~~ preciate it if you would fill out the information ~~aksed~~ asked for on the

19   ~~questionaire.~~ questionnaire. ~~Youre~~ Your answers to these questions will be of great

20   ~~assistants~~ assistance to us.

21   ~~Gordilly Yours,~~ Cordially yours,

22   AMERICAN ~~SEGETARIES~~ SECRETARIES CLUB

23   ~~HAM.YOI~~ HM: Helene Melnick
      enclosure

24   Contest ~~Editre~~ Editor

25

26

1

2   March 4, 19--

3   ~~Messers~~. Messrs. Grant and Hill

4   10 San ~~Francisko~~ Francisco Avenue

5   ~~Berkley~~, Berkeley, CA   94746

6   Attention of Leonard Grant

7   ~~Dear Mr. Grant~~ Gentlemen:

8   Why are you ~~witholding~~ withholding payment of our ~~onvoice~~ invoice of November 30

9   for $4,173.29? ~~Wen~~ When you ~~place~~ placed the order, we told Mr. Howard, your ~~production~~ pro-

10   ~~oduction~~ duction manager, that ~~ew~~ we could make a ~~shippent~~ shipment of about ~~ninty~~ ninety cartons

11   of ~~stationary~~ stationery in ~~Novembre~~ November and the rest of the ~~cartoons~~ cartons on the order by

12   the middle of December. Inasmuch as the last cartons were ~~shiped~~ shipped on

13   the ~~nineth~~ ninth of ~~Decembr~~, December, you ~~shoud~~ should have ~~recieve~~ received all that you ~~order~~ ordered well

14   before the date promised.

15   We assume that all the ~~stationary~~ stationery received was satisfactory ~~be-~~

16   because we have not ~~herd~~ heard from you to the contrary. ~~Incidently~~, Incidentally you

17   ~~you~~ never owed us so much in the ~~passed~~, past, and we are ~~somewat~~ somewhat ~~suprised~~ surprised

18   by ~~you~~ your failure to pay this rather large bill of ~~$4,172.29~~. $4,173.29.

19   Your credit with us is good, and ~~Im~~ I'm sure you want it to stay that

20   ~~weigh~~ way. Will you, ~~therfore~~, therefore, please ~~foward~~ forward ~~you~~ your check to us as early ~~as~~

21   as ~~possibel~~. possible.

22   ~~Your~~ Yours very ~~truely~~, truly,
                                     CALIFORNIA STATIONERY
23   ~~CALAFORNIA STATIONARY~~ SUPPLIERS

24   HB:YOI   Harry Buckley,

25   Credit ~~Manger~~ Manager

26

1

2   December
                                       ~~Decembr~~ 2, 19--

3   Mr. Leonard Kaufman

4   Bridgeport Gas Company

        Connecticut
5   53 ~~Conneticut~~ Avenue

      Bridgeport, CT
6   ~~Bridgport, CT~~ 06647

      Dear Mr. Kaufman:
7   ~~Gentlemen:~~

                         your   acceptance
8   Thank you for ~~you acceptence~~ of our invitation to speak at the Town

                                    organization,   Control
9   Hall Meeting sponsored by our ~~organisation~~ the Air ~~Cpntrol~~ Committee.

                                                       Tuesday, January
10   We have just had to change the date of the meeting from ~~Tuesdy January~~

        Wednesday, January   appreciate   your
11   3, to ~~Wensday January~~ 4. I would ~~appresiate~~ it if you could have ~~you~~

      secretary   able
12   ~~seeotary~~ telephone me to confirm the fact that you will be ~~abel~~ to

                    fourth   the
13   speak on the ~~forth~~ instead of on ~~teh~~ third.

                                          minimum   formal
14   At this meeting, we hope to have a ~~minium~~ of ~~formel~~ speeches and a

                         allowed   answers.   therefore,
15   maximum of time ~~aloud~~ for questions and ~~answeres.~~ Will you, ~~therefor~~

                        address   Recognizing
16   please limit your ~~adress~~ to about 20 minutes. ~~Reconizing~~ your skill

                    Mr. Kaufman,   your   across
17   as a speaker, ~~Mr Kaufmann~~ I am sure that you can get ~~you're~~ points ~~ac-~~

                                      time. Then,   further
18   ~~cross~~ in that short period of ~~time?~~ ~~Than,~~ any ~~futher~~ points you would

                         added   response
19   like to make can be ~~aded~~ in ~~responce~~ to questions.

      Incidentally,   forward
20   ~~Incidently,~~ we are looking ~~foward~~ to having a large crowd again,

           therefore,   repetition   when
21   and we, ~~theirfore~~ expect a ~~repitition~~ of the lively program we had ~~wen~~

          appearance   similar
22   you made an ~~appearence~~ last year at a ~~similiar~~ meeting.

                                       sincerely,
23   Yours ~~Sincerely,~~

                                       COMMITTEE
24   AIR CONTROL ~~GOMITTEE~~

25   JC:YOI   Jennifer Corwin

26   Program Chairperson

1

2   August
                                                          ~~Agust~~ 4,   19--

3   Messrs.
     ~~Messers.~~ Burton and Barr

4   Winston-Salem
     1 ~~Winston-Salem~~ Place

5   Asheville,
     ~~Ashville,~~ NC   28848

6   Gentlemen:
     ~~Gentleman:~~

7   Congratulations   cancellation   bankruptcy
           ~~Congradulations~~ on winning the ~~cancelation~~ of the ~~bankrupcy~~ pro-

8   ceedings last   won   was
     ~~ceedings~~ ~~las t~~ week in court! That you ~~one~~ against such high odds ~~wsa~~

9   surprising   attorneys   among
     amazing but not ~~supriizing~~ because your ~~attornies~~ are ~~amoung~~ the best in

10   Carolina   proved
     the State of North ~~Garalina.~~ One of the features of the case ~~prooved~~

11   interesting   you
     very ~~intresting~~ to me, and I would like to discuss it with ~~jue~~ with a

12   minimum
     ~~minimumm~~ of publicity.

13   meet   restaurants,
           I should like to ~~meeet~~ you for lunch at one of my favorite ~~res-~~

14   Asheville   convenient   realize
     ~~tarants,~~ the ~~Ashville~~ Inn, one day ~~convient~~ to you. I ~~realise~~ that you

15   somewhat   there
     must be ~~somewat~~ busy inasmuchas ~~their~~ is still a great deal of work

16   cancellation
     that must be done in connection with ~~with~~ the ~~cancelation~~ of the bank-

17   ruptcy,   believe   recognize   meeting
     ~~rupcy,~~ but I ~~beleive~~ you will ~~reconize~~ the importance of having a ~~meeti-~~

18   which   puzzles
     ~~ng~~ early after we have gone over the feature ~~wich~~ still ~~puzzle~~ me.

19   Incidentally,   would   arrangements
     ~~Incidently,~~ I ~~woud~~ prefer that we make ~~arrangments~~ for this ap-

20   pointment   than
     ~~ointment~~ by your calling me at home rather ~~then~~ at my office.

21   Cordially   yours,
                                               ~~Cordilly~~ ~~yours;~~

22   EDWARDS & EDWARDS

23   ABE:
     ~~EWE:~~YOI   Amy Beth Edwards

24

25

26

1

2   December ~~Decembr~~ 29, 19--

3 ~~Deluth~~ Duluth Paper Company

4 414 ~~Minnisota~~ Minnesota Avenue

5 ~~Deluth,~~ Duluth, MN   55849

6   Attention of Mr. Dana Brill, Vice President

7 ~~Dear Mr. Brill~~ Gentlemen:

8   We are ~~somewaht~~ somewhat ~~suprised~~ surprised and ~~dissappointed~~ disappointed by the fact that we

9 have not yet ~~recived~~ received the ~~shippment~~ shipment of ~~stationary~~ stationery ~~whih~~ which we ~~order~~ ordered more ~~then~~ than

10 ~~to~~ two months ago, on ~~Octobre~~ October 17. Before we ~~place~~ placed the order, we told you

11 the ~~following,~~ following: "We need this ~~stationary~~ stationery inorder to complete a big

12 printing order we have for ~~pamplets~~ pamphlets and ~~broshures~~ brochures for ~~won~~ one of our

13 ~~costumers".~~ customers." If we donot ~~haev~~ have the order completed on time, it will

14 ~~certinly effect~~ certainly affect the relationship that we have with this ~~improtant~~ important cus-

15 ~~tomar,~~ customer, and we are very ~~ankshus~~ anxious about the entire situation.

16   We feel that we gave you ~~adquate~~ adequate notice of our ~~requirments.~~ requirements. When

17 ~~your representive~~ your representative, Mr. Joliet, spoke to me, he said ~~taht~~ that the ~~shiping~~ shipping date

18 would be no ~~latter then Decembre~~ later than December 15. I ~~relize~~ realize that sometimes delays

19 are caused ~~buy~~ by unexpected events, but ~~aparently~~ apparently this is not ~~sew~~ so in this

20 instance. ~~Wohn ever~~ Whenever I have ~~telephone,~~ telephoned, I ~~hav~~ have been ~~assure~~ assured that ours is

21 ~~amoung~~ among the first orders yet to be filled, but sofar we have neither

22 ~~neither recieved~~ received the ~~stationary~~ stationery nor have we been given a ~~deffinate~~ definite date

23 for ~~shippment.~~ shipment. We are ~~allways~~ always ready to make ~~to alowances;~~ allowances; however, in

24 this case it is extremely difficult to do ~~sew.~~ so.

25   If we had ~~know taht their~~ known that there would have been such a long delay, we

26 would have ~~try~~ tried to get ~~sum assistence~~ some assistance from one or more of our other

27 suppliers. Often we can order ~~seperately~~ separately and ~~by~~ buy some paper from one

28 company and the rest ~~fromm~~ from another. This time we did not do this be-

29 ~~cuse~~ cause we were ~~assure~~ assured by your salesman, Mr. Joliet, that it would be ~~be~~

30 ~~unecessary~~ unnecessary to do ~~sew~~ so.

31   I would ~~appriciate~~ appreciate it if you ~~wod~~ would ~~personnelly~~ personally investigate this ~~ent-~~ entire

32 ~~ire~~ transaction. An ~~analisys~~ analysis of all the ~~facks~~ facts will ~~prooove~~ prove to you that

33 all my statements are ~~acurate~~ accurate.

34   Unless I ~~here~~ hear from you by next ~~Wosnesday,~~ Wednesday, I shall take up this

35 ~~this~~ matter with ~~may attornies~~ my attorneys to see what ~~theirr opinon~~ their opinion is. In the

36 ~~passed~~ past when this has ~~occured~~ occurred with other suppliers, they have ~~recomended~~ recommended

37 complete ~~cancelation~~ cancellation of ~~a~~ an order. We should hate to have to ~~insitute~~ institute

38 a lawsuit for the damages we will have ~~sufferred~~ suffered if the ~~stationary~~ stationery is

39 not ready for us ~~allmost immediatly,~~ almost immediately, but that will be a ~~desision Ill~~ decision I'll

40 have to make based on the ~~judgement~~ judgment and ~~advise~~ advice of my ~~attornies~~ attorneys.

41   Very ~~Truly Yours,~~ truly yours,

42   WESTERN PUBLISHERS, INC.

43 JBE:YOI   Jeffrey B. Ely, Sr.

44   ~~Presidennt~~ President

45

46

47

48

49

50

51

52

October 1, 19--

Ms. Lois Medner

2333 Nebraska Street

Omaha, NE   68150

Dear Ms. Medner:

  We are enclosing the results of a questionnaire which we recently sent to a somewhat large group of representatives of various organizations dealing with travel. They're very interesting because they give the opinions of people who recognize the need for excellent service at a minimum expense.

  After you have looked through this material, I know that you will want to use our services whenever you travel again. You were one of our earliest clients, and the fact that you still make your arrangements through us is proof that we give outstanding assistance to all of our friends.

  Under separate cover, we are sending you the latest ads that we have prepared for trips to Europe next spring. Look them over, Ms. Medner, and find out which trip will meet your requirements. Then, communicate with me personally, and I will be happy to give you the benefit of my advice.

        Cordially yours,

        NEBRASKA TRAVEL AGENCY

        Beverly Chazon

        President

BC:YOI

Enclosure

1

2   July
                                                                     ~~Juyl~~ 1, 19--

3   Mr. Herman Held

4   207 ~~Mew Jersy~~ New Jersey Avenue

5   ~~Patterson,~~ Patterson, NJ   07551

6   Dear ~~Mr Held~~ Mr. Held:

7   Of ~~cause,~~ course, I was very ~~gald~~ glad to write a letter of recommendation

8   for ~~yo u~~ you when I ~~recieved~~ received a request for ~~infromation form~~ information from the New ~~Jorsy~~ Jersey

9   ~~Insurence~~ Insurance Company. I am ~~confidant~~ confident that my ~~discription~~ description of your activ-

10   ities while you ~~work~~ worked for our ~~organization~~ organization will be ~~helpfull~~ helpful to you.

11   As I ~~tole~~ told you when you ~~choose~~ chose to leave our firm and ~~retrun~~ return to

12   college, I ~~woud~~ would be happy to ~~higher~~ hire you again. The high quality of

13   ~~you're~~ your work and your ~~curteous~~ courteous manner ~~alwways~~ always impressed me and our

14   ~~costumers.~~ customers.

15   I ~~regreat~~ regret that you ~~desided~~ decided to stay in New ~~Jersy~~ Jersey and, ~~therfore,~~ therefore,

16   ~~can not~~ cannot work for us now that you ~~hve receive~~ have received your college degree.

17   However, I ~~no~~ know that you will be ~~comming~~ coming home to visit ~~you~~ your family soon,

18   and I ~~hop~~ hope you will ~~stopp~~ stop in to see me. I ~~belive~~ believe you will be very

19   much ~~intrested~~ interested in the new ~~developements~~ developments that have ~~occured~~ occurred in our

20   company.

21   Good luck on ~~you~~ your new job!

22   ~~Sincerly~~ Sincerely yours,

23   HAMILTON ~~EQUIPTMENT~~ EQUIPMENT COMPANY

24   ~~RHA~~ RAH:YOI   Roy A. Hamilton

25   President

26

1

2   March 15, 19--

3   Mr. David Duval

4   976 California Street

5   Sacramento, CA   95852

6   Dear Mr. Duval:

7   I hope that you had a good trip back to Sacramento last Fri-

8   day, March 9. The weather here since then has been fine, and we are

9   looking forward to a pleasant spring.

10   I'm sorry that we could not have allowed sufficient time to discuss more

11   fully the controversy that has developed in our industry. As you know,

12   I am dependent upon your advice when a situation like this arises.

13   However, we simply didn't have enough time to go over all of the aspects

14   of the criticisms that have been raised.

15   I wonder if you could check your calendar to see whether the

16   second week of April would be convenient for you to spend some time with

17   me. I shall be in San Francisco on the ninth of the month, and I can

18   fly to Sacramento the next day. Since I really don't think that a de-

19   cision on the controversy can be deferred much beyond that time, I would

20   like the benefit of your advice and thinking on the subject.

21   Yours very sincerely,

22   MS:YOI   Maurice Stempler

23

24

25

26

1

2   May 25, 19--

3   Mr. Gregory Fallon

4   1233 ~~Buffallo~~ *Buffalo* Avenue

5   ~~Siracuse~~ *Syracuse,* NY   13253

6   Dear Mr. ~~Falon~~ *Fallon:*

7   Our company has attempted to ~~incourage~~ *encourage* the ~~developement~~ *development* of the

8   arts by having ~~mony alloted~~ *money allotted* for ~~advertisments~~ *advertisements* in many ~~newspaper~~ *newspapers* an

9   ~~magizines thruout~~ *magazines throughout* the country. A ~~disciption~~ *description* of the ~~soms~~ *sums* we have ~~aloted~~ *allotted*

10   is ~~goin~~ *going* to be ~~publish~~ *published* in a ~~bullitin~~ *bulletin* ~~wich~~ *which* we are ~~planint~~ *planning* to issue ~~wit-~~ *within*

11   ~~hin~~ the next month or ~~to.~~ *two.*

12   We are doing ~~thsi~~ *this* ~~becuse~~ *because* ~~their~~ *there* has been ~~som critisism~~ *some criticism* by a number

13   of ~~are~~ *our* stockholders about the fact that we are spending this money.

14   We will, therefore, communicate with all our stockholders to ~~fine~~ *find* out

15   ~~weather~~ *whether* they agree with those who ~~critisize~~ *criticize* our policy.

16   After you have read the ~~disciption~~ *description* of how ~~hte~~ *the* money is being

17   ~~spend~~ *spent,* we are ~~confidant~~ *confident* that you will be ~~amoung~~ *among* the ~~stock-holders~~ *stockholders* who

18   will be of ~~assistants~~ *assistance* to us ~~wen~~ *when* this matter is ~~discuss~~ *discussed* at ~~comittee~~ *committee*

19   meetings and at the meeting of the stockholders on ~~Wensday~~ *Wednesday,* July ~~1st.~~ *1.*

20   Because of ~~you~~ *your* long association with us, I ~~wouldd appriciate you ad-~~ *would appreciate your advice*

21   ~~vise~~ after you have ~~anilyzed~~ *analyzed* what we are ~~planing~~ *planning* to place in the

22   ~~bullitin.~~ *bulletin.*

23   Very ~~Truly Yours,~~ *truly yours,*

24   MEADOW COMPANY

25   AW:YOI   Alex West

26   Public Affairs Manager

September 17, 19--

Ms. Charlotte Schwarz

909 Schenectady Avenue

Rochester, NY   14654

Dear Ms. Schwarz:

Do you speak aloud to yourself while you are working at home? Do you have anxious feelings about your goals in life? Do you feel that the months on the calendar are coming and going too quickly? Do you feel dissatisfied with how you are occupying your time? Are you conscious that tension is always present?

If you believe that the questions we have asked above give a good description of your feelings, we have the answers to some of your problems. Just fill out the enclosed questionnaire, and we will put you on our mailing list to receive copies of the pamphlets we prepare each month. After you have subscribed to these pamphlets for two or three months, we believe that the advice you will receive from our columns will make the coming year a much happier one for you than the last one has been.

When you return the enclosed questionnaire, send us only $9, the low annual rate, and you will get the first pamphlet before the beginning of the year.

Yours sincerely,

MODERN HEALTH PUBLICATIONS

Victor Madden, Editor

VM:YOI

Enclosure

1

2   ~~November~~ *November* 20, 19--

3   Miss Carrie Hope

4   271 ~~Indianna~~ *Indiana* Avenue

5   ~~Indiannapolis,~~ *Indianapolis,* IN   46255

6   Dear ~~Ms.~~ *Miss* Hope:

7   Are you ~~alltgether~~ *altogether* sure ~~taht~~ *that* you are using all of ~~yur~~ *your* skills and

8   ~~personnel~~ *personal* assets in your present career~~.~~ *?* Have you ~~spend~~ *spent* a number of

9   years on a job where each day is a ~~ropitition~~ *repetition* of the ~~proceeding~~ *preceding* one~~.~~ *?*

10   Are you confident ~~you~~ that ~~coud~~ *you could* secure another position easily if, for

11   some reason, ~~uoyr~~ *your* position is ~~effected~~ *affected* by a change in company policy~~.~~ *?*

12   Our agency is ~~begining~~ *beginning* a series of small meetings each ~~Wensday~~ *Wednesday*

13   ~~evning~~ *evening* at 7 p.m. at the ~~too addreses~~ *two addresses* shown above on our letterhead. We

14   ~~belive~~ *believe* we can be of ~~asistance~~ *assistance* to you. We shall go over the Want ~~Adds~~ *Ads,*

15   stress how skills can be ~~improve allmost immediatly~~ *improved almost immediately,* and how ~~courtoet~~ *courtesy*

16   can be used to make the day pass ~~buy~~ *by* more ~~plesontly.~~ *pleasantly.* Because we ~~no~~ *know* the

17   ~~bonifits~~ *benefits* to you ~~wil~~ *will* be ~~substancial~~ *substantial,* we urge you to attend the ~~first~~ *first*

18   session ~~whic~~ *which* will be on ~~Wensday~~ *Wednesday,* December 3. Of ~~cause, their~~ *course, there* is ~~know~~ *no*

19   fee for these ~~meeting.~~ *meetings.* If you would like to bring a ~~freind,~~ *friend,* do ~~sew.~~ *so.*

20   ~~Incidently,~~ *Incidentally,* we chose ~~Wensday~~ *Wednesday* nights ~~beoase~~ *because* we ~~belived~~ *believed* a night in

21   the middle of the ~~weak woud~~ *week would* be most ~~conveinent.~~ *convenient.* However, if you have a

22   ~~preferrence~~ *preference* for another night, we can attempt to change our sessions ~~two~~ *to*

23   a night of your ~~choise.~~ *choice.*

24   ~~Sincerly~~ *Sincerely* yours,

25   ROBERTS EMPLOYMENT AGENCY

26   GF:YOI   Gloria Feit, ~~Personel~~ *Personnel* Director

1

2   January
                          ~~Janery~~ 19, 19--

3   Dr. Gary Clatworth

4   202 Michigan Avenue
        ~~Michagan Avenu~~

5   Detroit, MI
    ~~Detriot, MI.~~ 48256

6   Dear Dr. Clatworth:
    ~~Mr. Clattworth.~~

7   I appreciate ~~apprioiate~~ your efforts in behalf of the defendant ~~defendent~~ I am

8   representing, ~~respresenting~~ Glenn Johannes. As a result of the medical attention ~~atention~~

9   you gave him, he is much more ~~mire~~ at ease than ~~then~~ he had been previously. ~~previsly.~~ As

10 you know, before you ~~ou~~ saw him, he was dependent ~~dependant~~ on drugs to lessen the

11 anxious feelings ~~ankshus feels~~ he had. However, after you treated him twice, he became

12 much ~~mcuh~~ more independent. ~~independentt.~~ Now ~~is~~ he is able to go through ~~thru~~ each day without

13 resorting to drugs ~~durgs~~ or other medication.

14   I know ~~no~~ that you said that you would allow ~~allwo~~ him to withhold ~~withold~~ payment ~~paymennt~~

15 until ~~untill~~ he is better able to afford ~~affort~~ the costs of treatment. As one ~~won~~

16 of his attorneys, ~~attornies~~ I am doing the same thing.

17   In my judgment ~~judgement~~ Mr. Johannes ~~Hohanes~~ is innocent, and I hope to prove ~~proove~~

18 this at the trial ~~trail~~ which ~~whihe~~ will start at the ~~teh~~ beginning ~~begining~~ of next week. ~~weak.~~

19   Sincerely yours,

20   ROMANO AND JARVIS

21 TR:YOI   Tony Romano

22

23

24

25

26

1

2   March 1, 19--

3   Mr. Jerome Heller

4   207 ~~Massachusettes~~ Massachusetts Avenue

5   Washington, DC   20057

6   Dear Mr. ~~Heler:~~ Heller:

7   Now that the cold ~~whether~~ weather is on ~~it's~~ its way out, are you ~~planing~~ planning im-

8   ~~provments~~ improvements around the house? If you are, we are ~~confidant~~ confident that the

9   short ~~discription~~ description of our ~~servises~~ services listed below ~~ill~~ will be of great

10   ~~asistance~~ assistance to you.

11   ~~Hav~~ Have you been ~~disatisfied~~ dissatisfied with ~~you~~ your kitchen and not ~~knew~~ known what to

12   do about ~~ti.~~ it? As you ~~probable no,~~ probably know, we have remodeled kitchens for ~~to~~ two

13   of ~~you~~ your neighbors, and they were very ~~meuh please wit teh~~ much pleased with the results. We

14   can ~~remoove~~ remove all of your present appliances to make room for more ~~comp-~~ com-

15   ~~act appliences~~ pact appliances and cabinets. A ~~knew~~ new floor covering would ~~allso~~ also make

16   a ~~substanciai diference~~ substantial difference in the way ~~you~~ your kitchen ~~look.~~ looks.

17   Are you ~~dependant~~ dependent on ~~you~~ your playroom for peace and relaxation?

18   If you are, look at it closely. ~~Anilize weather~~ Analyze whether or not it is ~~adaquete~~ adequate

19   for ~~you~~ your needs now that ~~you~~ your family is larger than it ~~wsa wen~~ was when you bought

20   the house.

21   ~~Wen~~ When you come up to your ~~hosue~~ house are you ~~prowd~~ proud of ~~it's appearence.~~ its appearance?

22   Is the paint fresh? Do you still ~~fine~~ find it ~~convient~~ convenient to put the storm

23   windows on each fall and ~~remoove~~ remove them in the spring, or ~~wouldd~~ would you

24   like to ~~maok~~ make life easier and simpler by having the combination windows

25   we sell and install?

26   Now look at the garden, Mr. Heller. In the spring and the summer,

27 will you be ~~anxios~~ anxious about the lawn, flowers, trees, and shrubs? Will you

28 ~~loook~~ look at the ~~calender~~ calendar in April and think that you should have done some-

29 ~~thin~~ thing about the garden? In ~~Aprill~~ April it will be ~~to~~ too late! Now is the time

30 to be ~~planing~~ planning for a ~~beautifull~~ beautiful and gracious garden.

31   Now is ^the time to fill in the enclosed card and mail it to us. Our

32 ~~representive~~ representative will ~~than~~ then get in touch with you so that you can make ~~a~~ an

33 ~~appoitntment~~ appointment to discuss ~~you~~ your requirements.

34   Full payment can be ~~defered~~ deferred with the ~~balence~~ balance to be paid in

35 low, monthly ~~instalments~~ installments. If it is more ~~convient~~ convenient for you to pay in

36 full, of ~~cause,~~ course, we shall give you a ~~substantil~~ substantial ~~discoutn.~~ discount. We ~~aliso~~ also

37 ~~except~~ accept major credit cards.

38   ~~Won~~ One of our ~~curteous~~ courteous ~~salesman~~ salesmen will call on you in ~~responce~~ response to ~~you~~ your

39 postcard. Put it in the mail today, March 1.

40   Very truly ~~Yours,~~ yours,

41   GOLD CONTRACTORS, INC.
                Gilbert
42 GG:Yol   ~~Gilbert~~ Gold

43 ~~Encl:~~ Encl.

44

45

46

47

48

49

50

51

52

1

2   November
                                                               ~~Novembr~~ 13, 19--

3   Mr.
         ~~Mister~~ Arnold Kapp, Manager

4   Happy Hours Bookstore
                   Kentucky
5   57 ~~Kentuky~~ Street

         Louisville,
6   ~~Louieville,~~ KY   40258
                     Kapp:
7   Dear Mr. ~~Kap!~~
                                                                      allotted
8   In ~~response~~ to ~~you~~ request of October 20, we have ~~alotted~~ the
         response   your
              sum   of your   Although
9   ~~some~~ of $40,000 for the repairs and modernization ~~to you~~ store. We
         know   damage   Although
10   ~~no~~ that the fire caused a great deal of ~~damage~~ to the store. ~~Altho~~
                 insurance   allowed   believe
11   the ~~insurence~~ company has ~~loud~~ us only $20,000, we ~~beliv~~ that it is
         essential   additional
12   ~~essencial~~ that we spend ~~aditional~~ money in order to rebuild the store.
         Please send   description   would
13   ~~Pleas sent~~ me a full ~~decription~~ of what basic changes you ~~woud~~
         like   the   structural
14   ~~liek~~ to make in ~~teh~~ store, but remember that you must keep the ~~st-~~
                         minimum because   have become
15   ~~ructural~~ changes to a ~~minium~~ ~~becuse~~ repair costs ~~has~~ ~~becomme~~ so high.
                     altogether pleased   advice   received
16   I am not ~~alltogether~~ ~~please~~ with the ~~advise~~ I have ~~receive~~ from
                                           here   Cincinnati.
17   the contractors I have spoken to ~~hear~~ in ~~Ginncinnati.~~ I should ~~ap-~~
         appreciate   attempt   assistance from two   three
18   ~~pliciate~~ it if you would ~~attemt~~ to secure ~~assistence~~ ~~form to~~ or ~~threee~~
                                                  contract
19   local contractors before we sign a ~~contrack~~ to have the work done.
               I'm   Louisville   then discuss
20   Since ~~Im~~ going to be in ~~Louiville~~ shortly, we can ~~than~~ ~~discus~~

21   the situation more fully.
                                          Cordially
22   ~~Cordilly~~ yours,

23   HAPPY HOURS BOOKSTORES
                                                           President
24   QT:YOI   Quentin Tracy, ~~Presiden-~~

25

26

1

2   July 14, 19--

3   Ms. Pamela Peterson

4   309 ~~Wisconsan~~ *Wisconsin* Street

5   ~~Milwalkee~~ *Milwaukee,* WI   53259

6   ~~Dear Mrs. Peterson,~~ *Dear Ms. Peterson:*

7   I have ~~defered~~ *deferred* writing to you ~~becuse~~ *because* I ~~didnt~~ *didn't* want to ~~critisize~~ *criticize* you

8   ~~unfarely~~ *unfairly* before I had all the facts, and I am ~~gald taht~~ *glad that* I did so. New

9   ~~developements~~ *developments* show that you ~~was alltogether~~ *were altogether* correct in claiming that

10 ~~that~~ you had met the deadline for submitting the ~~manuscrip~~ *manuscript* for the

11 ~~artical~~ *article.* I was disagreeably ~~suprised~~ *surprised* to learn that your ~~arangements~~ *arrangements*

12 with ~~Mr~~ *Mr.* Thompson were not communicated ~~ot~~ *to* me. I was, ~~therfore,~~ *therefore,* under ~~teh~~ *the*

13 ~~the~~ impression ~~atht~~ *that* you and Mr. ~~Thompson~~ *Thompson* had ~~allso agreeed~~ *also agreed* on May ~~1st,~~ *1,*

14 but now he has told me that the deadline was changed to ~~Agust 1st.~~ *August 1.*

15   I ~~apoligize~~ *apologize* for the ~~inconvience~~ *inconvenience* caused you. Now I am ~~confidantly~~ *confidently*

16 looking ~~foward~~ *forward* to seeing the manuscript by ~~Agust~~ *August* 1.

17   ~~Cordilly your,~~ *Cordially yours,*

18   JEFFERSON PUBLISHERS, INC.

19 HG:YoI   Harold Grover

20   Editor

21

22

23

24

25

26

1

2   ~~Novembre~~ November 1, 19--

3   Mr. Leon Loeb

4   557 Ocean ~~Parkwya~~ Parkway

5   ~~Honollulu, HA~~ Honolulu, HI   96860

6   Dear ~~Mister Loeb,~~ Mr. Loeb:

7   ~~Their~~ There are many ~~columms~~ columns in the ~~wekly~~ weekly ~~magizines~~ magazines which ~~attemt~~ attempt to

8   give you ~~knoeledge~~ Knowledge of what is happening in the world; however, no

9   ~~magazie~~ magazine has the number and quality of columnists ~~we~~ that we have.

10   ~~Wen~~ When you have ~~look~~ looked at the sample copy that ~~shoud~~ should be ~~ariving~~ arriving at ~~you~~ your

11   house soon, you will be ~~aggreeably supprised~~ agreeably surprised at our superior coverage

12   of the up-to-the-minute news of ~~teh~~ the world. You ~~wil~~ will want to read some

13   ~~some~~ of the ~~columnns~~ columns ~~allowed~~ aloud to ~~you~~ your family ~~becuase~~ because of the new develop-

14   ~~oments~~ ments in the capitals of the world.

15   It is all right to say that you ~~do'nt~~ don't think that you need another

16   ~~magizine comming~~ magazine coming into your house, but it really is not all right not

17   to read carefully the ~~copie~~ copy we are ~~senting.~~ sending.

18   We are ~~confidant~~ confident that after you have ~~red~~ read this issue, you ~~wil~~ will want

19   ~~want to us~~ send to us the subscription blank for a six-month trial sub-

20   scription.

21   Yours ~~truely,~~ truly,

22   CURTIS ~~PUBLICTIONS~~ PUBLICATIONS

23   ~~DE:~~ DBE: YOI

24   ~~Enclosure~~

25

26

1

2   March 14, 19--

3   Thomas ~~Stationary~~ Stationery Company

4   235 ~~Tenesee~~ Tennessee Street

5   ~~Memfis,~~ Memphis, TN   38161

6   ATTENTION: Mr. Harvey Weiss

7   ~~Gentleman:~~ Gentlemen:

8   ~~Than~~ Thank you for sending ~~you're remittence~~ your remittance for $473.29, which is

9   in ~~parshul~~ partial payment of your acount. ~~Wen are bookeeper recieve~~ When our bookkeeper received your

10 check, she noted that ~~their~~ there seemed to be a ~~discrpency,~~ discrepancy between what

11 was ~~fowarded,~~ forwarded and the ~~ammount~~ amount on our books. She ~~refered~~ referred the matter

12 to me, and my ~~invesigation~~ investigation shows ~~tht~~ that what ~~probabley~~ probably happened is that

13 you did not use our current pricelist. If you look at the pricelist

14 in your ~~posession~~ possession, you will see ~~weather~~ whether or not it is the spring list

15 or the fall list. You ~~shoud~~ should be using the ~~won~~ one that is dated ~~"October".~~ "October."

16   ~~Insted~~ Instead of sending us ~~$873.29,~~ $473.29, you should ~~of snt $523,29.~~ have sent $523.29. We

17 ~~woul apreciate~~ would appreciate it if you could ~~male~~ mail us the ~~balanse~~ balance due within ten

18 ~~ten~~ days, which will help you take ~~avantage~~ advantage of the discount ~~offered~~ offered

19 for ~~promt~~ prompt payment.

20   ~~Your very truely,~~ Yours truly,

21   GENERAL SUPPLY COMPANY

22 RH:YOI   Richard Herbers

23   ~~Colection~~ Collection Manager

24

25

26

1

2   December 17, 19--

3   Mr. Michael Greco, Credit Manager

4   Independence Plumbing Company

5   375 Pennsylvania Avenue

6   Harrisburg, PA   17162

7   Dear Mr. Greco:

8   SUBJECT: OVERDUE ACOUNT OF ROY MARTIN

9   In answer to your inquiry of December 4, I am writing to let you know

10   that I have had practically no success in trying to persuade Mr. Martin

11   to take care of his overdue account.

12   I regret that I think we will have to pursue legal action because

13   Mr. Martin is unwilling to acknowledge the fact that he must pay for

14   that part of the goods, which was damaged in shipment from Har-

15   risburg to Cincinnati. He refuses to accept full responsibility

16   for the damages although this was clearly one of the terms of the sale.

17   He says that while he would pay for half of the goods that were

18   damaged, that is as far as he will go.

19   I referred to the terms of the original contract, but he says

20   that the damage was caused by poor packaging. Please let me know if

21   you would like me to continue my efforts with Mr. Martin, or whether

22   you would now like to turn the matter over to your attorneys.

23   Very truly yours,

24   JD:YOI   John Davis

25   Collection Specialist

26

1

2   September 14, 19--

3   Ms. Jane Milton

4   203 New Jersey Street

5   Jersey City, NJ   07363

6   Dear Ms. Milton:

7   Now that you are leaving Jersey City permanently to settle in

8   Italy, have you any possessions that you would like to sell? Our shop

9   is noted for the high prices it pays to estates and individuals for

10 valuables, including original oil paintings, silver and china.

11   If you are interested in selling any of these items, our representative

12 will come to your home at a time that will suit your convenience. He

13 will be able to assume all responsibility for decisions he makes in

14 setting prices for what he purchases.

15   Of course, I regret that you are leaving Jersey City after so many

16 years, but I am confident that you will be very happy in your new home in

17 Rome.

18   Sincerely yours,

19   JERSEY ANTIQUE SHOP

20 BL:YOI   Bertha Losey

21

22

23

24

25

26

1

2   July 7, 19--

                                  President
3   Mr. James Messer, Vice ~~Presideent~~

     Lincoln
4   ~~Linclon~~ Federal Savings Bank and Loan Association

            Nebraska
5   4987 ~~Nobraska~~ Street

     Lincoln,
6   ~~Linclon,~~ NE   68564

            Mr.   Messer:
7   Dear ~~Mister Messer:~~

                              Lincoln Shopping
8   RE: Branch Bank at ~~Linclon Shoping~~ Center

                       withholding   since   last
9   You have been ~~witholding~~ $500 on this project ~~sinse~~ early ~~las~~

     December   yet
10   ~~Desember~~ for work that had not ~~yte~~ been completed.

                  believe   all
11   We now ~~belive~~ that ~~wll~~ work has been completed, and we are in

     possession   effect.
12   ~~possesion~~ of documents to this ~~affect.~~

                          balance promptly   our accounts
13   Please send us this ~~balanse promply~~ so that we can close ~~cacounts~~
                                                                        ^
          development.   regret   inconvenience
14   ~~our~~ on this ~~develepement.~~ We ~~regreat~~ any ~~inconvience~~ that this delay

                           you,   until   persuade
15   ~~delay~~ may have caused ~~byou~~ but ~~untill~~ now our efforts to ~~pursuade~~ the

     electricians   were successful.   finally
16   ~~electricials~~ to complete the work ~~was~~ not ~~sucessfull.~~ They have ~~finaly~~

         their responsibilities,   should
17   met ~~there responsabilities~~ and everything ~~shoud~~ be in good shape now.

                                    Very truly
18   ~~Ver Truly~~ yours,
                                       CONSTRUCTION
19   TUCKER ~~CONSTRUCKTION~~ COMPANY
     RT:
20   ~~RT,YOI~~   Robert Tucker

                                    Treasurer
21   ~~Tresurer~~

22

23

24

25

26

1

2   April
                                                       ~~Arpil~~ 24, 19--

3   Ms. Joan Zeller

4   Wells and Raymond

5   Post Office Box 750
                 Hartford, CT
6   ~~Hardford, Ct~~ 06165
          Ms. Zeller:
7   Dear ~~Mrs. Zellar:~~
              Connecticut
8   RE: ~~Conneticut~~ Bank and Trust Company Balance
            response   ninth
9   In ~~responce~~ to your letter of the ~~nineth~~ of this month to
                                                  (front
10   Mr. Fred Gomez, I am inclosing photocopies ~~)front~~ and back) of our
                                        September
11   checks numbered 1027 and 1079, dated ~~Septembre~~ 13 and 20 respectively.
                               able   whatever errors
12   We hope that now you will be ~~abel~~ to correct ~~what ever~~ ~~error~~ exist
                    balance due   agree with   figures.
13   ~~exist~~ so that the ~~balanse do~~ will ~~aggree wiht~~ our ~~figurres.~~
                      previously, referred your   bookkeeper.
14   As I wrote you ~~previsly~~ I ~~refered you~~ letter to our ~~beookkeeper.~~
        checked   extreme   certain   responsibility
15   He ~~check~~ his records with ~~extream~~ care and is ~~certin~~ the ~~responsability~~
                              believes   occurred because
16   for the error is not his. He ~~beleives~~ that the error ~~occured~~ ~~becuse~~
           two   weren't   your
17   these ~~to~~ checks ~~worent~~ posted properly on ~~you~~ records.
                         further inquiries
18   If you have any ~~furthere inquireys~~ about this matter, please
     refer them Mr.   bookkeeper,   vacation
19   ~~referr it~~ to ~~Mr~~ Gerald Zak, our ~~bokeeper~~ because I will be on ~~vaction~~
                next month.
20   for ~~for~~ the ~~nex monthe.~~
                                     sincerely
21   Yours ~~Sincerely~~

22   SUTTER COMPANY
     AT:
23   ~~AS,YOI~~   Arnold Tatum
     Inclosures   Accounting
24   ~~Enclosure~~   ~~Accounting~~ Department

25

26

1

2   January
                                                             ~~January~~ 22, 19--

3   Arthur Hill, Esq.

4   French & Thomas

5   980 ~~Louisianna~~ Louisiana Street

6   ~~Baton Roug;~~ Baton Rouge, LA   70866

7   Dear Mr. ~~Hill,~~ Hill:

8   RE: KILLEWARE INDUSTRIAL PARK

9   In ~~acordance~~ accordance with ~~you~~ your request for a statement on the above

10 construction loan as of ~~January~~ January 26, please be ~~adviced~~ advised as ~~follows;~~ follows:

11   ~~Princ;le~~ Principal $300000.00

12   ~~Intrest~~ Interest Due   2135.41
                                                        41
13   TOTAL $302,135.~~42~~

14   The above figures represent the ~~ammount nesessary~~ amount necessary to make ~~repaym-~~ repayment

15 ~~ent~~ of the loan, assuming credit is ~~recieved~~ received (via transfer ~~thru~~ through the

16 Federal Reserve Bank of New ~~York.~~ York).

17   In ~~teh~~ the event that credit is not ~~recieved~~ received by ~~January~~ January 26, ~~a intrest~~ an interest

18 charge of ~~$85,42~~ $85.42 per day will be ~~incured untill~~ incurred until repayment is ~~affected.~~ effected.

19 ~~Pleas~~ Please note that if payment is made by check, ~~intrest~~ interest will accrue ~~untill~~ until

20 the check is ~~recieved~~ received by us and subsequently cleared ~~throug~~ through banking

21 channels. We are inclosing the ~~folowing~~ following documents to be held by you

22 ~~you~~ in escrow pending the payment of the loan in ~~full,~~ full:

23   1) Assignment of ~~Morgage~~ Mortgage from First ~~Natinal~~ National State Bank to Metro-

24 ~~politaan Insurence~~ politan Insurance Company, dated ~~January~~ January 22.

25   2. Income Loan Note from the Borrower to the Bank, dated

26 ~~Decembre~~ December 22.

27   3) Construction ~~Morgage~~ Mortgage Note from the Borrowers to the Bank, dated

28   ~~Novembr~~ November 13, in the amount of $170,000.00.

29   4) ~~Construcktion~~ Construction ~~Morgage~~ Mortgage from the Borrowers to the Bank, dated

30   November 13, in the ~~ammount~~ amount of $170,000.00.

31   5) Modification and ~~Extention Aggreement~~ Extension Agreement between Killeware ~~Ind-~~ Industrial

32   ~~ustrial~~ Park and First National ~~state~~ State Bank, dated May 15.

33   6) Financial ~~Statment~~ Statement and ~~Acknowledgement~~ Acknowledgment filed in the ~~Secetary~~ Secretary

34   of ~~States~~ State's Office on ~~Agust~~ August 7, File No. 1373.

35   7) Standard Fire ~~Insurence~~ Insurance Policy of ~~Commerical Insurence~~ Commercial Insurance Company,

36   No. 3WT-023-596.

37   ~~9)~~ 8) Hazard ~~Insurence~~ Insurance Policy of ~~Independance Insurence~~ Independence Insurance Company,

38   No. FF4-51-68-93.

39   The Construction ~~Morgage~~ Mortgage, Modification and ~~Extention Aggreement~~ Extension Agreement

40   ~~been~~ have been endorsed for ~~cancelation~~ cancellation, the ~~Construcktiin note~~ Construction Note has been

41   stamped ~~"Paid"~~ "Paid," and we have executed the termination ~~statments~~ statements on ~~teh~~ the

42   ~~the finnancial statment.~~ Financial Statement.

43   ~~Pleas acknoledge reciet~~ Please acknowledge receipt and ~~exceptence~~ acceptance of the above by signing ~~an~~ and

44   returning the ~~enclosed~~ inclosed copy of ~~tihs~~ this letter.

45   Very ~~truely~~ truly yours,

46   WMC:
      ~~WC:~~YOI

47   inclosures

48   William M. Clark
      ~~Assistent~~ Assistant Cashier

1

2   June
                                                                   ~~Juen~~ 4, 19--

3   Ms.
     ~~Ms~~ Rita Hunter

4   Ohio Boulevard
     1046 ~~Ohhio Boulevad~~

5   Toledo,
     ~~Tolledo,~~ OH   43667

6   Dear Ms. Hunter:

7   possession   places
          You are in ~~posession~~ of this letter. This ~~placess~~ you in the

8   an   Ms. Hunter.
     ~~the~~ middle of ~~a~~ exciting mystery, ~~Miss Hunt.~~

9   mystery   valuable
          First, there is to be the ~~mistery~~ of the ~~valueable~~ package that

10   Toledo   1046
     the ~~Tolledo~~ mailman is soon to deliver to you at ~~1045~~ Ohio Boulevard.

11   Then there   the money   whether
     ~~Than their~~ is the mystery of ~~teh money,~~ and ~~weather~~ you will win the

12   $50,000 grand prize.

13   have a
          We ~~hav an~~ mystery gift all wrapped and ready to deliver to you as

14   your shipping label.   gift   free   when
     ~~as~~ soon as you return ~~you shiping lable.~~ This ~~gif~~ is yours ~~free,~~ ~~wehn~~

15   catalog.   merchandise for   least
     you order from our ~~catolog.~~ You must order ~~merchandize of~~ at ~~lease~~

16   $5.   addition,   issued   your
     ~~5$.~~ In ~~edition,~~ we have ~~issue~~ a $50,000 prize entry ticket in ~~you~~ name.

17   cannot emphasize too   how   purchase
          We ~~can not emphazize two~~ much ~~hoew~~ very much pleasure the ~~pruchase~~

18   products   yield   look   original
     of our ~~producks~~ will ~~yeild~~ to you. Just ~~loook~~ at all of the ~~originel~~

19   practical   persuaded
     and ~~practicel~~ products we offer, and you will not have to be ~~pursuaded~~

20   purchase some   right
     to ~~purchas sem~~ of them ~~write~~ now.

21   Don't   remittance $5,
          ~~Dont~~ forget to send your ~~remittence~~ for at least ~~5$~~ and you will

22   eligible   today!
     be ~~elligible~~ for the grand prize. Act ~~today?~~

23   yours,
                                Very truly ~~your,~~

24   MAS:
     ~~MA:YOI~~   Mary Ann Spence

25

26

January 9, 19--

Miss Harriet Kaplan

598 Tennessee Lane

Chattanooga, TN   37468

Dear Miss Kaplan:

    We have devised a new system which we use to dye shoes. Never again will you dye your shoes and be embarrassed because the dye has run on your feet or on your stockings. The difference between our system and those systems used in the past is that we eliminate the removal of the original color. You just apply our polish, and the job is done quickly, efficiently and smoothly. We accept responsibility if you aren't satisfied with the results. Your shoes will have an attractive permanent finish, and, of course, it will not be noticeable that you used a dye to change the color.

    We are enclosing our latest price list. Please note that we don't accept partial payments. Please send us a remittance in full.

    We know that you you will not regret taking advantage of this opportunity to have "new shoes" at little cost.

Very sincerely yours,

CHATTANOOGA POLISH COMPANY

Sales Manager

YOI
enclosure

1

2   September
                                          ~~Septembr~~ 2, 19--

3   Mr. Kenneth B. Marlin
                Arizona
4   208 A~~rizonna~~ Avenue
         Tucson,
5   ~~Tuscon,~~ AZ   85769
               Mr. Marlin:
6   Dear ~~Mr Martin~~

                         your inquiry   Insurance
7   Thank you for ~~you inquirey~~ about Savings Bank Life ~~Insurence~~
       (SBLI).   Here
8   ~~(SBLI.)~~ ~~Hear~~ are some of the facts on low-cost SBLI:

                                  because   buy direct from
9   1) SBLI is low in cost ~~boouse~~ you ~~by~~ it ~~direckt form~~ the bank.
                           an   able
10   By not having ~~a~~ outside sales force, we are ~~abel~~ to keep our costs and
               overhead   minimum.
11   ~~and over head~~ to a ~~minium.~~
            SBLI   personnel   passed
12   2) ~~SBLI~~ has trained salaried ~~personal~~ who have ~~past~~ the same
                                    insurance   have
13   state examination as anyone selling ~~insurence~~ in this state. They ~~hav~~
                      knowledge   analyze   recommenda-
14   the time and the ~~knowlege~~ to ~~analize~~ your needs and make ~~reccommenda-~~
              There   buy.
15   tions. ~~Their~~ is no obligation and no pressure to ~~by.~~
            3)   plans;   available   amounts
16   ~~4)~~ SBLI has a variety of ~~plans;~~ which are ~~avalable~~ in ~~ammounts~~ up

17   to $30,000. The low-cost plans include straight life, term, limited pay-
             mortgage   beginning
18   ment, ~~morgage~~ and others. All plans pay dividends ~~begining~~ the first

19   year.
                       interested   buying substantial amounts
20   If you are ~~interest~~ in ~~bying substancial ammounts~~ of protection
                             necessary   an inquiry
21   at a low cost, it is not ~~nesassry~~ for you to make ~~a inquirey~~ about it
                                                  Further information   will
22   at the bank. Just mail the enclosed card, and ~~furthur infromation wil-~~
           your possession   return mail.
23   be in ~~you posession~~ by ~~rotrun mail/~~
                             truly
24   Yours ~~truely~~
                       ARIZONA
25   ~~ARIZONNA~~ STATE BANK
       RT:
26   ~~RY:YOI~~   Ray Terrasi, Customer Service
       enclosure

March 4, 19--

Mr. Randolph Webb

2037 Nebraska Street

Lincoln, NE   68570

Dear Mr. Webb,

If you were to die tomorrow, would your family regret that you didn't take the responsibility of providing enough funds for them after you have died? We cannot emphasize too strongly, that you should not have to be persuaded to carry enough life insurance to eliminate financial embarrassment to your survivors.

The enclosed brochure contains a partial listing of the types of policies we offer. As you can see, you are eligible for some types of insurance up to the age of 70. Choose one that is practical for your needs, and then you should telephone us so that we can make an appointment with one of our experienced, expert and courteous representatives for you. He will tell you which policy yields the most benefits for a person in your circumstances.

We hope to hear from you shortly. If you have an immediate inquiry which you would like answered by telephone, just call me at the number listed above.

Yours very truly,
NEBRASKA INSURANCE COMPANY

Albert Rossiter
District Manager

AR:Yol
enclosure

1

2   August
                                                    ~~Agust~~ 3, 19--

3   Mr. Eugene Hellers
                 Illinois
4   10 ~~Illinoise~~ Street
          Chicago, IL
5   ~~Chicago IL.~~ 60671
                 Hellers:
6   Dear Mr. ~~Heller:~~

           answer   inquiry   Accounts
7   In ~~anser~~ to your ~~inquirey~~ about Individual Retirement ~~Acounts~~
      (IRA),   pamphlet which   necessary
8   ~~(IRA)~~ I am happy to send you a ~~pamhplet wich~~ gives all the ~~nesessary~~
      information
9   ~~ihfromation~~ about IRA.

                   eligible   an   bank's
10   If you are ~~elligble~~ for ~~a~~ IRA plan, stop in at any of this ~~banks~~

                          convenient   so,
11   branches. If it is more ~~convient~~ for you to do ~~sew~~ mail the enclosed

                        envelope which   correspondence,
12   forms to us in the ~~envelop wich~~ we are sending with this ~~correspondents.~~

                      care
13   and we will take ~~car~~ of the rest.

          Please   your contributions cannot exceed $1,500 annually.
14   ~~Pleas~~ note your that ~~contrkbutions can not execde $1500 anually.~~

               choose   your
15   You may ~~chose~~ to have ~~you~~ funds earn the same high dividend rates
      paid   accounts,
16   ~~payed~~ by the bank on other savings ~~acounts~~ or you may build even
            IRA
17   larger ~~RIA~~ funds by using one of the many ~~higher-yeilding~~ higher-yielding time deposit
      accounts available
18   ~~acounts vailablbe~~ at our bank.

                                               don't
19   If you have any further questions, please ~~dont~~ hesitate to com-
      municate   me.
20   ~~unicate~~ with ~~m.e~~

                                           truly
21   Yours ~~truely~~
                              ILLINOIS
22   ~~ILLINOISE~~ NATIONAL BANK

23   JB:yol   John Berry, Cashier
      encls.
24

25

26

1

2   August
                                           ~~Agust~~ 5, 19--

3   Mr. Leslie Caban
                  Florida
4   390 ~~Florada~~ Highway

5   Miami, FL
      ~~Miama, FL,~~ 33172
                Mr. Caban:
6   Dear ~~Mr. Kaban:~~
              answer   your inquiry
7   In ~~anser~~ to ~~you inquirey~~ of July 25, I am happy to give you in-
      formation   Fares   fare   forty
8   ~~fromation~~ about the bus ~~fairs~~ in this city. The present ~~fair~~ of ~~fourty~~
                      existence   February. February,
9   cents has been in ~~existance~~ since last ~~Febuery.~~ In ~~Febuery,~~ the bus
                     indebtedness   necessary   fare
10   company had an ~~indebtness~~ which made it ~~nessassary~~ to raise the ~~fair~~
               Fourth   two   no   guarantee
11   for the ~~forth~~ time ~~to~~ in years. The bus company made ~~know~~ ~~garantee~~
               Fares   they   able
12   that the ~~fairs~~ would not be raised again soon, but ~~tohy~~ hope to be ~~abel~~
          exercise   Maybe
13   to ~~exeercise~~ good management, caution and economy. ~~May be~~ the present
      fare   effect   quite   will
14   ~~fair~~ will stay in ~~affect~~ for ~~quit~~ some time, but it maybe that it ~~wil~~
                   be   again.
15   ~~will~~ have ~~be~~ to increased once ~~agin.~~
                know, transportation   indispensable
16   As you ~~no~~ bus ~~transportion~~ is ~~indispensible~~ in our community. All
         equipment   well equipped   well serviced.   except
17   the ~~equipoment~~ is ~~well-equiped~~ and ~~well-serviced.~~ All lines ~~accept~~
          Fourth   until midnight,   extension
18   the ~~Forth~~ Avenue Line run ~~untill midneiht~~ and an ~~extention~~ of service
                          considered.
19   on that line is being ~~ensider.~~

                                       helpful   preparing
20   I hope that this information will be ~~helpfull~~ to you in ~~prepairing~~
      brochure
21   the ~~broshure~~ you are writing.
                                     Cordially
22   ~~Cordial~~ yours,

23   CHAMBER OF COMMERCE

24   BM:YOI   Brian Murray, Director

25

26

1

2   ~~April~~ April 9, 19--

3   Mr. James C. Amara, Jr.

4   Real Estate and ~~Contsruction~~ Construction Division

5   Amara ~~Equippment~~ Equipment Company

6   606 ~~Alibama~~ Alabama Avenue

7   ~~Mobile,,~~ Mobile, AL   36673

8   ~~Gentelemen:~~ Dear Mr. Amara:

9   I ~~appriciate~~ appreciate your keeping me ~~up-to-date~~ up to date on your office relocation

10   project. We ~~certinly~~ certainly would like to have you as a ~~tenaant~~ tenant in our new

11   building. I am ~~confidant~~ confident that we ~~coud~~ could work out the ~~frieght~~ freight and loading

12   ~~arrangments~~ arrangements to meet ~~you requirments.~~ your requirements.

13   We ~~can not~~ cannot ~~garantee~~ guarantee that the traffic situation will have ~~clear~~ cleared

14   up by the summer. ~~the~~ The Parkway Authority is building ~~a~~ an ~~extention~~ extension of

15   the State Parkway, and I ~~blieve~~ believe that this ~~will~~ work will be completed ~~buy~~ by

16   early summer.

17   Thank you very much for the ~~curtesies~~ courtesies you extended to me and to

18   ~~to~~ Mr. Fuller on our last visit. We ~~if~~ If we can ~~provied~~ provide you with any ~~furthur~~ further

19   ~~assistence~~ assistance, please ~~d'ont~~ don't hesitate to call on me.

20   ~~Sincery Yours,~~ Sincerely yours,

21   CHASE CONSTRUCTION COMPANY

22   JL:YOI   Joseph Localio, Vice President

23   Real Estate ~~Developement~~ Development

24

25

26

1

2   August 18, 19--

3   Armstrong ~~Frieght~~ Freight ~~Conpany~~ Company

4   27 ~~Minnisota~~ Minnesota Avenue

5   ~~Minneapilis~~ Minneapolis, MN   55474

6   ATT: Mr. Fred Burk, ~~Assistent~~ Assistant Vice ~~Prisident~~ President

7   ~~Genttelmen:~~ Gentlemen:

8   This is the ~~forth~~ fourth time I have had to write you about your in-

9   ~~debtness~~ debtedness of $14,327.29 to our ~~organzation.~~ organization. It is urgent that you make

10   payment by ~~Agust~~ August 29 ~~in as much~~ inasmuch as at that time we are ~~planing~~ planning to turn

11   the ~~acount~~ account over to our ~~attornies.~~ attorneys.

12   I am sure ~~taht~~ that you are ~~concious~~ conscious of the fact that we are as de-

13   ~~pendant~~ pendent upon collecting money owed ~~us,~~ us, as you are. We want to ~~ellimi-~~ elimi-

14   nate ~~finantial embarasment when ever~~ financial embarrassment whenever it is ~~posible~~ possible to do ~~sow~~ so, and the

15   ~~decicion~~ decision to turn the matter over for ~~leagal procedings~~ legal proceedings is the last

16   resort. Our business ~~existense~~ existence is ~~effected~~ affected by not ~~reciving remittancs~~ receiving remittances

17   ~~promply~~ promptly, and we ~~do'nt~~ don't want to be ~~finantially inconvienienced~~ financially inconvenienced because of

18   very high ~~Acounts Reeivable.~~ Accounts Receivable.

19   I am enclosing a stamped, ~~selfadressed envelop~~ self-addressed envelope with this letter.

20   I ~~genuinly~~ genuinely hope that we shall not be ~~force~~ forced to communicate with

21   ~~our attornies.~~ our attorneys. You can prevent this by mailing us a check in full for

22   ~~you~~ your debts which you have ~~incured~~ incurred $14,327.29.

23   Very truly ~~yours,~~ yours,

24   JENKINS BOX ~~CONPANY~~ COMPANY

25   YOI   ~~Assistent~~ Assistant Treasurer
     enclosure

26

October 8, 19--

Ms. Ina Clarke

43 Niagara Falls Avenue

Buffalo, NY 14275

Dear Ms. Clarke:

In reference to your inquiry about a stationary model of a sewing machine to replace your portable one, I am genuinely sorry to tell you that we no longer are the manufacturers of these larger units. Inasmuch as the demand for this type of sewing machine has almost entirely disappeared, it was no longer profitable to manufacture them.

When our company came into existence about forty years ago, we manufactured only the stationary model. Within the last few years, we analyzed our sales figures and made the decision that it would be foolish to continue manufacturing the stationary model, since we were losing money on it. We have had excellent reports from purchasers about our new model, the D-147, with its many new devices.

We are enclosing with this letter copies of our latest advertisements, catalogs and price lists. In addition, if you would like to stop in at one of our local stores, one of our courteous and helpful salesmen will be all ready for you. He will show you that owning our Model D-147 will make it pleasant, easy and efficient for you to make your own clothes.

Cordially yours,

Manuel Ortiz

MO:YOI
Enclosures

1

2   April 4, 19-- ~~Arpil~~

3   Mr. Gerald Koppel

4   437 ~~Indianna~~ *Indiana* Avenue

5   ~~Indianipolis~~ *Indianapolis,* IN 46276

6   *Dear Mr. Koppel:* ~~Gentlemen:~~

7   "*Who's* ~~Whos~~ ready for a drive in the country?" is a question that is of-

8   ~~fen ask~~ *ten asked* at this time of year. However, if your car is not ~~equiped~~ *equipped* with

9   ~~a efficint~~ *an efficient* air-conditioning system, you ~~regret~~ may *regret* that drive in the

10   ~~country,~~ *country* if the ~~weater~~ *weather* turns very hot, as it is ~~likly~~ *likely* to do. While ~~a~~ *an*

11   air-conditioner may not be ~~indispensible~~ *indispensable* now, by the time July and ~~Agust~~ *August*

12   roll around, you will be ~~consience~~ *conscious* of the fact that air-conditioning

13   ~~ads~~ *adds* to ~~you~~ *your* ~~convience~~ *convenience* and ~~confort~~ *comfort* while you are riding ~~troughout~~ *throughout* the

14   countryside.

15   ~~Investagate~~ *Investigate* the newest ~~dovoloopments~~ *developments* in ~~air-cpnditioning~~ *air-conditioning* for ~~you~~ *your*

16   car. We are ~~enclossing broshures~~ *enclosing brochures* and our price list. In ~~edition~~ *addition,* look

17   at the ~~adds~~ *ads* which will be ~~place~~ *placed* in the Sunday papers for the ~~nex to~~ *next two*

18   weeks.

19   Remember, if you are driving the ~~Forth~~ *Fourth* of July, you will not have a

20   happy ~~Indopendance~~ *Independence* Day if you are badly ~~effected~~ *affected* by the breezes, heat

21   and ~~humiditity.~~ *humidity.* Make a ~~defanite decison~~ *definite decision* now, and you will be ~~gratful~~ *grateful* for

22   this ~~adviso,~~ *advice* as you drive this summer. Our ~~curteous~~ *courteous* mechanics will

23   do the work ~~efficently~~ *efficiently,* and all work is ~~throughly garanteed~~ *thoroughly guaranteed.*

24   *Sincerely* ~~Sincerly~~ yours,

25   INDIANAPOLIS AIR-CONDITIONING, ~~INDIANNAPOLIS AIR-CONDIONING,~~ INC.

26   Art Forrest, *Assistant* ~~Assistent~~ Manager

AF: ~~APF:~~ YOI

enclosures

1

2   March
                                                         ~~Marroh~~ 14, 19--

3   Miss Mae Lovett

                Bridgeport
4   2964 ~~Bridgport~~ Road

      Waterbury,
5   ~~Waterberry~~, CT   06771

            Miss Lovett:
6   Dear ~~Mrs. Lovitt~~

                  omission   exercise   look
7   Does the ~~ommission~~ of daily ~~exersize~~ bother you? Do you ~~loook~~ at

            calendar   will   like   your
8   the ~~calender~~ and think of what you ~~wil~~ look ~~liek~~ in ~~you~~ bathing outfit

                        ?   everyone   your   except   at-
9   this summer? Will ~~every one~~ in ~~you~~ group ~~accept~~ you look slim and ~~attr-~~

                          embarrassed   exceeds   your
10   ~~tractive~~. Will you be ~~embarassed~~ because your weight ~~exceedes~~ ~~you~~ best

      weight?   for an improvement   your
11   ~~wait?~~ Are you looking ~~fro~~ a ~~improvment~~ in ~~you~~ self-image?

                       answers   "Yes,"
12   If your ~~ansers~~ to all of the questions listed above are ~~"Yes"~~, I

      recommend   an appointment   very
13   ~~recommend~~ very strongly that you make ~~a apointment~~ with us in the ~~vor~~

           future.   At   find   women   doing
14   near ~~futrue~~. ~~Ta~~ our gyms you will ~~fine~~ many men and ~~woman~~ who are ~~doi~~

                    guarantee   Filled   excite-
15   something to ~~grantee~~ that they will have a summer ~~fill~~ with fun, ~~excit-~~

                            judgment,   omitted
16   ment, and pleasure. In our ~~judgement~~ nothing has been ~~ommitted~~ to meet

      your requirements.   addition   equipment,
17   ~~you requirments.~~ In ~~edition~~ to the ~~equipmenet~~ there are experts who

      advise   self-improvement.
18   ~~advice~~ you about ~~self improvment.~~

            make   principle
19   We ~~mack~~ it a ~~principal~~ to keep our fees so moderate that they will

          exceed   budget.   dissatisfied
20   not ~~exceede~~ the limits of your ~~budgt.~~ If you are ~~disatisfied~~ in any

                                           forfeit
21   way after your first visit, you do not ~~forfiet~~ your deposit. It will be

         refunded   promptly   cheerfully.
22   ~~be refund~~ to you ~~promply~~ and ~~cheerfuly.~~

23   Cordially ~~your,~~ yours,

24   EASTERN GYMS, INC.

      JWE:
25   ~~JE:~~YOI   June W. Esposito, Manager

26

July 14, 19--

Fried and Gross

437 New Haven Avenue

Hartford, CT   06178

Attention: Maynard Fried

Gentlemen:

Milton Spieler suggested that I call you in reference to office space you need here in New Jersey.

We are owners and developers of industrial, commercial and office buildings throughout New Jersey and we would certainly like to be helpful to you in satisfying your office requirements.

At present we have space available in our Davis Metropark Building, which is located at the Garden State Parkway Extension and the Metropark Rail Station. This affords direct train access into New York, Philadelphia, and Washington as well as excellent and convenient highway connections. In addition, train and bus connections are more than adequate, and the fares are reasonable. We are hoping that the building will definitely be available in November of this year. In this building we will have some very desirable office suites on the third and fourth floors.

In Springfield, Jersey, which is in the Morristown district, we have nearly completed the construction of a forty-story building which is already being talked about as one of the outstanding structures in the entire state. It is located at the intersection of Route 10 and Route 287. This also provides good access throughout the metropolitan

27 area. This building is scheduled for completion by the first of next

28 year.

29 I'm enclosing floor plans of these two buildings. Inasmuch as so

30 much space has already been rented, I urge you to look at these floor

31 plans immediately, if you think that you might be interested in setting

32 up offices in this part of New Jersey. In case you are not familiar with

33 this section of the state, I am enclosing a map which indicates the

34 locations of these two buildings.

35   I am also enclosing a copy of our company's brochure which lists

36 the buildings we manage. This brochure describes our principal buildings.

37 They're practically all rented at the present time, but it is possible that

38 there will be vacancies soon because some tenants have expressed a

39 preference for larger quarters. We shall try to meet their requirements

40 in our two new buildings.

41   In addition to reading our literature, you're welcome to visit me at

42 any time which is mutually convenient. Maybe a Saturday in August would

43 prove to be the best time that we can get together here. It will be

44 unnecessary for you to make an appointment more than a few days in advance

45 because that month is the one which I am least busy.

46   If you believe our organization can be of assistance to you, please

47 don't hesitate to get in touch with me.

48   Sincerely yours,

49   DAVIS CONSTRUCTION COMPANY

50 JTA:YOI   Joseph T. Albertson

51 Enclosures   Assistant Manager

52

1

2 January 16, 19--

3 Mr. Roy Potter

4 241 Milwaukee Avenue

5 Racine, WI 53479

6 Dear Mr. Potter:

7   I am returning your check for this month's rent because you omitted

8 your signature. I am enclosing an envelope addressed to me so that after you

9 have signed the check, you can return it to me promptly.

10   Except for three or four tenants, everyone else has renewed his lease.

11 I'm encouraged by this fact, because everyone seems to realize that

12 the maintenance problems that we had while the superintendent was ill

13 were not permanent. In our tenants' opinion, efficiency has returned to its

14 formerly high state. As soon as the freight elevator has been equipped

15 with new doors, the building should be back to its original condition.

16   Last year you said you would be interested in moving to a smaller

17 apartment, and that this move would be dependent on its location.

18 Among the tenants who are apparently not renewing their leases are

19 two with apartments on the fourth floor. These apartments should be

20 available in the near future. I suggest, therefore, that you speak to

21 the superintendent immediately, to see whether or not these apartments

22 would meet your requirements.

23   Sincerely yours,

24   INDEPENDENCE MANAGEMENT CO.

25 FB:yol
encls.   Foster Bailey

26

1

2   November
                                              ~~NOvember~~ 2, 19--

3   Mrs. Joan Alexander

                Fortieth
4   271 ~~Fourtieth~~ Street

        Gary, IN
5   ~~Garry, In~~ 46480

           Mrs. Alexander:
6   Dear ~~Ms. Alexander,~~

                             Sewing   all ready   fourth
7   The new American ~~Sewing~~ Machines are ~~already~~ for you on the ~~forth~~

                        store.   equipped   forty
8   floor of our ~~store,~~ Each machine is ~~equiped~~ with about ~~fourty~~ features

                   indispensable
9   which will be ~~indispensible~~ to you in making clothing, curtains, and

                                          your house.   manufacturers   omitted
10   decorative items for each room in ~~you hous.~~ The ~~manufactures~~ have ~~om-~~

              which   add   your convenience   machine.
11   ~~mitted~~ nothing ~~wich~~ will ~~add~~ to ~~you convience~~ in operating this ~~mac-~~

              It's   genuine   opinion   there   sewing
12   ~~hine.~~ ~~Its~~ our ~~genuinne opinon~~ that ~~their~~ is no other ~~sowing~~ machine in

     existence   its
13   ~~existance~~ which does ~~it's~~ work as well as the American.

                                                                            persuaded
14   Once you have seen the machine, you will not have to be ~~persuaded~~

           it's practical   addition
15   that ~~its~~ a ~~practicel edition~~ to your sewing room. The machine may be

                                                                  partial
16   bought for cash, with a credit card, or by means of a ~~parcial~~ payment.

     Don't lose
17   ~~Dont loose~~ any time in coming to our store to look at the various

     models   Inasmuch   annual November
18   ~~models~~ we have on display. ~~In asmuch~~ as we are having our ~~anuol No-~~

                            able   buy   what
19   ~~vembr~~ sale, you will be ~~ablel~~ to ~~by~~ a machine at about half of ~~wat~~ you

     formerly   courteous, efficient
20   ~~formally~~ would have had to pay. Our ~~curteous efficent~~ and well-trained

                        glad   assistance
21   sales force will be ~~gald~~ to be of ~~assistante~~ to you.

                                  Cordially
22   ~~Cprdially~~ yours,

                                     DEPARTMENT
23   MORTON ~~DEPARTMMENT~~ STORE

24   TT:YOI   Tina Throck, Sewing Department

25

26

1

                                                                October
2   ~~Octobr~~ 4, 19--

        Cincinnati   Equipment
3   ~~Cinncinati~~ ~~Equipoment~~ Company

            Cleveland
4   4090 ~~Clevland~~ Road

        Akron, OH
5   ~~Ackron Oh~~   44381

6   Attention of Mr. Herbert Lewes, Treasurer

        Gentlemen:
7   ~~Dear Mr. Lewis:~~

            maintenance   indispensable
8   The ~~maintainance~~ of ~~of~~ a good credit rating is ~~indispensible~~ to

        responsible   When your indebtedness exceeds   usual
9   any ~~responsable~~ businessman. ~~Wehn you indebtness excedes~~ your ~~usull~~

                            You're   losing   benefits received
10   credit limit, ~~your'e~~ in danger of ~~loosing~~ the credit ~~benifits receive~~

                   past.
11   in the ~~passed.~~

              genuinely   have   write   to   I
12   I am ~~genuinnely~~ sorry to ~~hvae~~ to ~~writ~~ this letter ~~tu~~ you but ~~i~~

             deferred writing   possible.   analyzed
13   have ~~defered writting~~ it as long as ~~possible.~~ I have ~~anilized~~ our

           records   find   allowed   indebtedness $17,423.67
14   ~~our records,~~ and ~~fine~~ that we have ~~aloud~~ your ~~indetness~~ of ~~$17423,67~~

                        too   sent   usual
15   to last much ~~to~~ long. We have ~~send~~ you the ~~usul~~ collection letters,

                        no response from   wrote   letter
16   but we have had ~~know responce form~~ you. As we ~~wroet~~ you in our ~~lett-~~

             September   partial   overdue account
17   ~~er~~ of ~~Septembr~~ 17, even a ~~paroial~~ payment for the ~~overdo acount~~ would

                   an encouraging   partial payment
18   have been ~~a incouraging~~ development. However, even this ~~parshal paym-~~

                            withheld.
19   ~~ent~~ has been ~~witheld.~~

                       one   customers almost
20   As you have been ~~won~~ of our ~~costumers all most~~ since our organi-

        zation   existence,   regret   that
21   ~~sation~~ has been in ~~existance~~ we ~~regreat~~ very much ~~thta~~ we can wait

        wait   one   recent customers,
22   ~~wait~~ no longer. If ~~If~~ you had been ~~won~~ of our ~~resent costumers~~ we

                     instituted   proceedings   didn't
23   would have ~~insituted~~ legal ~~procedings~~ many months ago. We ~~did'nt~~ do

        this   conscias   fact   and
24   ~~this,~~ because we are ~~concious~~ of the ~~fack~~ that we have had a long ~~an~~

        pleasant
25   ~~pleasent~~ association.

                   forced   write   an immediate response
26   I am now ~~force~~ to ~~right~~ that unless we get ~~a imediate responce~~

310   Corrected Letter 81

27 ~~form~~ [from] you with at ~~lease~~ [least] a ~~partiall~~ [partial] ~~payement~~ [payment] of what is ~~ode~~ [owed] us, we shall

28 ~~hve~~ [have] to turn the ~~acont~~ [account] over to a collection agency. This is a very

29 ~~disaggreable~~ [disagreeable] action to have to take, but ~~Im certin~~ [I'm certain] that you will ~~aggree~~ [agree]

30 that we have been more than ~~fare~~ [fair] and patient.

31   ~~Dont~~ [Don't] make us take ~~htis~~ [this] step. ~~INStead~~ [Instead,] use the enclosed self-

32 ~~addresed~~ [addressed] ~~envelop~~ [envelope] and ~~foward~~ [forward] your check to us ~~buy retrun~~ [by return] mail. Once

33 we have ~~receive~~ [received] a ~~parsial~~ [partial] payment, we can give ~~a extention~~ [an extension] of about

34 ~~ninty~~ [ninety] days for paying ~~teh balense~~ [the balance.] However, ~~untill~~ [until] you have ~~payed~~ [paid] us

35 ~~sum~~ [some] of the ~~some~~ [sum] owing, we ~~wo'nt attemt~~ [won't attempt] to discuss the payment of the

36 ~~balence.~~ [balance.]

37   At the risk of endless ~~repitition~~ [repetition,] I am once again ~~sayint~~ [saying] that ~~its~~ [it's]

38 ~~essencial~~ [essential] that you mail us a check ~~imediately.~~ [immediately.] Otherwise, the ~~acount~~ [account]

39 will ~~bee~~ [be] in the hands of the collection ~~agency~~ [agency;] and you will ~~here form~~ [hear from]

40 them or from their ~~attornies~~ [attorneys] rather ~~then~~ [than] from me.

41   Very ~~Truley~~ [truly] yours,

42   OHIO ~~STATIONARY~~ [STATIONERY] COMPANY

43 ~~AAA:YOI~~ [AA:]
     Enc.   Amos Andrews

44   Comptroller

45

46

47

48

49

50

51

52

1

2   August 11, 19--

3   Mr. Bruce Raymond

4   205 Minnesota Avenue

5   Saint Paul, MN   55182

6   Dear Mr. Raymond:

7   Under separate cover we are sending you the six invitations to

8   the luncheon which will be held on Saturday, November 12, at the

9   Minneapolis Restaurant at noon. The principal speaker at the luncheon

10 will be the Superintendent of Schools, Dr. Benjamin Marlowe.

11 Dr. Marlowe is honoring a group of teachers, assistant principals,

12 principals and librarians who have retired or transferred to other school

13 districts. Since you know that many of them have given valuable servi-

14 ces and have been responsible for the improvement of learning and teaching,

15 I know that you and some of the members of your organization will

16 want to attend. Of course, you will be our guests because you have helped

17 to sponsor so many joint activities with us in the past.

18   I would be very grateful if you would send me the names of those who

19 will attend so that our program can be prepared promptly, efficiently and

20 accurately. Incidentally, we regret that we cannot send more than six

21 invitations. As you undoubtedly know, our budget has to be strictly ad-

22 hered to.

23   Sincerely yours,

24 JP:yo1   Joseph Paxton

25

26

1

2   October ~~Octobr~~ 14, 19--

3   Pennsylvania Stationery ~~Pennsyllvania Stationary~~ Store

4   489 Pittsburgh ~~Pittsburg~~ Avenue

5   Philadelphia, ~~Philidelphia,~~ PA   19183

6   Gentlemen: ~~Gentleman~~

7   An analysis ~~analisis~~ of our records ~~recordds~~ by our head bookkeeper ~~bookeeper~~ shows that you

8   have not yet paid ~~payed~~ your overdue account ~~overdo acount,~~ in spite ~~inspite~~ of the letters we have

9   ~~have~~ sent ~~send~~ and the telephone ~~tolphone~~ calls we made have made within ~~withing~~ the last two ~~to~~

10   months. ~~month.~~ If you would ~~woud~~ like to eliminate ~~ellimiante~~ the embarrassment ~~embarassment~~ of legal pro-~~proc-~~

11   ceedings, ~~eedings~~ we suggest ~~sugest~~ that you use the enclosed stamped, self-addressed ~~self-adressed~~ en-

12   velope and place your remittance ~~remittence~~ of $143.29 ~~$143.29~~ in it.

13   To you the amount ~~ammount~~ of $143.29 ~~$142.29~~ may not seem to be a large sum. ~~some.~~

14   Nevertheless, ~~Never-the-less~~ we could not attempt ~~attemp~~ to have such ~~suhe~~ low prices if payments

15   were withheld ~~witheld~~ for more than two ~~then to~~ months. We have devised ~~deviced~~ a thorough ~~through~~ system

16   for notifying our customers ~~costomers~~ when they have unpaid balances ~~unpayed ballances~~ in their ~~there~~

17   accounts, ~~acounts we~~ and we have gone through ~~thru~~ all these steps in this system with you.

18   Apparently, ~~Apatently~~ the only solution we have is to ~~too~~ turn ~~turn~~ over to our

19   attorneys ~~attornies~~ copies of our correspondence ~~corospondence~~ with you, and they will take the ~~teh~~

20   necessary ~~necessary~~ steps to see that the debt you have incurred ~~incured~~ is paid ~~payed~~ promptly. ~~promply.~~

21   We are hoping ~~hopping~~ that we will receive ~~recieve~~ your check in the mail ~~male~~ by the

22   beginning ~~beginnig~~ of next week so that we don't ~~do'nt~~ have to take the step described ~~discribe~~

23   above.

24   Yours very truly ~~Very Truly~~

25   YOI   Miriam Paine

     enclosure   Collection

26   ~~Colection~~ Manager

June 4, 19--

Coolidge Vacuum Cleaners, Inc.

4596 San Francisco Street

Berkeley, CA 94784

Attention: Mr. Wilson Forbes

Gentlemen:

    We are very unhappy with the shipping company you're using in shipping the vacuum cleaners we buy from you. As a responsible manufacturer you know "The customer is always right." In this case we believe that we are entirely right.

    When we removed the vacuum cleaners from the cartons for the last two shipments we received, we found that two of the vacuum cleaners were damaged. Since this occurrence took place on two separate occasions, we believe that the time and expense involved for you and for us is too valuable to have to spend on unnecessary damage. We suggest, therefore, that you consider changing to another freight agency which will be more careful, efficient and satisfactory.

    Enclosed are the original and duplicate shipping documents. They're complete and correct. After you have read them, you undoubtedly will tell us what to do with the damaged vacuum cleaners. Of course, we would like you to investigate thoroughly the causes of the damage so that you can place the responsibility for these occurrences.

                    Yours truly,

                    CALIFORNIA MERCHANDISE COMPANY

                    Ted Elkins, Manager

TE:YO1
enclosures

1

2   March 4,
                                              ~~March 4~~ 19--

3   ~~Miss.~~ **Miss** Mary Lou Parton

4   498 ~~Syracuse~~ **Syracuse** Avenue

5   ~~Rochostar, NY.~~ **Rochester, NY** 14685

6   Dear Miss ~~Partonn:~~ **Parton:**

7   Please ~~begian~~ **begin** to make ~~arangements~~ **arrangements** for the end-of-year ~~lunchon~~ **luncheon** for

8   our volunteers. The ~~principle~~ **principal** purpose of this affair is to show our

9   ~~appreciation~~ **appreciation** to the ~~voluntears~~ **volunteers** for the ~~ecellent~~ **excellent** quality of their ~~baluable~~ **valuable**

10   services ~~throughowt~~ **throughout** the year. The last ~~to~~ **two** affairs ~~weich~~ **which** you ~~planed~~ **planned**

11   ~~yeilded~~ **yielded** many ~~bonifits~~ **benefits,** and messages of ~~congradulations~~ **congratulations** resulted. I ~~no~~ **know**

12   you will ~~exeercise~~ **exercise** the same good ~~judgement~~ **judgment** that you have ~~use~~ **used** in the past.

13   ~~In as much~~ **Inasmuch** as I ~~no~~ **know** that you ~~allways~~ **always** do such ~~a efficeint~~ **an efficient** job, I am

14   ~~greatful~~ **grateful** that I ~~dont~~ **don't** have to spend ~~unecessary~~ **unnecessary** time trying to ~~pursuade~~ **persuade**

15   you to ~~except~~ **accept** this ~~aditional~~ **additional** chore.

16   ~~Alltogether~~ **Altogether,** the ~~some~~ **sum** of ~~$1000~~ **$1,000** has been ~~alotted~~ **allotted** to this function.

17   We can expect about 75 ~~aceptances~~ **acceptances** so that there should be ~~sufficent~~ **sufficient**

18   funds. It ~~maybe~~ **may be** that we will ~~exeede~~ **exceed** our ~~budjet~~ **budget,** but we can ~~allways~~ **always**

19   find funds to make up the ~~diffarance.~~ **difference.**

20   Please see me ~~witin~~ **within** the next two ~~of~~ **or** three days so that we can

21   ~~discus possibel~~ **discuss possible** dates. If we wait ~~untill~~ **until** the ~~whether~~ **weather** ~~beeommes~~ **becomes** much

22   milder**,** many of the ~~restarants~~ **restaurants** with outdoor facilities will ~~allready~~ **already**

23   have been booked.

24   ~~Sincerly~~ **Sincerely** yours

25   ~~YOI:LAP~~ **LP:YOI**   Lillie Popp, Administrator

26

1

2   December
                                           ~~Decemmber~~ 7, 19--

3   Mr. George ~~Marго,~~ Margo

4   1253 ~~Washinngton~~ Washington Avenue

5   ~~Seatle,~~ Seattle, WA   98186

6   Dear ~~Mister Marggo,~~ Mr. Margo:

7   We ~~genuinly beleive~~ genuinely believe that our bank offers ~~indispensible~~ indispensable service to

8   ~~its' custommers.~~ Its customers. We have been in ~~existance~~ existence for more ~~then fourly~~ than forty years,

9   and we are the ~~forth~~ fourth largest bank in the entire state. Our deposits

10   ~~exceed~~ exceed more than ~~$4500000000~~ $4,500,000,000 and we offer more kinds of services ~~tohn~~ than

11   any other bank in ~~in~~ this city.

12   ~~Alltogether~~ Altogether, we have eight ~~diffrent~~ different kinds of savings ~~accouns.~~ accounts. We

13   have ~~to~~ two kinds of interest-paying club ~~accounts~~ accounts and offer many general

14   ~~general~~ services.

15   As a ~~speial~~ special offer at this time, we offer free safe-deposit boxes

16   in every branch ~~accept~~ except the ~~Galafornia~~ California Highway branch. The only re-

17   ~~quirment~~ quirement is the ~~maintainance~~ maintenance of a ~~minimum balence~~ minimum balance of at least ~~$5000,~~ $5,000

18   while you have the safe-deposit box.

19   For ~~you convinence,~~ your convenience, we are ~~enclossing~~ enclosing a free ~~clendar~~ calendar and a ~~specia;~~ special

20   ~~bullitin~~ bulletin which lists ~~sum~~ some of our services.

21   ~~Sincerly~~ Sincerely yours,

22   SEATTLE TRUST COMPANY

23   ~~JA:YOI~~ JAA:YOI   John A. Anderson, Vice President
     enclosures

24

25

26

1

2   October 5, ~~Octobar 5,,~~ 19--

3   Mrs. Adrienne Danforth

4   98 Ninth ~~Nineth~~ Avenue

5   Louisville, ~~Louivillo,~~ KY   40287

6   Dear Mrs. ~~Miss~~ Danforth:

7   What are you doing to encourage ~~incourage~~ your children's ~~childrens~~ food preferences ~~prefarances~~

8   so that you're certain ~~your'e certin~~ that they're ~~theyr'e~~ getting all the essential ~~essencial~~ nutrition

9   to develop ~~develope~~ strong, healthy bodies? Do you find ~~fine~~ that you have to remove ~~remoove~~

10   the so-called "junk" foods from your shopping ~~shoping~~ lists so that your chil- ~~you're child-~~

11   dren don't ~~ren dont~~ become dependent ~~dependant~~ upon snacks instead ~~insted~~ of food which ~~ofood wich~~ will bring

12   improvement ~~improvment~~ to their ~~they're~~ health?

13   We suggest ~~sugest~~ that you check the special columns in ~~colums ni~~ our magazine ~~magizine~~

14   which are devoted to simple snacks which yield ~~yeild~~ exceptionally fine ~~find~~

15   benefits. ~~benifits.~~ We also ~~alsow~~ think that you should send ~~sent~~ for copies of our

16   pamphlets ~~phamphlets~~ which contain suggestions ~~suggestions~~ which have been successful ~~successful~~ in pre-

17   previous years.

18   Send $1 and a self-addressed ~~self-address~~ envelope, ~~envelop~~ and we will rush two of ~~to fo~~ our

19   pamphlets ~~pamphlets~~ to you by return ~~rotrun~~ mail.

20   Very truly yours, ~~your,~~

21   GOOD HOMEMAKING

22   JM ~~JAM:~~YOI   Jane Martinson, Food Editor ~~Editr~~

23

24

25

26

1

2   February 27, 19--

3   Mrs. Janet Deborah Collings

4   9701 ~~Misouri~~ Missouri Parkway

5   ~~Saint Louis~~ St. Louis, MO   63188

6   Dear ~~Ms. Collins~~ Mrs. Collings:

7   Do ~~yuo~~ you have the feeling that the ~~redocoratting~~ redecorating of ~~you~~ your home is

8   ~~is~~ long ~~overdo,~~ overdue? Do you ~~loook~~ look at ~~advertisments~~ advertisements in the ~~newspaers~~ newspapers and

9   ~~magizines~~ magazines and ~~also~~ ask yourself if your ~~prefferances~~ preferences and ~~tastse~~ tastes of 10 or

10   15 years ago have ~~change.~~ changed? Do you have the feeling that what you ~~thoug~~ thought

11   of as ~~perminent~~ permanent when you bought it has ~~outlive~~ outlived its ~~usefullness?~~ usefulness? Are

12   you ~~embarassed~~ embarrassed when ~~froinds~~ friends and neighbors drop in? Do you ~~critioizo~~ criticize

13   ~~waht~~ what you see in your livingroom silently or ~~allowed?~~ aloud?

14   If you have ~~ansered~~ answered these questions with a ~~"Yes!"~~ "Yes," you ~~reoly~~ really ~~shoud~~ should

15   not have to be ~~pursuaded~~ persuaded to stop in ~~our~~ at our store ~~stoore.~~ As you ~~no~~ know, our

16   sales force is noted for ~~its'~~ its ~~curtesy~~ courtesy, patience and knowledge. One of

17   our salesmen will help you ~~chose~~ choose furnishings and accessories which will

18   ~~will~~ be ~~practicle~~ practical, beautiful and ~~up-to-date.~~ up to date.

19   We hope to see you ~~sooon.~~ soon.

20   ~~Coridally~~ Cordially yours,

21   ~~MISOURI~~ MISSOURI FURNITURE ~~S:ORE~~ STORE

22   ~~RXH:YOI~~ RH: Rex Harris, Manager

23

24

25

26

1

2   May 4, 19--

3   ~~Dr~~ Dr. Edward Samson

4   5987 ~~Nasheville~~ Nashville Avenue

5   ~~Chatanooga,~~ Chattanooga, TN   37489

6   Dear Dr. ~~Sampson:~~ Samson:

7   Are you al[l]ready for the ~~fare~~ fair and warm ~~whether~~ weather that has been ~~pred-~~ pre-

8   ~~icted~~ dicted for this spring and summer? Is your backyard ~~equiped~~ equipped with ~~ever-~~ every-

9   ~~ything~~ thing you will need to make outdoor living ~~pleasent~~ pleasant, easy and ~~comfor-~~ comfortable?

10 ~~table.~~

11   I ~~sugest~~ suggest that ~~you~~ after you have ~~refered~~ referred to our price list and ~~otalog~~ catalog,

12 you will have to ~~excercise~~ exercise restraint to ~~by~~ buy only what you require. In

13 the ~~passed,~~ past, we have ~~offorred~~ offered to take back any ~~merchandize~~ merchandise ~~witin~~ within ~~twwo~~ two

14 weeks, and that same offer still applies.

15   ~~Sence~~ Since you ~~hav~~ have been ~~won~~ one of our ~~costomers~~ customers for many years, a deposit

16 or a ~~parcial~~ partial ~~remittence~~ remittance will be ~~asceptable~~ acceptable to us for purchases up to

17 $500. Any charges ~~incured~~ incurred above that ~~ammont~~ amount can be ~~payed~~ paid for with any

18 ~~reconized~~ recognized credit card.

19   It is ~~essencial~~ essential that you shop now, while the ~~weatther~~ weather is still

20 cool. ~~Undoubtably,~~ Undoubtedly, as soon as it turns warmer, our ~~costomers~~ customers will rush

21 to the store. If you wait ~~to~~ too long, you may ~~regreat~~ regret the fact that what

22 ~~what~~ you want has ~~all ready~~ already been sold.

23   ~~yours~~ Yours very truly,

24   ~~TENESEE~~ TENNESSEE OUTDOOR FURNISHINGS

25 ~~TD:~~ TED:YOI   Thomas ~~o.~~ E. Drake, Manager

26

1

2   September 16, 19--

3 Shreveport Equipment Company

4 49 Louisiana Street

5 New Orleans, LA 70190

6 Gentlemen:

7   We were genuinely surprised when you wrote to us on August 30

8 that there is still an indebtedness of $170 on our account. We had made

9 partial payments of $85 for two successive weeks in August, and we were

10 certain that the account had been cleared up in its entirety.

11   Has your bookkeeper omitted to record these checks in his books?

12 Undoubtedly the error is in your books, because we have checked and

13 double checked our records and find that they're absolutely accurate.

14   As you say in your letter, we do know that the maintenance of a good

15 credit record is indispensable. We have always attempted to keep

16 this principle in mind, because we don't want to forfeit our excellent

17 credit rating.

18   Please check your records again and let me know what your findings

19 are.

20   Very truly yours,

21   LOUISIANA STATIONERY COMPANY

22 JJM:YOl

23   John Joseph Miller

                                Accounting Department

24

25

26

1

2   March 3, 19--

3   Mr. Arthur Maxwell

4   1248 Government Square

5   Washington, DC 20091

6   Dear Mr. Maxwell:

7   Though you are probably a success in the government bureau in which

8   you are employed have made you any noticeable improvement in your standard

9   of living? Is there a discrepancy between what you would like to be

10   earning and the amount you carry home each month? Do you resent the

11   fact that some of your friends are doing all right financially, while you're

12   finding it difficult to make ends meet?

13   Who's going to say to you, "Stay on your job until you retire or

14   die"? Whose resources should you use?

15   We believe you should make an appointment with one of our counselors

16   as soon as possible to discuss these important matters. Maybe some of

17   your fellow workers may have preferred to do nothing in the past, and

18   they have not benefited from the assistance and advice that you can

19   secure. We believe you should pursue this matter before it is too late.

20   Just fill in the enclosed form and mail it in the stamped self-

21   addressed envelope. One of our representatives will telephone to make an

22   appointment at a time mutually convenient.

23   Yours very truly,

24   WASHINGTON EMPLOYMENT AGENCY

25   RAJ:YOI   Ruth A. Jacoby
     Enclosure   President
26

1

2   June 3, 19--

3 Ms. Harriet Shipmann

4 249 Phoenix Street

5 Tucson, AZ   85792

6 Dear Ms. Shipmann:

7   Do you know that as a government employee, you are eligible for

8 miscellaneous allowances and benefits on the insurance policies offered

9 by our organization? They're all explained in the pamphlet which I'm

10 enclosing.

11   Do you want to eliminate the concern about unpaid or late

12 premiums? See page 19 of the pamphlet.

13   Have financial difficulties been occurring which make it difficult

14 for you to meet all of your expenses and obligations? See page 21.

15   Do you realize that the policies you originally chose five or ten

16 years ago may be unsuitable for your present needs? Perhaps an examina-

17 tion of your policies once again is long overdue. See page 26.

18   I suggest that you read through the pamphlet thoroughly. An analysis

19 of the information will convince you that you should fill out the

20 questionnaire which is on page 35. Return it to me immediately. I

21 will be all ready to come to see you with proof that you will benefit

22 from one of our insurance programs.

23   Very sincerely yours,

24   INDEPENDENCE INSURANCE ASSOCIATION

25 YOI   District Office Manager

26 Enclosure

January 14, 19--

Mr. Clark Gateson

5698 Ohio Avenue

Cincinnati, OH 45293

Dear Mr. Gateson:

At the suggestion of the attorneys for your sister, Lillian Wise, I have made a thorough analysis of the two volumes of testimony in the case in which she was the defendant last year in Cleveland. I agree with them that there were many omissions in Judge Smith's statement which served to prejudice the jury against her. Some of the procedures in the trial itself were questionable, and I do not disagree with her attorneys that further action be taken as soon as all areas have been investigated.

I believe that the best course we can take is to reach a decision soon as to whether or not to bring additional attorneys into the picture. It's my opinion that the original set of attorneys which your sister chose did an excellent job considering all the circumstances. Nevertheless, it may be wise to meet with them and with the attorneys to whom I referred you last month. It is essential that we be fair to the previous attorneys, but we must also try to avoid a repetition of what took place in Cleveland.

If anything develops, call me at once. In the meantime think about what your preferences would be about changing attorneys.

Cordially yours,

John D. Adams

JDA:YOI

1

2   October 19, 19--

3   Mr. Irwin Grill

4   109 Kentucky Avenue

5   Louisville, KY 40294

6   Dear Mr. Grill:

7   Has it been occurring to you that prices are finally beginning to

8   get more reasonable? Are you losing the feeling that you cannot af-

9   ford to buy the merchandise you want and need?

10   If the answers to these questions are in the affirmative, we re-

11   gard it as a real achievement that our ads in the columns of our local

12   papers may have brought these feelings about.

13   Let's talk about our Book Department and our Stationery Department.

14   Our Book Department was formerly under the direction of Miss Amy Coe.

15   However, she has been transferred to the Stationery Department. Before

16   she left, she arranged for a special purchase of first editions of the

17   classics, and our advertisements this week emphasize the fact that you

18   can make additions to your home library at reasonable prices.

19   Stop in to see Miss Coe and say, "Hello." She is thoroughly

20   familiar with both the personal and commercial stationery, and you will

21   also receive a courteous welcome from her.

22   Sincerely yours,

23   LOUISVILLE DEPARTMENT STORE

24   RB:YOI   Rose Barrett, Manager

25   Second Floor Departments

26

1

2   ~~Juen~~ June 25, 19--

3   ~~Messers.~~ Messrs. Harrison & Cooper

4   1398 ~~Conneticut~~ Connecticut Avenue

5   ~~Waterberry, Ct~~ Waterbury, CT   06795

6   ~~Gentleman:~~ Gentlemen:

7   RE: Building at 137 Fourth Street in ~~Springfeild~~ Springfield

8   In the ~~bsence~~ absence of any ~~commmunications form~~ communications from you, I am going ahead

9   with my ~~planns~~ plans to ~~remoove~~ remove the ~~lose~~ loose shingles from our building at

10   137 ~~Forth~~ Fourth Street. This is in ~~acordance~~ accordance with my letter of June ~~15th~~ 15,

11   which was sent to you ~~formerly~~ formally by registered mail. The return ~~reciept~~ receipt

12   we ~~recieved~~ received was signed by "John ~~Parker~~ Parker."

13   Frankly I ~~dont~~ don't think that we should be in a ~~possition~~ position to have ~~ot~~ to

14   ~~apoligize~~ apologize for the ~~apearance~~ appearance of our property. Yet this has been neces-

15   ~~sarie becuse~~ sary because of the way in which the shingles were ~~replace.~~ replaced. We thought

16   that with all the ~~expences~~ expenses we ~~incured~~ incurred in the modernization of ~~toh~~ the

17   property, the ~~improvment~~ improvement would be ~~notioable.~~ noticeable. In ~~som~~ Some instances it was,

18   but the ~~shinkles~~ shingles which you ~~attach aded~~ attached added no ~~improvment~~ improvement to the ~~aperance~~ appearance,

19   of the ~~prprty, becase~~ property because they were not ~~attach strickly acording~~ attached strictly according to the

20   specifications of our ~~contract~~ contract with you.

21   As soon as the shingles have been ~~remooved~~ removed and replaced, we shall

22   send you the bill which ~~result form~~ results from this work.

23   Very truly ~~your,~~ Yours,

24   MORGAN GENERAL STORE

25   ~~TM:YOI~~ TAM: Thomas A. Morgan

26   Proprietor

1

2   May 4,
                                                        ~~Mya 4th,~~ 19--

                        Barrow
3   Mr. Lester ~~Barrow,~~

          Massachusetts
4   475 ~~Massachusettes~~ Avenue

     Worcester,
5   ~~Worchester~~ MA   01696

                  Barrow:
6   Dear Mr. ~~Barow,~~

            interested   buying commercial   suggest that
7   If you are ~~introsted~~ in ~~bying~~ ~~commerical~~ property, we ~~sugest~~ ~~thta~~

             one   representatives.   organization
8   you see ~~won~~ of our ~~represontives.~~ Our ~~orgnization~~ handles property

     across   except
9   ~~accross~~ the entire state ~~accept~~ for the Cape Cod area.

          believe   right   be-
10   We ~~blieve~~ that this may be the ~~write~~ time for you to see us ~~boo~~

     cause   coming
11   ~~ause~~ during the ~~comming~~ months we expect to be handling some property

         firms which   just   bankruptcy. It's   opinion
12   for ~~frims~~ ~~whihe~~ have ~~jus~~ gone into ~~bankrupcy.~~ ~~Its~~ our ~~opinon~~ that

            properties   have be   reasonable
13   these ~~proportiees~~ will ~~hav~~ be to sold at very ~~resonable~~ prices. If

     there   Massachusetts   which
14   ~~their~~ are any special sections of ~~Massachusettes~~ in ~~wich~~ you are

                    interested,   efficient, courteous   helpful
15   particularly ~~introsted~~ one of our ~~efficent~~ ~~curteous~~ and ~~helpfull~~

     salesmen   pursue   with
16   ~~salesman~~ will ~~persue~~ the matter ~~wit~~ you.

            you're interested   don't forfeit   secure
17   If ~~your'e~~ ~~introsted~~ in low prices, ~~dont~~ ~~forfiet~~ your chance to ~~see~~

                         bargain   It's essential
18   ~~ure~~ property at these ~~bargin~~ prices. ~~Its essencial~~ that you get in

                   immediately   opportunities
19   touch with us ~~imediately,~~ because these ~~opportunitie's~~ are temporary

     ones,   permanent ones.
20   ~~one's~~ not ~~permonent~~ ~~one's.~~

            won   fairly   excellence
21   We have ~~one~~ our reputation ~~farely~~ because of the ~~excellance~~ of the

                 offered   ninety years.   assistance.
22   service we have ~~offerred~~ for over ~~nint~~ ~~yors.~~ Let us be of ~~assistants.~~

                               yours,
23   Very truly ~~yours,~~

24   RELIABLE REALTY CORPORATION

                                    Manager
25   PW:YOI   Paul Walters, ~~Manager~~

26

1

2   September   19--
                                                           ~~Septeber 4, 91~~

3   Mrs. ~~Harreit~~ Harriet Rosenborg

4   4954 North ~~Caroline~~ Carolina Avenue

5   ~~Winstonsalem~~ Winston-Salem, NC 27197

6   Dear ~~Ms. Rosenberg~~ Mrs. Rosenborg:

7   ~~Congradulations.~~ Congratulations! It is a ~~priviledge~~ privilege for us to let you ~~knwe~~ know that

8   you have been ~~sponsored~~ sponsored by Mr. Seymour White, 432 Sixth Avenue, Spring-

9   ~~foild Massachusettes~~ field, Massachusetts 01103, for membership in the American ~~Libary~~ Library

10   Society. He has ~~payed~~ paid the one-year membership ~~feee~~ fee for you. You may be

11   sure that membership in our ~~oganization~~ organization will enable you to secure

12   ~~posessions~~ possessions which ~~ad~~ add will to the joys of life.

13   The ~~folowing~~ following are ~~sum~~ some of the ~~advantiges~~ advantages of ~~you membership;~~ your membership:

14   1) Each month you will ~~recieve~~ receive the ~~LIBERY~~ LIBRARY BULLETIN, a publication

15   which reviews the up-to-the-minute books being published ~~buy~~ by leading

16   publishers ~~raound~~ around the country.

17   ~~2(~~ 2) All books listed in the ~~LIBERY BULLETTIN~~ LIBRARY BULLETIN may be ~~purchase~~ purchased at

18   ~~resonable~~ reasonable prices. ~~Proceedures~~ Procedures for ordering books ~~is~~ are given on Page 17

19   of the ~~BULLITIN~~ BULLETIN each month.

20   3) In ~~edition~~ addition to the ~~curent~~ current books, each ~~months~~ month's issue of the ~~LIBRARY~~ LIBRARY

21   ~~BULLETINN list~~ BULLETIN lists new ~~addtions~~ editions of some favorite books ~~form~~ from the ~~passed.~~ past.

22   These ~~boooks~~ books are ~~attractivly~~ attractively bound in leather and are limited ~~ad-~~ editions.

23   ~~ditions. Proceedures~~ Procedures for ordering ~~thoes~~ these books ~~is~~ are also given on

24   ~~page~~ Page 17.

25   ~~4-~~ 4) ~~Attendence~~ Attendance at lectures ~~iw won~~ is one of the ~~benifits~~ benefits you will ~~recieve.~~ receive.

26   Twice a year, leading writers ~~adress~~ address our ~~mobership~~ membership meetings. The

27 arrangements for their personal appearances are made well in advance, and

28 publicity is given ahead of time. The July meeting is always held at a

29 vacation spot. You can, therefore, combine a vacation with a stimulating

30 meeting. Each member is allowed one guest at these lectures, and there

31 is no charge for the guest or for the member.

32   5) The annual dinner is held in a restaurant in one of the exclusive

33 hotels in Washington. Last year's dinner was a great success. Not

34 only was the food exceptional, but our speakers were two writers who had

35 just won important literary awards. Although many of the guests dress

36 formally, it is unnecessary to do so, since dress is "Optional". As

37 you're no doubt familiar with the costs of similar dinners, I'm sure

38 you realize that the cost of $20 for this dinner is extremely reasonable.

39 This year we hope to have the winner of the Bancroft Award, Julia Morse.

40   6) The maintenance of your membership doesn't depend upon the num-

41 ber of books you buy. Instead, you merely have to spend $50 annually, and

42 your membership will stay in effect. If you spend more than $100

43 annually, you will be eligible for some of the special dividends which

44 are listed monthly in the BULLETIN. When you look at the BULLETIN, you

45 will see that the plan we have devised for dividend allowances is fair

46 and simple.

47   After you have been a member, we should appreciate receiving sug-

48 gestions, or criticisms for helping us improve our services.

49   Sincerely yours,

50   AMERICAN LIBRARY SOCIETY

51 JB:YOI   Janet Baker

52

1

2   February
                                                        ~~Fobuary~~ 4, 19--

3   Akron
      ~~Ackron~~ Filing Company, Inc.

4   Toledo
      296 ~~Tolledo~~ Avenue

5   Cincinnati,
      ~~Cincinnatti~~ OH   45298

6   Gentlemen:
      ~~Gentllemen~~

7   There   controversy   criticism
      ~~Tohro~~ has been a great deal of ~~contraversy~~ and ~~critisism~~ about the

8   sums   allotted   Bureau   our organization.
      ~~sumes~~ of money ~~alloted~~ to the ~~Boureau~~ of Files in ~~out organzation.~~

9   Among   one   files
      ~~Amoung~~ the complaints is the frequent ~~won~~ that the ~~filles~~ hav been so

10   kept   almost impossible   correspondence
      poorly ~~kep~~ that it is ~~allmost~~ ~~imposible~~ to find ~~corresponence~~ which has

11   transferred. Miscellaneous government   essential
      been ~~transfered.~~ ~~Miscellaneous govoment~~ papers, which are so ~~essencial~~

12   efficient   institute often cannot   It's
      to the ~~efficent~~ running of our ~~insitute offen can not~~ be found. ~~Its~~ a

13   occurrence   can't
      frequent ~~occurence~~ for one of the file clerks to say, "I just ~~cant~~

14   find what you are looking for."

15   Since your   filing   equipment
      ~~Sinse you~~ firm sold us most of our ~~filling equipoment~~ during the

16   past two or   suggested   one   representatives
      ~~passed to of~~ three years, it has been ~~suggest~~ that ~~won~~ of your ~~represe-~~

17   encourage   personnel
      ~~ntives~~ visit our filing department. He can ~~incourage~~ our ~~personal~~

18   necessary   criticize where necessary.   commercial
      where ~~necessary~~ and ~~critsize wher necesssary.~~ Both our ~~commorical~~

19   government   improvement,   believe
      and ~~govoment~~ files are in need of ~~improvmont~~ and we ~~beleive~~ that only

20   an   succeed being   assistance
      ~~a~~ expert will ~~suceed~~ in ~~boih~~ of ~~assistence~~

21   that   an appointment
      Please call me so ~~cant~~ we can make ~~and appoinment~~ to go over

22   thoroughly.
      this matter ~~throughly.~~

23   Very   yours,
                                       ~~very~~ truly ~~Yours,~~

24   OHIO INSTITUTE
                                       ~~OHHIO~~ ~~INSITUTE~~ OF EDUCATION

25   JE:YOI   Office
                                       Jan Edwards, ~~Ofice~~ Manager

26

1

2   October
                                                ~~Octobr~~ 19, 19--

3 Mr. Glenn Johansen, President

4 Johansen Electrical Components Company

5 986 ~~Pensylvania~~ Pennsylvania Turnpike

6 ~~Wilkesbarre, Pa.~~ Wilkes-Barre, PA   18799

7 Dear Mr. ~~Johanson:~~ Johansen:

8   Have ~~bankrupoies~~ bankruptcis been ~~occuring~~ occurring with regularity in ~~you insustry?~~ your industry?

9 Is it ~~noticeable~~ noticeable that they are ~~incresing~~ increasing each year? Is ~~their somewon~~ there someone in

10 ~~you orrganization~~ your organization who is ~~responsable~~ responsible for the ~~analysys~~ analysis of ~~unpayed~~ unpaid debts

11 and ~~over due acounts.~~ overdue accounts? Have you ~~recently incured lossses~~ recently incurred losses which you

12 did not anticipate?

13   We ~~can not emphazize to~~ cannot emphasize too strongly that though ~~strick~~ strict precautions

14 are ~~offen~~ often taken, things ~~sometings accidently "go wrong".~~ sometimes accidentally "go wrong." If you look

15 at ~~som~~ some of the ~~columens~~ columns in the ~~magizines~~ magazines in your industry, you ~~probaly~~ probably

16 ~~realise~~ realize that ~~their~~ there are many things ~~taht~~ that "go ~~wrong~~ wrong" even in the largest

17 firms. ~~Prooof~~ Proof of this can be easily seen on Page 95 of this ~~months~~ month's

18 issue of MODERN ELECTRONICS.

19   We ~~d'ont~~ don't mean to ~~criticise you~~ criticize your present policies. ~~Never the less~~ Nevertheless,

20 they should be ~~check throughly.~~ checked thoroughly. Fill in the enclosed ~~questionaire~~ questionnaire and

21 return it to me ~~immediatoley~~ immediately in the stamped, ~~self=addressed envelop.~~ self-addressed envelope. I

22 will ~~than~~ then get in ~~tuch~~ touch with you to discuss ~~proooedures~~ procedures we would ~~recomend.~~ recommend.

23   Very truly ~~your,~~ yours,

24   ELECTRONICS ~~FINTIAL~~ FINANCIAL ADVISORS

25 MA:YOI   Mark Austin, ~~Anilyst~~ Analyst
   enclosures

26

1

2   ~~Agost~~ August 4, 19--

3   Illinois ~~Illinoise~~ Button Company

4   495 ~~Chicago Drive,~~ Chicago Drive.

5   ~~Springfeild,~~ Springfield, IL   62701

6   ~~Gentleman:~~ Gentlemen:

7   SUBJECT: ~~Profered Devises~~ Preferred Devices for Door Locks

8   This letter is in ~~refarance~~ reference to the letter you ~~rote~~ wrote to our firm

9   on ~~Juyl~~ July 14.

10   In ~~anser~~ answer to ~~you inqures,~~ your inquiries, I can assure you that we are the

11   ~~manufactures~~ manufactures of ~~devises~~ devices ~~wich~~ which have ~~succeded~~ succeeded more ~~then~~ than any others at

12   present ~~the~~ the on market. ~~Prove~~ Proof of this can be found in the ~~phamphlet~~ pamphlet we

13   are ~~enelosin wiht~~ enclosing with this letter.

14   Your ~~desision~~ decision on installing new locks ~~can not~~ cannot be ~~delaied unlesss,~~ delayed unless

15   you want to wait ~~untill~~ until your offices ~~is~~ are robbed. We ~~can not emphizise~~ cannot emphasize

16   ~~to~~ too strongly that the ~~ommision~~ omission of ~~adaquate~~ adequate protection ~~wil~~ will result in

17   disaster.

18   ~~Form~~ From your letter ~~Ibelive~~ I believe that you are in need of our ~~assistence~~ assistance

19   ~~imediately.~~ immediately. Telephone me at 896-0933 so that we can set up ~~a apointment.~~ an appointment.

20   ~~ent.~~

21   Yours very ~~truely,~~ truly,

22   ~~ILLINOISE~~ ILLINOIS LOCK COMPANY

23   KI:YoI   Karl Irwinson
     Enclosure

24   Sales Manager

25

26